Microsoft® Office PowerPoint 2010

A SKILLS APPROACH, COMPLETE

Cheri Manning

Catherine Manning Swinson

Triad Interactive, Inc.

Connect
Learn
Succeed™

Connect
Learn
Succeed™

MICROSOFT® OFFICE POWERPOINT 2010: A SKILLS APPROACH, COMPLETE
Published by McGraw-Hill, a business unit of The McGraw-Hill Companies, Inc., 1221 Avenue of the Americas,
New York, NY, 10020. Copyright © 2012 by The McGraw-Hill Companies, Inc. All rights reserved. No part of this
publication may be reproduced or distributed in any form or by any means, or stored in a database or retrieval system,
without the prior written consent of The McGraw-Hill Companies, Inc., including, but not limited to, in any network
or other electronic storage or transmission, or broadcast for distance learning.

Some ancillaries, including electronic and print components, may not be available to customers outside the
United States.

This book is printed on acid-free paper.

1 2 3 4 5 6 7 8 9 0 RMN/RMN 1 0 9 8 7 6 5 4 3 2 1

ISBN 978-0-07-739502-5
MHID 0-07-739502-6

Vice president/Director of marketing: *Alice Harra*
Publisher: *Scott Davidson*
Sponsoring editor: *Paul Altier*
Director, digital products: *Crystal Szewczyk*
Development editor: *Alan Palmer*
Editorial coordinator: *Allison McCabe*
Marketing manager: *Tiffany Russell*
Digital development editor: *Kevin White*
Director, Editing/Design/Production: *Jess Ann Kosic*
Project manager: *Marlena Pechan*
Buyer II: *Laura M. Fuller*
Senior designer: *Srdjan Savanovic*
Senior photo research coordinator: *Keri Johnson*
Manager, digital production: *Janean A. Utley*
Media project manager: *Brent dela Cruz*
Media project manager: *Cathy L. Tepper*
Outside development house: *Barrett Lyon*
Typeface: *10.5/13 Garamond Premier Pro*
Compositor: *Laserwords Private Limited*
Printer: *R. R. Donnelley*
Cover credit: © Plainview, iStockphoto; bcakcover: © Okea, iStockphoto
Credits: The credits section for this book begins on page PPC-1 and is considered an extension of the copyright page.

Printed in the United States of America.

Library of Congress Cataloging-in-Publication Data
Manning, Cheryl.
   Microsoft Office Powerpoint 2010 : a skills approach, complete / Cheri Manning, Catherine
Manning Swinson.
      p. cm.
   Includes bibliographical references and index.
   ISBN-13: 978-0-07-739502-5 (alk. paper)
   ISBN-10: 0-07-739502-6 (alk. paper)
   1. Presentation graphics software. 2. Microsoft PowerPoint (Computer file) I. Swinson,
Catherine Manning. II. Title.
T385.M3617 2012
005.5'8—dc23
                                                                    2011023868

The Internet addresses listed in the text were accurate at the time of publication. The inclusion of a Web site does not
indicate an endorsement by the authors or McGraw-Hill, and McGraw-Hill does not guarantee the accuracy of the
information presented at these sites.

www.mhhe.com

contents

office and powerpoint 2010

Essential Skills for Microsoft Office and PowerPoint 2010 — PP-ii

Skill **0.1** Introduction to Microsoft Office 2010 — PP-iii

Skill **0.2** Exploring the PowerPoint 2010 User Interface — PP-vi

Skill **0.3** Customizing PowerPoint — PP-xi

Skill **0.4** Designing Presentations — PP-xii

Skill **0.5** Opening an Existing Presentation — PP-xiii

Skill **0.6** Understanding Security Warnings in PowerPoint — PP-xiv

Skill **0.7** Creating a New Blank Presentation — PP-xv

Skill **0.8** Creating a New Presentation Using a Template — PP-xvi

Skill **0.9** Modifying Presentation Properties — PP-xvii

Skill **0.10** Using Cut, Copy, and Paste — PP-xviii

Skill **0.11** Using Paste Special — PP-xix

Skill **0.12** Using Undo and Redo — PP-xx

Skill **0.13** Using Find and Replace — PP-xxi

Skill **0.14** Checking Spelling — PP-xxii

Skill **0.15** Saving a Presentation — PP-xxiii

Skill **0.16** Using Help — PP-xxiv

Skill **0.17** Closing a Presentation — PP-xxv

Skill **0.18** Exiting PowerPoint — PP-xxvi

Projects — PP-xxvii

powerpoint 2010

chapter 1
Getting Started with PowerPoint 2010 — PP-2

Skill **1.1** Introduction to PowerPoint 2010 — PP-3

Skill **1.2** Understanding Views — PP-4

Skill **1.3** Using the Slides Tab — PP-6

Skill **1.4** Using the Outline Tab — PP-7

Skill **1.5** Adding Slides to Presentations — PP-8

Skill **1.6** Adding Sections to Presentations — PP-9

Skill **1.7** Changing Slide Layouts — PP-10

Skill **1.8** Applying Slide Transitions — PP-11

Skill **1.9** Working with the Slide Master — PP-12

Skill **1.10** Inserting Headers and Footers — PP-13

Skill **1.11** Adding and Printing Notes — PP-14

Projects — PP-16

chapter 2
Adding Content to Slides — PP-24

Skill **2.1** Adding Text to Slides — PP-25

Skill **2.2** Adding Bulleted and Numbered Lists — PP-26

Skill **2.3** Opening a Word Outline as a Presentation — PP-28

Skill **2.4** Adding WordArt to Slides — PP-30

Skill **2.5** Understand the Content Placeholder — PP-32

Skill **2.6** Creating Tables in Presentations — PP-33

Skill **2.7**	Adding Charts to Slides	PP-34
Skill **2.8**	Adding SmartArt to Slides	PP-35
Skill **2.9**	Adding Shapes to Slides	PP-36
Skill **2.10**	Adding Text to Shapes	PP-37
Skill **2.11**	Adding Clip Art Images to Slides	PP-38
Skill **2.12**	Adding Screenshots to Slides	PP-39
Skill **2.13**	Adding Pictures to Slides	PP-40
Skill **2.14**	Adding Sounds to Slides	PP-41
Skill **2.15**	Adding Movies to Slides	PP-42
	Projects	PP-43

chapter **3**
Formatting Presentations — PP-56

Skill **3.1**	Changing the Presentation Theme	PP-57
Skill **3.2**	Changing the Color Theme	PP-58
Skill **3.3**	Changing the Theme Effects	PP-59
Skill **3.4**	Changing the Slide Background	PP-60
Skill **3.5**	Changing Fonts	PP-61
Skill **3.6**	Changing the Look of Text Boxes	PP-62
Skill **3.7**	Applying Quick Styles to Text Boxes	PP-63
Skill **3.8**	Applying Quick Styles to Tables	PP-64
Skill **3.9**	Using the Shape Styles Gallery	PP-65
Skill **3.10**	Changing the Layout of SmartArt	PP-66
Skill **3.11**	Using the Picture Styles Gallery	PP-67
Skill **3.12**	Showing the Ruler and Gridlines	PP-68
Skill **3.13**	Changing the Size of Images	PP-69
Skill **3.14**	Changing the Size of a Placeholder	PP-70
Skill **3.15**	Aligning, Grouping, and Rotating Images	PP-71
Skill **3.16**	Applying Animation Effects	PP-73
Skill **3.17**	Modifying Animations	PP-74
	Projects	PP-75

chapter **4**
Managing and Delivering Presentations — PP-85

Skill **4.1**	Deleting Slides from Presentations	PP-86
Skill **4.2**	Changing the Order of Slides	PP-87
Skill **4.3**	Copying and Pasting Slides	PP-88
Skill **4.4**	Using the Office Clipboard	PP-89
Skill **4.5**	Defining a Custom Show	PP-90
Skill **4.6**	Hiding Slides	PP-91
Skill **4.7**	Adding Hyperlinks to Slides	PP-92
Skill **4.8**	Adding Comments	PP-93
Skill **4.9**	Rehearsing Timings	PP-94
Skill **4.10**	Starting the Slide Show	PP-95
Skill **4.11**	Using Presentation Tools	PP-96
Skill **4.12**	Printing Presentations	PP-98
Skill **4.13**	Customizing Handout Masters	PP-99
Skill **4.14**	Previewing and Printing Handouts	PP-100
	Projects	PP-101

chapter **5**
Exploring Advanced Graphics, Tables, and Charts — PP-109

Skill **5.1**	Applying Artistic Effects to Pictures	PP-110
Skill **5.2**	Removing the Background from Pictures	PP-111
Skill **5.3**	Correcting Pictures	PP-112
Skill **5.4**	Changing the Color of Pictures	PP-113
Skill **5.5**	Cropping Graphics	PP-114
Skill **5.6**	Compressing Pictures	PP-115

Skill **5.7** Resetting Pictures PP-116

Skill **5.8** Aligning Text in Tables PP-117

Skill **5.9** Inserting and Deleting Rows and Columns in Tables PP-119

Skill **5.10** Modifying Charts PP-120

Skill **5.11** Animating Charts PP-121

Skill **5.12** Creating Multipart Animations PP-122

Skill **5.13** Setting Animation Timings PP-123

Skill **5.14** Creating an Action Button PP-124

Skill **5.15** Recording a Slide Show PP-125

Skill **5.16** Editing Audio on a Slide PP-126

Skill **5.17** Editing Video on a Slide PP-128

Skill **5.18** Creating a Photo Album PP-129

Projects PP-130

chapter **6**
Polishing and Finishing the Presentation

PP-137

Skill **6.1** Adding Slides from Another Presentation PP-138

Skill **6.2** Applying Character Effects PP-139

Skill **6.3** Aligning Text PP-140

Skill **6.4** Adding Columns to Text Placeholders PP-141

Skill **6.5** Changing Line Spacing PP-142

Skill **6.6** Using the Format Painter PP-143

Skill **6.7** Clearing Formatting PP-144

Skill **6.8** Using Animation Painter PP-145

Skill **6.9** Modifying the Slide Master PP-146

Skill **6.10** Adding New Layouts and Placeholders to the Slide Master PP-149

Skill **6.11** Checking for Compatibility with Previous Versions of PowerPoint PP-151

Skill **6.12** Saving Slides as Graphics PP-153

Skill **6.13** Saving a Presentation as a PDF PP-155

Skill **6.14** Saving a Presentation as a Template PP-156

Skill **6.15** Packaging a Presentation for CD PP-158

Skill **6.16** Broadcasting a Presentation PP-160

Skill **6.17** Publishing Slides to a Slide Library PP-162

Skill **6.18** Saving a Presentation as a Video PP-164

Projects PP-165

Glossary PPG-1

Index PPI-1

preface

How well do you know Microsoft Office? Many students can follow specific step-by-step directions to re-create a document, spreadsheet, presentation, or database, but do they truly understand the skills it takes to create these on their own? Just as simply following a recipe does not make you a professional chef, re-creating a project step by step does not make you an Office expert.

The purpose of this book is to teach you the skills to master Microsoft PowerPoint 2010 in a straightforward and easy-to-follow manner. But *Microsoft® Office PowerPoint 2010: A Skills Approach, Complete* goes beyond the ***how*** and equips you with a deeper understanding of the ***what*** and the ***why.*** Too many times books have little value beyond the classroom. The *Skills Approach* series has been designed to be not only a complete textbook but also a reference tool for you to use as you move beyond academics and into the workplace.

ABOUT TRIAD INTERACTIVE

Triad Interactive is a small business and a District of Columbia Qualified High Technology Company specializing in online education and training products.

Triad's flagship program is SimNet®—a simulated Microsoft Office learning and assessment application developed for the McGraw-Hill Companies. SimNet development began in 1999 with SimNet 2000, a CD-ROM-based program used to measure students' understanding of the Microsoft Office 2000 applications. In 2000, for Office XP, Triad expanded the SimNet platform to include a learning component with lessons written by Cheri Manning and Catherine Manning Swinson. Over the past 10 years, the SimNet series has continued to evolve from a simple CD-ROM program into a robust online learning and assessment system. More than 500,000 students worldwide have used SimNet to learn the skills necessary to master Microsoft Office.

Triad is also actively involved in cancer education and in research projects to assess the usefulness of technology for helping high-risk populations make decisions about managing their cancer risk and treatment.

about the **authors**

CHERI MANNING

Cheri Manning is the president and co-owner of Triad Interactive. She is the author of the Microsoft Excel and Microsoft Access content for the SimNet series of online assessment and learning programs. She has been authoring instructional content for these applications for over 10 years. Cheri is also the co-author of McGraw-Hill's *What's New in Microsoft Office 2003* and *What's New in Microsoft Office 2007*.

Cheri began her career as an Aerospace Education Specialist with the Education Division of the National Aeronautics and Space Administration (NASA), where she produced materials for K–12 instructors and students. Prior to founding Triad Interactive, Cheri was a project manager with Compact Publishing, where she managed the development of McGraw-Hill's Multimedia MBA CD-ROM series.

CATHERINE MANNING SWINSON

Catherine Manning Swinson is the vice president and co-owner of Triad Interactive. She is the author of the Microsoft Word, Microsoft PowerPoint, and Microsoft Outlook content for the SimNet series of online assessment and learning programs. She has been authoring instructional content for these applications for over 10 years. Catherine is also the co-author of *What's New in Microsoft Office 2003* and *What's New in Microsoft Office 2007*.

Catherine began her career at Compact Publishing, one of the pioneers in educational CD-ROM-based software. She was the lead designer at Compact and designed every edition of the *TIME Magazine Compact Almanac* from 1992 through 1996. In addition, she designed a number of other products with Compact, including the *TIME Man of the Year* program and the *TIME 20th Century Almanac*.

The authors would like to extend a special thank-you to the Triad staff especially to Torger Wuellner for keeping the show running while we were writing the text and to Katie Lawson and Jodi Sandvick for staying late and coming in on the weekends to help with graphics. Thanks to Marlena Pechan, Barrett Lyon, and Alan Palmer for their patience working with two authors new to the print world. Thanks to Liz Haefele and Scott Davidson for the opportunity to expand our digital collaboration into print. And a final thanks to Paul Altier for his extraordinary vision of what this series could be and for all of his encouragement and support throughout the process. We deeply appreciate all of the hard work by the contributors, technical editors, reviewers, and everyone at McGraw-Hill to develop this new series.

contributors

powerpoint projects

Debra Fells
Mesa Community College

Melissa Prinzing
Sierra College

Diane Santurri
Johnson & Wales University

from the perspective of

Marlene Roden
Asheville-Buncombe Technical Community College

Bonnie Smith
Fresno City College

technical editors

Elliot Cherner
Mesa Community College

Michael Dunklebarger
Alamance Community College

Susan Fuschetto
Cerritos College

Brenda Nielsen
Mesa Community College

Vicky Seehusen
Metropolitan State College of Denver

Judy Settle
Central Georgia Technical College

Candace Spangler
Columbus State Community College

reviewers

OUR THANKS GO TO ALL WHO PARTICIPATED IN THE DEVELOPMENT OF
MICROSOFT® OFFICE POWERPOINT 2010: A SKILLS APPROACH, COMPLETE.

Rosalyn Amaro
Florida State College at Jacksonville

Beverly Amer
Northern Arizona University

Wilma Andrews
Virginia Commonwealth University

Tom Ashby
Oklahoma City Community College

Robert Balicki
Cleary University

Diana Baran
Henry Ford Community College

Nathan Barker
Southern Utah University

Alfred Basta
Kaplan University

Judy Bennett
Sam Houston State University

Jan Bentley
Utah Valley University

Judy Brierley
Seminole State College

Eva Brown
San Jacinto College

Judy Brown
The University of Memphis

Katharine Brown
University of North Florida

Menka Brown
Piedmont Technical College

Sylvia Brown
Midland College

Peter Cardon
University of South Carolina

Patricia Casey
Trident Technical College

Gerianne Chapman
Johnson & Wales University

Dan Combellick
Scottsdale Community College

Paulette Comet
Community College of Baltimore County

Sissy Copeland
Piedmont Technical College

Jami Cotler
Siena College

Penny Cypert
Tarrant County College

Don Danner
San Francisco State University

Raphael De Arazoza
Miami Dade College

Darren Denenberg
University of Nevada–Las Vegas

Joy DePover
Minneapolis Community and Technical College

Charles DeSassure
Tarrant County College

Kim Ellis
Virginia Western Community College

Jean Finley
Asheville Buncombe Technical Community College

Dave Fitzgerald
Jackson Community College

Deborah Franklin
Bryant & Stratton College

Susan Fuschetto
Cerritos College

Amy Giddens
Central Alabama Community College

Fred Goldberg
Community College of Philadelphia

Barbara Gombetto
Bryant & Stratton College

Kemit Grafton
Oklahoma State University–Oklahoma City

Marilyn Griffin
Virginia Tech

Andrew Hardin
University of Nevada–Las Vegas

Michael Haugrud
Minnesota State University Moorhead

Terri Hayes
Broward College

Cheryl Heemstra
Anne Arundel Community College

Marilyn Hibbert
Salt Lake Community College

Mary Carole Hollingsworth
Georgia Perimeter College

Lister Horn
Pensacola State College

Jennifer Ivey
Central Carolina Community College

Linda Johnsonius
Murray State University

Barbara Jones
Golden West College

Sally Kaskocsak
Sinclair Community College

Hazel Kates
Miami Dade College Kendall Campus

Judith Keenan
Salve Regina University

Hal Kingsley
Trocaire College

Linda Kliston
Broward College

Kitty Koepping
Shepherd University

Charles Lake
Faulkner State

Jackie Lamoureux
Central New Mexico Community College

Nanette Lareau
University of Arkansas Community College at Morrilton

Kevin Lee
Guilford Technical Community College

Patricia Lee
Florida State College at Jacksonville

Kate LeGrand
Broward College

Mary Locke
Greenville Technical College

Donna Lohn
Lakeland Community College

Nicki Maines
Mesa Community College

Daniela Marghitu
Auburn University

Juan Marquez
Mesa Community College

Phil Marshall
University of South Carolina

Prosenjit Mazumdar
George Mason University

Robert McCloud
Sacred Heart University

Sue McCrory
Missouri State University

Daniel McKee
Mansfield University of PA

Patricia McMurray
Kaplan Career Institute ICM Campus

Dawn Medlin
Appalachian State University

Alanah Mitchell
Appalachian State University

Susan Mitchell
Davenport University

Kathleen Morris
University of Alabama

Carmen Morrison
North Central State College

Melissa Nemeth
Kelley School of Business Indianapolis

Brenda Nielsen
Mesa Community College

Philip Nielson
Salt Lake Community College

Maria Osterhoudt
St. Petersburg College

Judy Pento
Seacoast Career School

Rene Polanco
Austin Community College

Don Rhyne
San Joaquin Valley College

Steven Rosen
Keiser University

Kathy Ruggieri
Lansdale School of Business

Charles Salazar
Clackamas Community College

Diane Santurri
Johnson & Wales University

Paul Schwager
East Carolina University

Vicky Seehusen
Metro State College of Denver

Steven A. Singer
Kapiolani Community College

Cindi Smatt
Texas A&M University

Bonnie Smith
Fresno City College

Thomas Michael Smith
Austin Community College

Candice Spangler
Columbus State Community College

Diane Stark
Phoenix College

Allen Truell
Ball State University

Kari Walters
Louisianna State University

Eric Weinstein
Suffolk County Community College

Stu Westin
University of Rhode Island

Billie Jo Whary
McCann School of Business and Technology Sunbury Campus

Melinda White
Seminole State College

Katherine Winters
University of Tennessee at Chattanooga

Judy Wynekoop
Florida Gulf Coast University

Laurie Zouharis
Suffolk University

Matthew Zullo
Wake Technical Community College

Instructor Walkthrough

Microsoft Office PowerPoint 2010: A Skills Approach, Complete

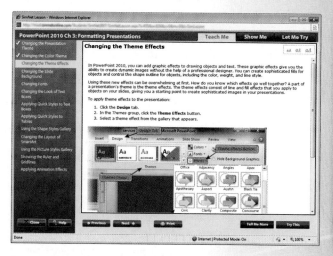

3.3 Changing the Theme Effects

In PowerPoint 2010, you can add graphic effects to drawing objects and text. These graphic effects give you the ability to create dynamic images without the help of a professional designer. You can create sophisticated fills for objects and control the shape outline for objects, including the color, weight, and line style.

Using these new effects can be overwhelming at first. How do you know which effects go well together? A part of a presentation's theme is the theme effects. The theme effects consist of line and fill effects that you apply to objects on your slides, giving you a starting point to create sophisticated images in your presentations.

To apply theme effects to the presentation:

1. Click the **Design** tab.
2. In the *Themes* group, click the **Theme Effects** button.
3. Select a theme effect from the gallery that appears.

FIGURE PP 3.3

> **1-1 Content in SimNet for Office 2010**

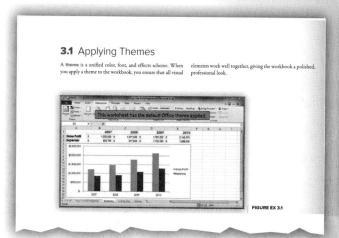

3.1 Applying Themes

A theme is a unified color, font, and effects scheme. When you apply a theme to the workbook, you ensure that all visual elements work well together, giving the workbook a polished, professional look.

FIGURE EX 3.1

> **At-a-glance PowerPoint 2010 skills**
>
> *Quick, easy-to-scan pages, for efficient learning*

---

chapter 4

Managing and Delivering Presentations

In this chapter, you will learn the following skills:

Skill **4.1** Deleting Slides from Presentations
Skill **4.2** Changing the Order of Slides
Skill **4.3** Copying and Pasting Slides
Skill **4.4** Using the Office Clipboard
Skill **4.5** Defining a Custom Show
Skill **4.6** Hiding Slides
Skill **4.7** Adding Hyperlinks to Slides
Skill **4.8** Adding Comments

> Delete, reorder, copy, and paste slides, and use the Office Clipboard
> Define a custom show and hide slides
> Add hyperlinks and comments
> Rehearse timings and use navigation tools
> Print presentations and handouts

> **Introduction—Learning Outcomes are clearly listed.**

> **Diverse end-of-chapter projects**

Projects that relate to a broad range of careers and perspectives, from nursing, education, business, and everyday personal uses.

Features:

Tips and Tricks

From the Perspective of...

from the perspective of . . .

DENTAL HYGIENIST

In my profession as a dental hygienist, I created a fun presentation showing good oral hygiene habits. Using presentation software, I was able to add clip art, music, and cartoons. My young patients love it.

After you have added WordArt to your document, you can modify it just as you would any other text. Use the *Font* box and *Font Size* box on the *Home* tab to change the font or font size of WordArt.

In previous versions of Microsoft Office, WordArt came with a predefined set of graphic styles that could be formatted, but on a very limited basis. Beginning with PowerPoint 2007, WordArt was changed to allow a wide range of stylization. When you add WordArt to a slide, the *Drawing Tools Format* contextual tab appears. In the *WordArt Styles* group you can apply Quick Styles to your WordArt, or modify it further by changing the text fill, text outline, and text effects.

Tips and Tricks

tips & tricks

If you typically use one type of chart for your presentations, you can set that chart type as the default chart type. In the *Insert Chart* dialog box, select the chart type you want to set as the default. Next, click the **Set as Default Chart** button. Now when you open the *Insert Chart* dialog box, that chart type will automatically be selected and you won't need to search through the different chart types to find the one you want to use.

Try This

try **this**

To change the font, right-click the text, click the arrow next to the **Font** box on the Mini toolbar, and select an option.

To change the font size, right-click the text, click the arrow next to the **Font Size** box on the Mini toolbar, and select an option.

To change the font color, right-click the text, click the arrow next to the **Font Color** button on the Mini toolbar, and select an option.

Tell Me More

tell me **more**

PowerPoint offers a number of transitions for you to choose from. There are simple fades and dissolves, any number of directional wipes (including shapes and rotations), pushes and covers, stripes and bars, and random transitions. When choosing transitions for your presentation, it is important to keep in mind who your audience will be. If you are presenting in a formal business environment, you will probably want to use more subtle transitions, such as fades and dissolves. If your audience expects more "sizzle" in the presentation, then you may want to choose a complex wipe, such as the Newsflash transition.

> **Instructor materials available on the online learning center, www.mhhe.com/office2010skills**

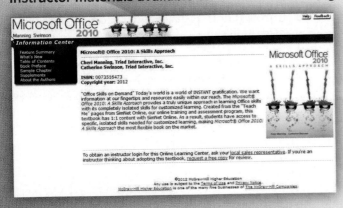

- Instructor Manual
- Instructor PowerPoints
- Test Bank
- Project Data and Solution Files

SimNet for Office 2010
Online training and assessment

Teach Me

Show Me

Let Me Try

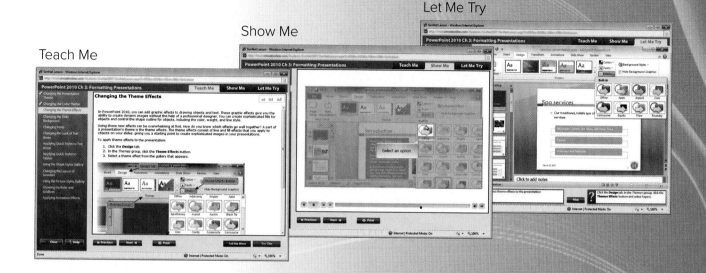

INCLUDES:

- Microsoft® Office Suite
- Microsoft® Outlook
- Windows XP
- Windows Vista
- Windows 7
- Internet Explorer 7
- Internet Explorer 8
- Computer Concepts

Since 1999, instructors have been using SimNet to measure student outcomes in a virtual Microsoft® Office environment. Now completely online, with nothing to install, students can practice and study their skills at home or in the school lab. Moreover, this resource is an ideal course solution, but even more valuable, as it can be used beyond the course for self-study! For more information, contact your McGraw-Hill sales representative or visit the SimNet Online Web site, **www.mhhe.com/simnet2010**

IT'S EASY!

SimNet is an EASY & INTUITIVE, true turnkey design. Instructors can quickly and efficiently assign content around the needs of your course, edit throughout the semester, and copy to multiple sections and instructors! SimNet is scannable so students can quickly scan the tasks in a lesson to identify the skills they know and the ones they don't…saving them time!

STUDENTS LEARN BEYOND THE BOOK!

SimNet offers a complete computer-based learning side that presents each skill or topic in several different modes:

- *Teach Me:* combines instructional text, graphics, and interactivity to present each skill.

- *Show Me:* uses animation with audio narration to show how the skill is implemented.
- *Let Me Try:* allows students to apply and practice what they have learned on their own to master the learning objective.

STUDENTS LEARN BEYOND THE COURSE!

SimNet allows students to perform their best in the course, and SimNet allows students to continue learning Office skills for future classes and beyond through its self-study material! Need to learn an advanced topic or a refresher on a certain skill? Use SimSearch to search or pull up specific content when you need it.

Essential Skills for Microsoft Office and PowerPoint 2010

Essential Skills for Microsoft Office and PowerPoint 2010

In this chapter, you will learn the following skills:

> Learn about Microsoft Office 2010 and its applications: Word, Excel, PowerPoint, and Access

> Recognize Microsoft PowerPoint 2010 common features and navigation elements

> Create new PowerPoint 2010 presentations

> Demonstrate how to open, save, print, and close PowerPoint presentations

> Use Microsoft Help

> Perform basic editing tasks

Skill **0.1**   Introduction to Microsoft Office 2010
Skill **0.2**   Exploring the PowerPoint 2010 User Interface
Skill **0.3**   Customizing PowerPoint
Skill **0.4**   Designing Presentations
Skill **0.5**   Opening an Existing Presentation
Skill **0.6**   Understanding Security Warnings in PowerPoint
Skill **0.7**   Creating a New Blank Presentation
Skill **0.8**   Creating a New Presentation Using a Template
Skill **0.9**   Modifying Presentation Properties
Skill **0.10** Using Cut, Copy, and Paste
Skill **0.11** Using Paste Special
Skill **0.12** Using Undo and Redo
Skill **0.13** Using Find and Replace
Skill **0.14** Checking Spelling
Skill **0.15** Saving a Presentation
Skill **0.16** Using Help
Skill **0.17** Closing a Presentation
Skill **0.18** Exiting PowerPoint

skills

introduction

This chapter introduces students to Microsoft Office and Microsoft PowerPoint 2010. Students will learn about the shared features across the applications of Microsoft Office 2010 and how to navigate common interface elements such as the Ribbon and status bar. Students will be introduced to basic design principles and become familiar with basic editing skills including checking spelling; using cut, copy, and paste; and finding and replacing text. Introductory features such as creating, opening, saving, and closing files and using Office Help are explained.

0.1 Introduction to Microsoft Office 2010

Microsoft® Office 2010 is a collection of business "productivity" applications (computer programs designed to make you more productive at work, school, and home). The most popular Office applications are:

Microsoft Word—a word processing program. Word processing software allows you to create text-based documents, similar to how you would type a document on a typewriter. However, word processing software offers more powerful formatting and design tools, allowing you to create complex documents including reports, résumés, brochures, and newsletters.

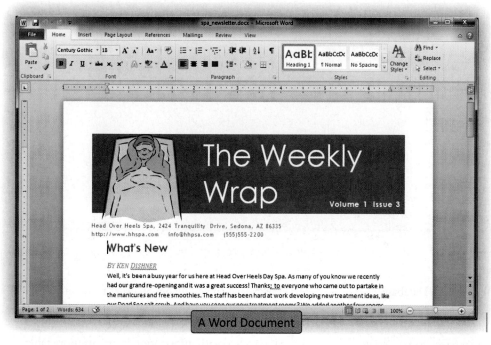

A Word Document

FIGURE PP 0.1

Microsoft Excel—a spreadsheet program. Originally, spreadsheet applications were viewed as electronic versions of an accountant's ledger. Today's spreadsheet applications can do much more than just calculate numbers—they include powerful charting and data analysis features. Spreadsheet programs can be used for everything from personal budgets to calculating loan payments.

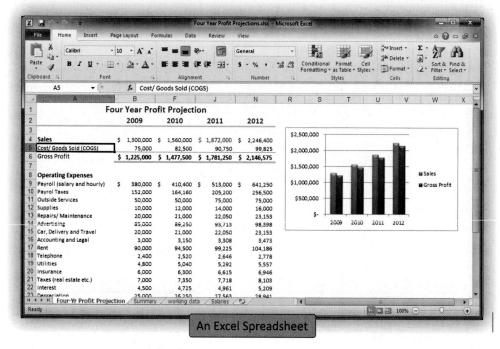

An Excel Spreadsheet

FIGURE PP 0.2

Microsoft PowerPoint—a presentation program. Presentation applications enable you to create robust, multimedia presentations. A presentation consists of a series of electronic slides. Each slide contains content, including text, images, charts, and other objects. You can add multimedia elements to slides, including animations, audio, and video.

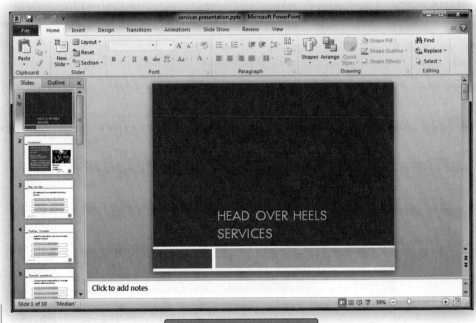

FIGURE PP 0.3

A PowerPoint Presentation

Microsoft Access—a database program. Database applications allow you to organize and manipulate large amounts of data. Databases that allow you to relate tables and databases to one another are referred to as *relational* databases. As a database user, you usually see only one aspect of the database—a *form*. Database forms use a graphical interface to allow a user to enter record data.

For example, when you fill out an order form online, you are probably interacting with a database. The information you enter becomes a record in a database *table*. Your order is matched with information in an inventory table (keeping track of which items are in stock) through a *query*. When your order is filled, a database *report* can be generated for use as an invoice or a bill of lading.

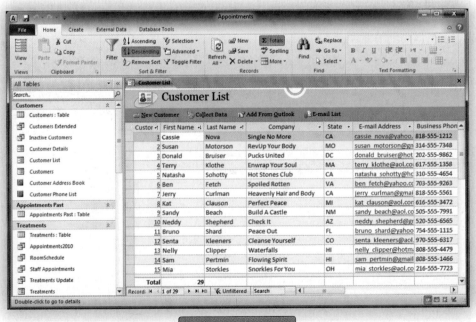

FIGURE PP 0.4

An Access Database

from the perspective of . . .

COMPUTER SUPPORT SPECIALIST

Setting up equipment for employee use, performing or ensuring proper installation of cable, operating systems, and appropriate software . . . wow! Training is a lot easier now since we have content on slideshows. Our employees are able to view materials when they need instead of giving me a call.

To open one of the Office applications:

1. Click the Windows **Start button** (located in the lower-left corner of your computer screen).
2. Click **All Programs.**
3. Click the **Microsoft Office** folder.
4. Click the application you want to open.

Word, Excel, and Power-Point open a new blank file automatically; Access opens to Backstage view, where you are asked to give the database a file name first.

tips & tricks

You can download a free trial version of Microsoft Office from Microsoft's Web site (http://office.microsoft.com). The trial allows you to try the applications before buying them. When your trial period ends, if you haven't purchased the full software license yet, you will no longer be able to use the applications (although you will continue to be able to open and view any files you previously created with the trial version).

tell me more

There are three popular versions of Microsoft Office, each offering a different combination of programs.

Office Home and Student—includes *Word 2010, Excel 2010, PowerPoint 2010,* and *OneNote 2010* (a note-taking and organizational program). This version of Office is intended for home use only. Use by commercial or nonprofit businesses is prohibited.

Office Home and Business—includes the same applications as the Home and Student version, and adds *Outlook 2010* for e-mail, contacts, and calendar management.

Office Professional—includes the same applications as the Home and Business version, and adds *Access 2010* and *Publisher 2010* (a desktop publishing application).

try **this**

A shortcut for starting one of the Office applications is to type the application name in the *Instant Search* box at the bottom of the *Start* menu:

1. Click the **Start** button.
2. In the *Instant Search* box, type `Access, Excel, PowerPoint,` or `Word,` and then press `←Enter`.
3. The application will open a new blank file.

0.2 Exploring the PowerPoint 2010 User Interface

THE RIBBON

If you have used a presentation program in the past, you may be surprised when you open PowerPoint 2010 for the first time. Beginning with PowerPoint 2007, Microsoft redesigned the user experience—replacing the familiar menu bar/toolbar interface with a Ribbon interface that makes it easier to find application functions and commands.

The **Ribbon** is located across the top of the application window and organizes common features and commands into tabs.

Each **tab** organizes commands further into related **groups.** When a specific type of object is selected (such as a picture, table, or chart), a contextual tab will appear. **Contextual tabs** contain commands specific to the type of object selected and are only visible when the commands might be useful.

The **Home tab** contains the most commonly used commands. In PowerPoint, the *Home* tab includes the following groups: *Clipboard, Slides, Font, Paragraph, Drawing,* and *Editing.*

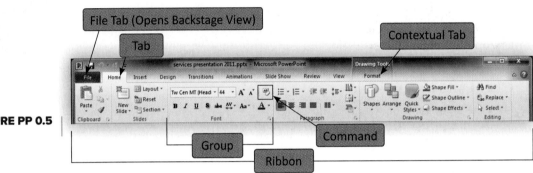

FIGURE PP 0.5

BACKSTAGE

The **File tab** appears at the far left side of the Ribbon. Clicking the *File* tab opens the **Microsoft Office Backstage™ view,** where you can access the commands for managing and

protecting your presentations including *Save, Open, Close, New,* and *Print.* Backstage replaces the *Office Button* menu from PowerPoint 2007 and the *File* menu from previous versions of PowerPoint.

---

tips & tricks

If you need more space for your presentation, you can minimize the Ribbon by clicking the **Minimize the Ribbon** button 🔲 in the upper-right corner of the Ribbon (or press Ctrl + F1). When the Ribbon is minimized, the tab names appear along the top of the window (similar to a menu bar). When you click a tab name, the Ribbon appears. After you select a command or click away from the Ribbon, the Ribbon hides again. To redisplay the Ribbon permanently, click the **Expand the Ribbon** button 🔲 in the upper-right corner of the window. Double-click the active tab to hide or display the Ribbon.

KEYBOARD SHORTCUTS

Many commands available through the Ribbon and Backstage are also accessible through keyboard shortcuts and shortcut menus.
Keyboard shortcuts are keys or combinations of keys that you press to execute a command. Some keyboard shortcuts refer to F keys or function keys. These are the keys that run across the top of the keyboard. Pressing these keys will execute

specific commands. For example, pressing the F1 key will open Help in any Microsoft Office application. Keyboard shortcuts typically use a combination of two keys, although some commands use a combination of three keys and others only one key. When a keyboard shortcut calls for a combination of key presses, such as Ctrl + V to paste an item from the Clipboard, you must first press the modifier key (Ctrl), holding it down while you press the V key on the keyboard.

FIGURE PP 0.6

Press and *hold* **Ctrl** and then press **V** to paste text or item in a document.

Many of the keyboard shortcuts are universal across applications—all applications, not just Microsoft Office applications. Some examples of universal shortcut keys include:

Ctrl + C = Copy

Ctrl + X = Cut

Ctrl + V = Paste

Ctrl + Z = Undo

Ctrl + O = Open

Ctrl + S = Save

SHORTCUT MENUS

Shortcut menus are menus of commands that display when you right-click an area of the application window. The area or object you right-click determines which menu appears.

For example, if you right-click on a text phrase, you will see a shortcut menu of commands for working with text; however, if you right-click an image, you will see a shortcut menu of commands for working with images.

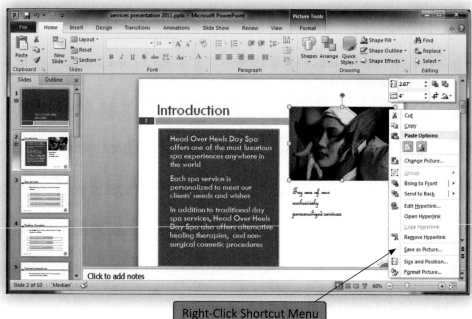

FIGURE PP 0.7

Right-Click Shortcut Menu

QUICK ACCESS TOOLBAR

The **Quick Access Toolbar** is located at the top of the application window above the *File* tab. The Quick Access Toolbar, as its name implies, gives you quick one-click access to common commands. You can add commands to and remove commands from the Quick Access Toolbar. One of the advantages of the Quick Access Toolbar is that it stays visible no matter what tab is active.

To modify the Quick Access Toolbar:

1. Click the **Customize Quick Access Toolbar** button located on the right side of the Quick Access Toolbar.
2. Options with check marks next to them are already displayed on the toolbar. Options with no check marks are not currently displayed.
3. Click an option to add it to or remove it from the Quick Access Toolbar.

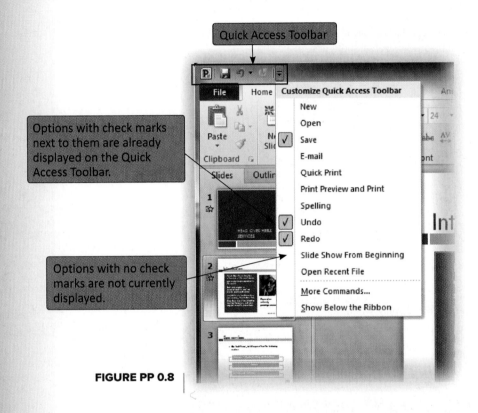

Quick Access Toolbar

Options with check marks next to them are already displayed on the Quick Access Toolbar.

Options with no check marks are not currently displayed.

FIGURE PP 0.8

tips & tricks   If you want to be able to print with a single mouse click, add the *Quick Print* button to the Quick Access Toolbar. If you do not need to change any print settings, this is by far the easiest method to print a file because it doesn't require opening Backstage view first.

THE MINI TOOLBAR

The **Mini toolbar** gives you access to common tools for working with text. When you select text and then rest your mouse over the text, the Mini toolbar fades in. You can then click a button to change the selected text just as you would on the Ribbon.

To display the Mini toolbar, you can also right-click the text. The Mini toolbar appears above the shortcut menu.

try **this**

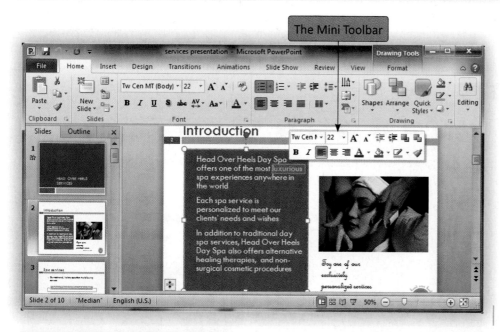

FIGURE PP 0.9

ENHANCED SCREENTIPS

A **ScreenTip** is a small information box that displays the name of the command when you rest your mouse over a button on the Ribbon. An **Enhanced ScreenTip** displays not only the name of the command but also the keyboard shortcut (if there is one) and a short description of what the button does and when it is used. Certain Enhanced ScreenTips also include an image along with a description of the command.

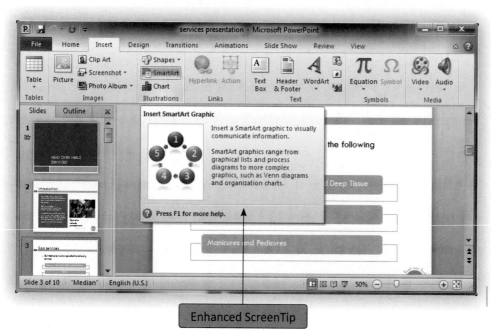

FIGURE PP 0.10

The **Live Preview** feature in Microsoft PowerPoint 2010 allows you to see formatting changes in your presentation before actually committing to the change. When Live Preview is active, rolling over a command on the Ribbon will temporarily apply the formatting to the currently active text or object. To apply the formatting, click the formatting option.

Use Live Preview to preview the following:

> **Font Formatting**—including the font, font size, and font color

> **Paragraph Formatting**—including numbering, bullets, and shading

> **Quick Styles and Themes**

> **Table Formatting**—including table styles and shading

> **Picture Formatting**—including correction and color options, picture styles, borders, effects, positioning, brightness, and contrast

> **SmartArt**—including layouts, styles, and colors

> **Shape Styles**—including borders, shading, and effects

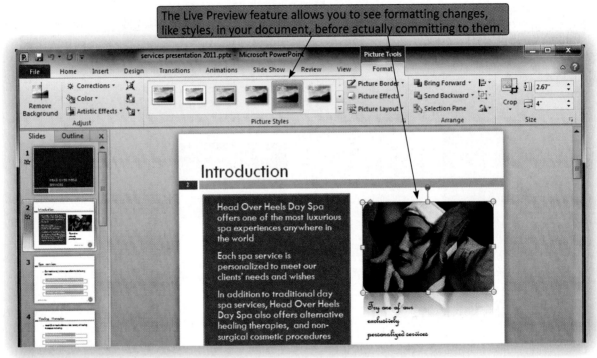

The Live Preview feature allows you to see formatting changes, like styles, in your document, before actually committing to them.

FIGURE PP 0.11

0.3 Customizing PowerPoint

When first installed, every version of PowerPoint has the same features enabled. However, you can enable and disable some of the user interface features through the *PowerPoint Options* dialog box. You can even change the colors used in the PowerPoint interface.

1. Click the **File** tab to open Backstage view.
2. Click **Options.**
3. Make the changes you want, and then click **OK** to save your changes.

   > Check or uncheck *Show Mini toolbar on selection* to control whether or not the Mini toolbar appears when you hover over selected text. (This does not affect the appearance of the Mini toolbar when you right-click.)

> Check or uncheck *Enable Live Preview* to turn the Live Preview feature on or off.

> Change the color scheme used for the PowerPoint interface by expanding the *Color scheme* list and selecting *Silver, Blue,* or *Black.*

> Make a selection from the *ScreenTip style* list:

   > *Show feature descriptions in ScreenTips* displays Enhanced ScreenTips when they are available.

   > *Don't show feature descriptions in ScreenTips* hides Enhanced ScreenTips. The ScreenTip will still include the keyboard shortcut if there is one available.

   > *Don't show ScreenTips* hides ScreenTips altogether, so if you hold your mouse over a button on the Ribbon, nothing will appear.

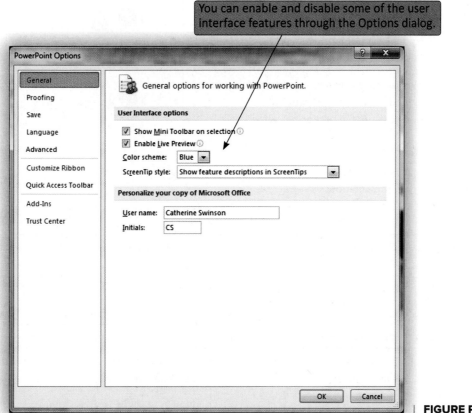

You can enable and disable some of the user interface features through the Options dialog.

FIGURE PP 0.12

The *PowerPoint Options* dialog also allows you to control such features as AutoCorrect, checking spelling as you type, and autosaving the presentation while you work.

tell me **more**

0.4 Designing Presentations

In this book, you will learn the skills needed to create Power-Point presentations. You will learn to create slides, add text and images, animate objects, and add transitions to slides. You also will learn how to run a presentation, using Power-Point's built-in navigation and presentation tools.

Before you learn the mechanics of creating and giving a presentation, there are some basic design principles that will help you create more effective PowerPoint presentations:

Balance, Distribute the elements on your slides in a balanced layout. Don't crowd the elements to one side or the other.	
Flow. Elements on your slides should guide your audience's eyes from one point to another in a natural progression. Think of reading a line of text on the page. Your eye is naturally led from one word to the next. Lay out the elements on a slide using the same principle of leading the eye smoothly from one element to another.	
Distinction. If all elements on your slides are the same size, nothing will stand out to your audience. Stress important elements by making them slightly larger than other elements.	
Recurrence. Repeat design elements (such as backgrounds, slide title styles, and bullet styles) throughout a presentation to give your presentation a unified and professional look.	

In addition to these design principles, there are some basic dos and don'ts to follow when designing presentations:

	Do	Don't
Color choice	Use PowerPoint's built-in color themes.	Use too many colors or colors that do not work well together.
Text amount	Use short bullet points.	Use long paragraphs of text.
Text size	Use large fonts.	Use 10 pt. or 11 pt. fonts.
Animation	Animate important elements for emphasis.	Animate every element on a slide.
Slides	Keep the number of slides to a minimum (10 to 20 slides at the most).	Create a slide for every minor point in the presentation.
Presentation	Make unrehearsed comments.	Read your slides word for word.

tips & tricks

Use the presentation templates available from Office.com as a starting point for your presentations. Many of these templates come with built-in styles and slides that incorporate the design principles discussed here. To learn more about PowerPoint templates see the topic *Creating a New Presentation Using a Template* later in this chapter.

tell me more

Guy Kawasaki, a well-known authority in the software field, developed the *10/20/30 rule* for PowerPoint design. This rule states that PowerPoint presentations should have no more than 10 slides, take no longer than 20 minutes, and should not use fonts smaller than 30 points. You can read his blog at http://blog.guykawasaki.com/.

0.5 Opening an Existing Presentation

Opening a presentation retrieves it from storage and displays it on your computer screen.

To open an existing presentation:

1. Click the **File** tab to open Backstage view.
2. Click **Open**.

3. The *Open* dialog box appears. If necessary, navigate to find the folder location where the presentation you want is stored.
4. Select the presentation name in the large list box.
5. Click the **Open** button in the dialog box.

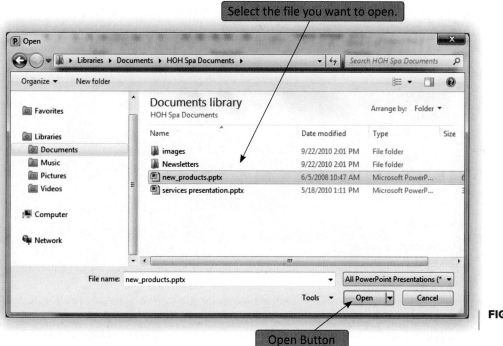

Select the file you want to open.

Open Button

FIGURE PP 0.13

0.6 Understanding Security Warnings in PowerPoint

When you download a presentation from a location that PowerPoint considers potentially unsafe, it opens automatically in Protected View. **Protected View** provides a read-only format that protects your computer from becoming infected by a virus or other malware. Potentially unsafe locations include the Internet, e-mail messages, or a network location.

Files that are opened in Protected View display a yellow warning bar at the top of the window, below the Ribbon. To disable Protected View, click the **Enable Editing** button in the yellow warning bar.

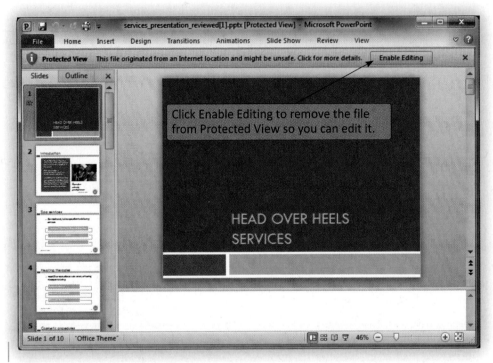

FIGURE PP 0.14

---

tips & tricks

To learn more about the security settings in PowerPoint 2010, open the Trust Center and review the options.

---

tell me **more**

You can modify the Protected View settings to add or delete specific locations or types of locations.

To review or modify the Protected View settings for PowerPoint:

1. Click the **File** tab.

2. If you are currently in Protected View, the *Info* tab will include a link to go to the Protected View settings. If you are not currently in Protected View, click the **Options** button to open the *PowerPoint Options* dialog.

3. Click **Trust Center,** and then click the **Trust Center Settings** button.

4. The *Trust Center* dialog opens. Click **Protected View** to enable or disable Protected View for different locations such as the Internet and Outlook attachments.

5. To exempt specific locations from Protected View, click **Trusted Locations,** and add the locations you trust (such as secure network locations).

0.7 Creating a New Blank Presentation

When you open Microsoft PowerPoint from the *Start* menu, a new blank presentation appears on your screen ready for you to begin work. But what if you want to create another new presentation? Will you need to exit the program and then launch it again? The **New** command allows you to create new presentations without exiting and reopening the program.

To create a new blank presentation:

1. Click the **File** tab to open Backstage view.
2. Click **New.**
3. Under the *Home* section, the *Blank presentation* option is selected by default. To create a new blank presentation, click the **Create** button beneath the preview of the blank presentation.

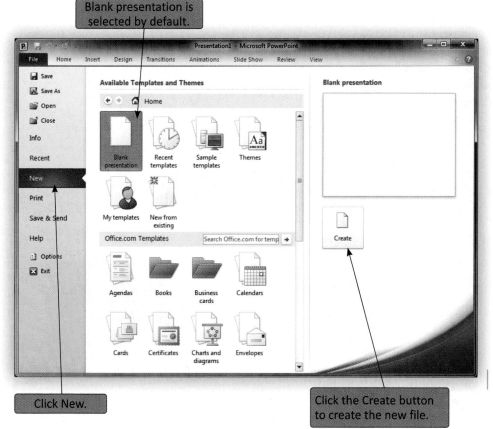

FIGURE PP 0.15

To bypass the Backstage view and create a new blank presentation, press Ctrl + N on the keyboard.

try **this**

0.8 Creating a New Presentation Using a Template

A **template** is a presentation with predefined settings that you can use as a pattern to create a new file of your own. Using a template makes creating a fully formatted and designed new presentation easy, saving you time and effort. There are templates available for full presentations or single slides. You can use templates to create business presentations, medical and health care presentations, and highly sophisticated slides.

To create a new presentation from a template:

1. Click the **File** tab to open Backstage view.
2. Click **New.**
3. Notice that the entire right pane is labeled *Available Templates.* Even the *Blank presentation* option is considered a template. The *Home* section gives you access to all the templates located on your computer. The *Office.com* section gives you access to hundreds of templates available from Office.com, but you must have an active Internet connection to download a template from this section.

4. To find a template from Office.com, click the **PowerPoint presentations and slides** category.
5. Click one of the subcategories to view its templates.
6. Click each template image to see a preview of the template.
7. When you find the template you want to use, click the **Download** button.
8. A new presentation opens, prepopulated with all of the template elements.

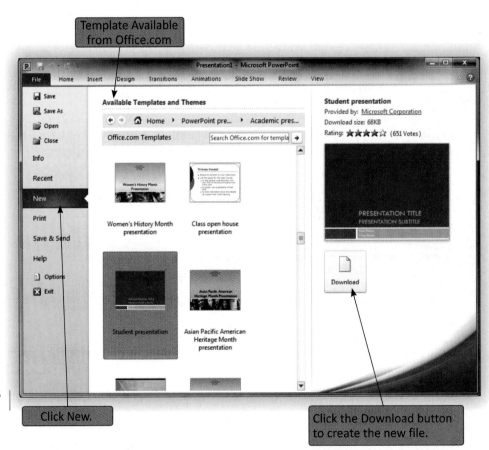

FIGURE PP 0.16

Template Available from Office.com

Click New.

Click the Download button to create the new file.

---

tell me **more**   Microsoft PowerPoint includes a set of templates that are copied to your computer when you install the application. These templates are always available from the *Home* section of the *Available Templates* page, in the *Sample templates* category.

0.9 Modifying Presentation Properties

Presentation Properties provide information about a presentation such as the location of the presentation, the number of slides in the presentation, when the presentation was created and when it was last modified, the title, and the author. Properties also include keywords, referred to as **tags,** that are useful for grouping common files together or for searching. All this information about a file is referred to as **metadata.**

To view a presentation's properties, click the **File** tab to open Backstage view. Properties are listed at the far right of the *Info* tab.

To add keywords to a presentation, click the text box next to *Tags* and type keywords that describe the presentation, separating each word with a comma.

The Author property is added automatically using the name entered when you installed and registered PowerPoint. You can change the author name or add more names by editing the Author property.

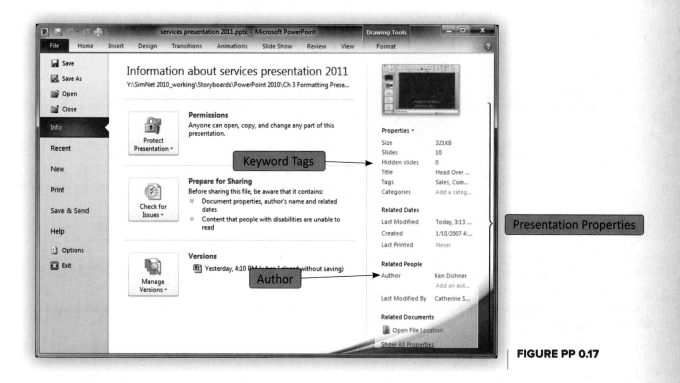

FIGURE PP 0.17

---

tips & tricks

Some presentation properties are generated automatically by Windows and cannot be edited by the user, such as the date the file was created and the size of the file.

tell me **more**

The Windows Vista and Windows 7 operating systems take advantage of the enhanced properties in Office 2010 documents by allowing you to search for files based on metadata, including author and keywords. When you select a file in the Explorer, its metadata are displayed in the *Details* pane.

0.10 Using Cut, Copy, and Paste

The *Cut, Copy,* and *Paste* commands are used to move text and other objects within a presentation and from one presentation to another. Text or an object that is **cut** is removed from the presentation and placed on the Office Clipboard for later use. The **Copy** command places a duplicate of the selected text or object on the Clipboard without changing the presentation. The **Paste** command is used to insert text or an object from the Clipboard into a presentation.

To move text within a presentation:

1. Select the text to be cut or copied.

    On the *Home* tab, in the *Clipboard* group, click the appropriate button:

Cut

or

Copy

2. Place the cursor where you want to insert the text from the Clipboard.

3. In the *Clipboard* group, click the **Paste** button.

These same steps apply whether you are cutting, copying, and pasting text, pictures, shapes, video files, or any type of object in a PowerPoint presentation.

FIGURE PP 0.18

When you cut or copy items, they are placed on the **Office Clipboard**. The Office Clipboard can store up to 24 items. When you use the *Paste* command, the item most recently added to the Clipboard is pasted into the current presentation. If you want to cut or copy multiple items and then paste them in different places in your presentation, open the Office Clipboard by clicking the **dialog launcher** in the *Clipboard* group. Next to each item in the Clipboard is an icon that identifies the application from which the item originated (Word, Excel, PowerPoint, etc.). From the *Clipboard* task pane, click any item to paste it into the current presentation.

tips & tricks

The Office Clipboard is common across all Office applications—so you can cut text from a Word document and then paste that text into an Excel spreadsheet or copy a chart from Excel into a PowerPoint presentation.

try **this**

To apply the *Cut, Copy,* or *Paste* command, you can also use the following shortcuts:

> **Cut** = Press `Ctrl` + `X` on the keyboard, or right-click and select **Cut.**
> **Copy** = Press `Ctrl` + `C` on the keyboard, or right-click and select **Copy.**
> **Paste** = Press `Ctrl` + `V` on the keyboard, or right-click and select **Paste.**

tell me **more**

The *Paste* button has two parts—the top part of the button pastes the topmost contents of the Clipboard into the current presentation. If you click the bottom part of the button (the *Paste* button arrow), you can control how the item is pasted. Each type of object has different paste options. For example, if you are pasting text, you may have options to keep the source formatting, use the current presentation's theme, or paste only the text without any formatting. Move your mouse over the icon for each paste option to see a preview of how the paste would look, and then click the icon for the paste option you want.

0.11 Using Paste Special

Using the **Paste Special** command, an object from another Office application (for example, an Excel spreadsheet) can be inserted into a PowerPoint slide. When pasting source material from another program, you have two choices:

Linked objects—Linked data are stored in the source file. Information in a linked object is updated if the source file is edited. The destination file stores only the location of the source file and displays a representation of the linked data. Double-click the linked object to open the source file.

Embedded objects—Once pasted into your PowerPoint presentation, the data are independent of the original source. Information in an embedded object does not change if you modify the source file. Double-click the embedded object to edit it within the PowerPoint presentation (using the source program, but not the source file).

To use the *Paste Special* command:

1. Copy the object you want to paste.
2. On the *Home* tab, in the *Clipboard* group, click the **Paste** button arrow and select **Paste Special. . .**
3. Select a format for pasting the object in the *As* box. Different formats are available depending on the source of the pasted material.
4. If you want to paste the material as a link, click the **Paste link** radio button.
5. Click **OK**.

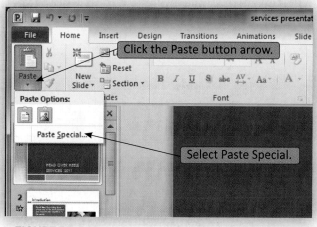

FIGURE PP 0.19

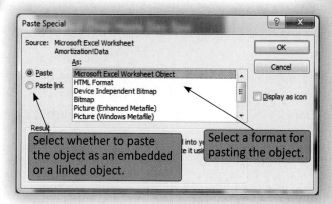

FIGURE PP 0.20

---

tips & tricks

The *Paste Special* options available vary depending on the type of source material. Some objects may only be available to paste as an embedded object, not a linked object.

tell me more

Information in a linked object is updated every time you open the presentation. To update an object manually, right-click the object and select **Update Link**.

0.12 Using Undo and Redo

If you make a mistake when working, the **Undo** command allows you to reverse the last action you performed. The **Redo** command allows you to reverse the *Undo* command and restore the file to its previous state. The Quick Access Toolbar gives you immediate access to both commands.

To undo the last action taken, click the **Undo** button on the Quick Access Toolbar.

To redo the last action taken, click the **Redo** button on the Quick Access Toolbar.

To undo multiple actions at the same time:

1. Click the arrow next to the *Undo* button to expand the list of your most recent actions.

2. Click an action in the list.

3. The action you click will be undone, along with all the actions completed after that. In other words, your presentation will revert to the state it was in before that action.

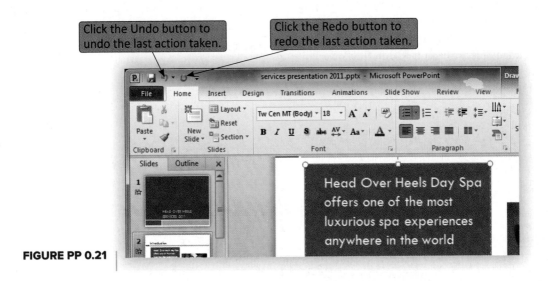

Click the Undo button to undo the last action taken.

Click the Redo button to redo the last action taken.

FIGURE PP 0.21

try **this**

To undo an action, you can also press Ctrl + Z on the keyboard.
To redo an action, you can also press Ctrl + Y on the keyboard.

0.13 Using Find and Replace

The **Find** command in PowerPoint allows you to locate specific instances of text in your presentation. With the *Find* command, you can find instances of a word or phrase throughout a presentation.

To find a word or phrase in a presentation:

1. On the *Home* tab, in the *Editing* group, click the **Find** button.
2. Type the word or phrase you want to find in the *Find what:* box.

3. Click **Find Next** to find the first instance of the word or phrase.
4. Click **Find Next** again to find the next instance.

The **Replace** command allows you to locate specific instances of text in your presentation and replace them with different text. With the *Replace* command, you can replace words or phrases one instance at a time or all at once throughout the presentation.

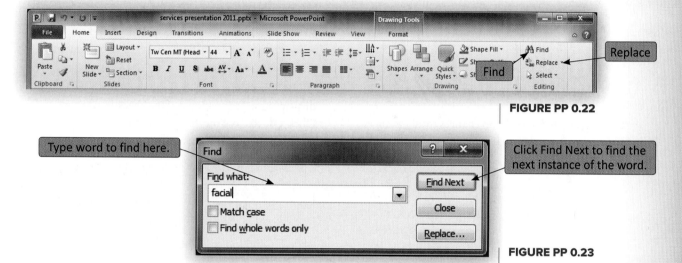

FIGURE PP 0.22

Type word to find here.

Click Find Next to find the next instance of the word.

FIGURE PP 0.23

To replace instances of a word in a presentation:

1. On the *Home* tab, in the *Editing* group, click the **Replace** button.
2. Type the word or phrase you want to change in the *Find what:* box.
3. Type the new text you want in the *Replace with:* box.
4. Click the **Find Next** button to find the first instance of the text.

5. Click **Replace** to replace just that one instance of the text.
6. Click **Replace All** to replace all instances of the text.
7. PowerPoint displays a message telling you how many replacements it made. Click **OK** in the message that appears.
8. To close the *Replace* dialog box, click the **Close** button.

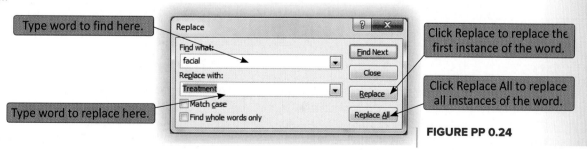

Type word to find here.

Type word to replace here.

Click Replace to replace the first instance of the word.

Click Replace All to replace all instances of the word.

FIGURE PP 0.24

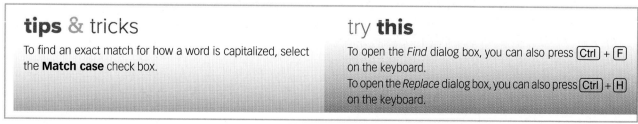

tips & tricks

To find an exact match for how a word is capitalized, select the **Match case** check box.

try **this**

To open the *Find* dialog box, you can also press Ctrl + F on the keyboard.

To open the *Replace* dialog box, you can also press Ctrl + H on the keyboard.

0.14 Checking Spelling

Regardless of the amount of work you put into a presentation, a spelling error or typo can make the entire presentation appear sloppy and unprofessional. All the Office applications include a built-in spelling checker. In PowerPoint, the *Spelling* command analyzes your entire presentation for spelling errors. It presents any errors it finds in a dialog box, enabling you to make decisions about how to handle each error or type of error in turn.

To check a presentation for spelling errors:

1. Click the **Review** tab.
2. In the *Proofing* group, click the **Spelling** button.
3. The first spelling error appears in the *Spelling* dialog box.
4. Review the spelling suggestions and then select an action:

   > Click **Ignore Once** to make no changes to this instance of the word.

   > Click **Ignore All** to make no changes to all instances of the word.

> Click **Add** to make no changes to this instance of the word and add it to the main dictionary, so future uses of this word will not show up as misspellings. When you add a word to the main dictionary, it is available for all of the Office applications.

> Click the correct spelling in the *Suggestions* list, and click **Change** to correct just this instance of the misspelling in your presentation.

> Click the correct spelling in the *Suggestions* list, and click **Change All** to correct all instances of the misspelling in your presentation.

5. After you select an action, the spelling checker automatically advances to the next suspected spelling error.

6. When the spelling checker finds no more errors, it displays a message telling you the check is complete. Click **OK** to close the dialog and return to your presentation.

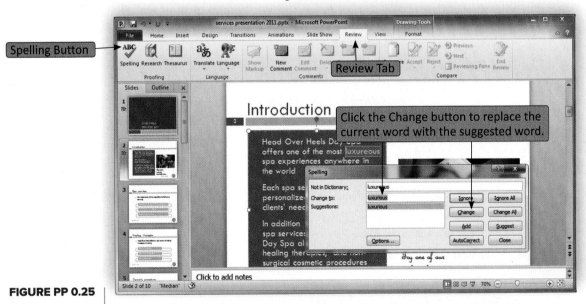

FIGURE PP 0.25

---

tips & tricks

Whether or not you use the Spelling tool, you should always proofread your files. Spelling checkers are not infallible, especially if you misuse a word yet spell it correctly—for instance, writing "bored" instead of "board."

If you misspell a word often, the next time the spelling checker catches the misspelling, use this trick: Click the correct spelling in the *Suggestions* list and then click the **Auto-Correct** button. Now, when you type the misspelled version of the word, it will be corrected automatically as you type.

tell me **more**

If you have repeated the same word in a sentence, Power-Point will flag the second instance of the word as a possible error. In the *Spelling* dialog box, the *Change* button will switch to a *Delete* button. Click the **Delete** button to remove the duplicate word.

try **this**

To open the *Spelling* dialog box, you can also press the F7 key.

0.15 Saving a Presentation

As you work on a new presentation, it is displayed on-screen and stored in your computer's memory. However, it is not permanently stored until you save it as a file to a specific location. The first time you save a presentation, the *Save As* dialog box will open. Here you can enter a file name, select the file type, and choose where to save the presentation.

To save a presentation for the first time:

1. Click the **Save** button on the Quick Access Toolbar.
2. The *Save As* dialog box appears.
3. If necessary, navigate to the location where you want to save the presentation.
4. Click in the *File name:* box and type a file name.
5. Click the **Save** button.

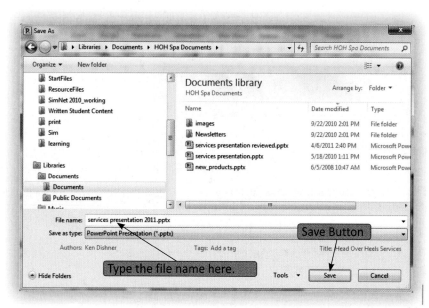

FIGURE PP 0.26

The next time you save this presentation, it will be saved with the same file name and to the same location automatically. The *Save As* dialog will not open again.

As you are working with presentations, be sure to *save often!* Although PowerPoint 2010 includes a recovery function, it is not foolproof. If you lose power or your computer crashes, you may lose all the work done on the presentation since the last save.

tips & tricks

The screenshot shown here is from PowerPoint 2010 running on the Microsoft Windows 7 operating system. Depending on the operating system you are using, the *Save As* dialog box will appear somewhat different. However, the basic steps for saving a presentation are the same regardless of which operating system you are using.

try this

To save a presentation, you can also:

> Press Ctrl + S on the keyboard.
> Click the **File** tab, and then select **Save**.

To open the *Save As* dialog box, you can also click the **File** tab, and then select **Save As.**

tell me more

Beginning with PowerPoint 2007, Microsoft changed the file format for PowerPoint presentations. Presentations created with PowerPoint 2007 and PowerPoint 2010 will not work with older versions of PowerPoint. If you want to share your presentations with people who are using PowerPoint 2003 or older, you should save the presentations in a different file format.

1. Click the **File** tab.
2. Click **Save As.**
3. The *Save As* dialog opens. Click the arrow at the end of the *Save as type:* box to expand the list of available file types.
4. To ensure compatibility with older versions of PowerPoint, select *PowerPoint 97-2003 Presentation.*

0.16 Using Help

If you don't know how to perform a task, you can look it up in the Microsoft PowerPoint Help system. The Help system includes several ways of displaying help topics, including articles, online training, and videos. When Microsoft Power-Point Help first opens, the Home page displays. From the Home page, you can click any of the links to learn more about that topic. If you are looking for specific information, use the search box at the top of the Help window.

To search for a topic using the Microsoft PowerPoint Help system:

1. Click the **Microsoft PowerPoint Help** button. It is located at the far right of the Ribbon.
2. In the *Type words to search for* box, type a word or phrase describing the topic you want help with.
3. Click the **Search** button.
4. A list of results appears.
5. Click a result to display the help topic.

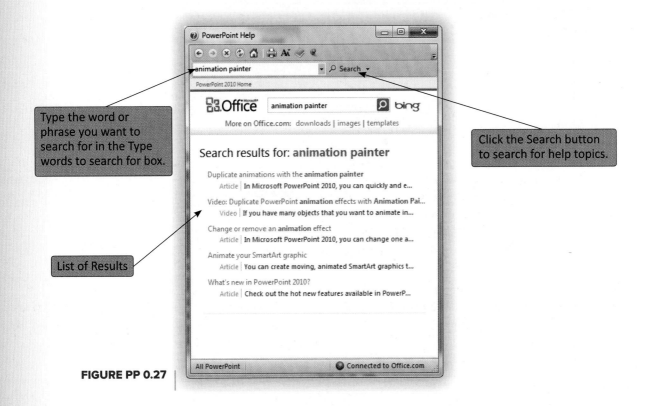

FIGURE PP 0.27

---

tips & tricks

At the bottom right of the Help window there is a button indicating whether you are connected to Office.com or whether you are working offline. If you are working offline (and not connected to Office.com), Help is still available, but it is limited to the topics that are installed as part of the Office applications. If you are connected to Office.com, the Help system adds material from the Office.com Web site including templates and links to other Web sites.

tell me **more**

The Help toolbar is located at the top of the Help window. This toolbar includes buttons for navigating between screens, reloading the current screen, and returning to the Help Home page. Click the printer icon on the toolbar to print the current topic. Click the pushpin icon to keep the Help window always on top of the Microsoft PowerPoint window.

try **this**

To open the Help window, you can also press F1 on the keyboard.

0.17 Closing a Presentation

Closing a presentation removes it from your computer screen and stores the last-saved version for future use. If you have not saved your latest changes, PowerPoint will prevent you from losing work by asking if you want to save the changes you made before closing.

To close a presentation and save your latest changes:

1. Click the **File** tab to open Backstage view.
2. Click the **Close** button.

3. If you have made no changes since the last time you saved the presentation, it will close immediately. If changes have been made, PowerPoint displays a message box asking if you want to save the changes you made before closing.

   〉 Click **Save** to save the changes.
   〉 Click **Don't Save** to close the presentation without saving your latest changes.
   〉 Click **Cancel** to keep the presentation open.

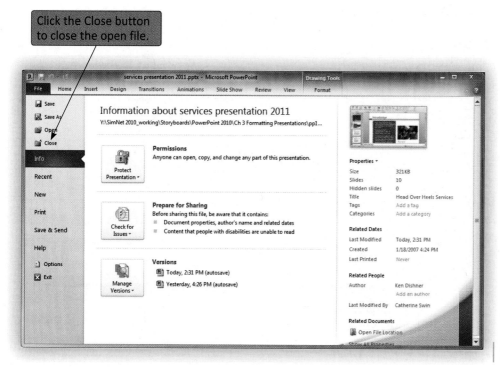

FIGURE PP 0.28

try **this**　　To close a presentation, you can also press Ctrl + W on the keyboard.

0.18 Exiting PowerPoint

When you close a presentation, Microsoft PowerPoint stays open so you can open another presentation to edit or begin a new presentation. Often, when you are finished working on a presentation, you want to close the presentation *and* close Microsoft PowerPoint at the same time. In this case, you will want to *exit* Microsoft PowerPoint.

To exit Microsoft PowerPoint:

1. Click the **File** tab to open Backstage view.
2. Click the **Exit** button.

3. If you have made no changes since the last time you saved the presentation, PowerPoint will close immediately. If changes have been made, PowerPoint displays a message box asking if you want to save the changes you made before exiting.

> Click **Save** to save the changes.
> Click **Don't Save** to exit PowerPoint without saving your latest changes.

FIGURE PP 0.29

Click the Exit button to close the application.

tips & tricks

Click **Cancel** in the message box to not exit the application. This action keeps PowerPoint and all presentations open.

try **this**

To exit PowerPoint, you can:

> Click the ▬X▬ in the upper-right corner of the application window.
> Right-click the title bar of the application window, and select **Close**.

projects

Skill Review 0.1

In this project you will be taking on the role of a high school teacher. You will be preparing a presentation for the first day of class to lay out for your students your classroom expectations.

1. Start Microsoft PowerPoint 2010 as follows:

   If a shortcut has been installed on your desktop, you can double-click the **PowerPoint** icon to launch the application.

   Or use the *Start* menu.

   If you have recently been using PowerPoint a lot, Microsoft PowerPoint 2010 will be on the *Start* menu, and you may click it.

   If you do not see Microsoft PowerPoint 2010 on the *Start* menu:

   a. In the *Start menu* search box, type: **PowerPoint**

   b. Click **Microsoft PowerPoint 2010.**

2. Use Microsoft PowerPoint 2010 Help:

   a. Click the **Microsoft PowerPoint Help** button. It is a blue circle with a question mark, located at the far right of the Ribbon.

   b. In the *Search* box at the top of the Help window, type **PowerPoint templates** and click the **Search** button.

   c. Click the article **What is a PowerPoint template?**

   d. Read the article to learn about PowerPoint templates. When you are finished, close the Help window.

3. Create a new presentation using a template:

   a. Click the **File** tab to open Backstage view.

   b. Click **New.**

   c. In the *Office.com* section you have access to hundreds of templates available from Office.com, but you must have an active Internet connection to download a template from this section. To find a template from Office.com, click the **PowerPoint presentations and slides** icon.

   d. Click the **Academic presentations** subcategory folder to view templates related to education.

   e. Click each template image to see a preview of the template. In this case, scroll down and click **Classroom expectations presentation.**

   f. If you don't find this template by browsing the folders, try using the *Search Office.com for templates* box. Type in: **classroom expectations**. Press the **Enter** key.

   g. When you find the template, *Classroom expectations presentation,* click the **Download** button. *Note:* Be sure to select the *Classroom expectations presentation* option and not the *Classroom Expectations* option.

   h. A new presentation opens, containing all the template elements.

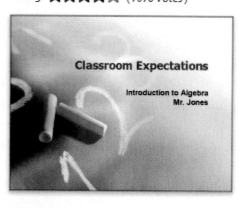

FIGURE PP 0.30

4. Save the presentation:

a. Click the **Save** button on the Quick Access Toolbar.

b. The *Save As* dialog box appears.

c. Navigate to the location where you will be saving your completed presentations.

d. Click in the *File name:* box, and type a file name:

`[your initials]PP_SkillReview_0-1.`

e. Click the **Save** button.

5. Use the Ribbon:

a. Select the title text: *Classroom Expectations.*

b. On the *Home* tab, in the *Font* group, click the **Increase Font Size** button.

6. Use find and replace:

a. On the *Home* tab, in the *Editing* group, click the **Replace** button.

b. In the *Find what:* box, type: `coursework`

c. In the *Replace with:* box, type: `homework`

d. Click the **Replace All** button. A message should appear noting two replacements were made. Click **OK.**

e. In the *Find what:* box, replace the existing text with: `due dates`

f. In the *Replace with:* box, replace the existing text with: `deadlines`

g. Click the **Replace All** button. A message should appear noting two replacements were made. Click **OK.**

h. Click the **Close** button to close the *Replace* dialog box.

7. Close and save the presentation, but leave PowerPoint open to continue the exercise.

a. Click the **File** tab to open Backstage view.

b. Click the **Close** button.

c. Click **Save** in the message box to save the changes.

8. Create a new blank presentation:

a. Click the **File** tab to open Backstage view.

b. Click **New.**

c. Under the *Home* section, the *Blank presentation* option is selected by default.

d. Click the **Create** button beneath the preview of the blank presentation.

e. Click in the slide. In the title box, click and enter your name. Use just your title and last name. Do not type your first name.

f. In the subtitle box, click and enter `Algebra I` as the course title.

9. Copy your name and course title to the Office Clipboard:

a. On the *Home* tab, in the *Clipboard* group, click the Clipboard dialog box launcher.

b. On your slide, select your name, click the **Copy** button or use the **Ctrl + C** shortcut. You should see your name on the Clipboard.

c. Select your course title, and click **Copy.** This too will show on the Clipboard.

10. Create another new presentation using a template:

a. Click the **File** tab to open Backstage view.

b. Click **New.**

c. In the *Search Office.com for templates* box, enter: `Churchill`

d. When you find the template you want to use, in this case, the *Winston Churchill quote slide,* click the **Download** button.

e. A new presentation opens containing the one Churchill quote slide.

11. Copy the Churchill quote slide:

    a. Click the thumbnail in the *Slides* pane on the left.

    b. On the *Home* tab, in the *Clipboard* group, click the **Copy** button.

12. Open *[your initials]PP_SkillReview_0-1* presentation:

    a. Click the **File** tab to open Backstage view. Click **Open.**

    b. The *Open* dialog box appears. If necessary, navigate to find the folder location where the presentation you want is stored.

    c. Select the presentation name in the large list box. In this case select *[your initials] PP_SkillReview_0-1*.

    d. Click the **Open** button in the dialog box.

13. Paste the Churchill quote slide into the *[your initials]PP_SkillReview_0-1* presentation:

    a. On the left, in the *Slides* pane, click the first slide.

    b. Click **Paste.** You will see that the white quote text does not work well on the white background of the slide design theme. Click the **Undo** button on the Quick Access Toolbar.

    c. On the left, in the *Slides* pane, click the first slide.

    d. Click the **small arrow** under the *Paste* button.

    e. Click second paste options button, **Keep Source Formatting.**

    f. The Churchill quote slide has been added to the presentation with its clearly readable, original black background and white text.

14. Paste from the Clipboard:

    a. If necessary, open the Clipboard: Click the Clipboard dialog box launcher on the *Home* tab.

    b. On the title slide, select the teacher's name.

    c. Click your name on the Clipboard to replace the teacher's name with your name.

    d. On the title slide, select the course name, and click your course name on the Clipboard.

15. Modify the presentation properties:

    a. Click the **File** tab to display Backstage view.

    b. The *Info* tab is displayed by default.

    c. On the right side of the window, click the **Add an author** box and type your name.

    d. Click the **Add a category** box and type `class notes`

    e. Click the **Home** tab again to return to your presentation.

16. Check spelling:

    a. Click the **Review** tab.

    b. Click the **Spelling** button in the *Proofing* group.

    c. The first spelling error appears in the *Spelling* dialog box.

    d. Review the spelling suggestions to determine which one is correct.

      • Click **Ignore Once** to skip just this instance of the word, such as your name.

      • Click **Ignore All** to skip all instances of the word, such as your name.

- Click the correct spelling in the *Suggestions:* list, and click **Change** to correct just this instance of this misspelling in your presentation.
- Click the correct spelling in the *Suggestions:* list, and click **Change All** to correct all instances of this misspelling in your presentation.

  e. A message appears to tell you that the spelling check is complete; click **OK.**

  Always proofread your presentations. The *Spell Check* feature is not infallible, especially if you misuse a word, yet spell it correctly.

17. View the presentation:

  a. Click the **Slide Show** tab.

  b. In the *Start Slide Show* group, click the **From Beginning** button.

  c. Click the slide to advance the show, and continue clicking to the end of the show.

18. Save the presentation: Click the **Save** button on the Quick Access Toolbar.

19. Exit PowerPoint and close the presentation:

  a. Click the **File** tab to open Backstage view.

  b. Click the **Exit** button. If prompted, do not save any other open files.

Skill Review **0.2**

In this project you will be taking on the role of a nutritionist. You will be preparing a presentation about good eating habits to use with clients.

1. Start Microsoft PowerPoint 2010 as follows:

  If a shortcut has been installed on your desktop, you can double-click the **PowerPoint** icon to launch the application.

  Or use the *Start* menu.

  If you have recently been using PowerPoint a lot, Microsoft PowerPoint 2010 will be on the *Start* menu, and you may click it. If you do not see Microsoft PowerPoint 2010 on the *Start* menu:

  a. In the *Start menu* search box, type: `PowerPoint`

  b. Click **Microsoft PowerPoint 2010.**

2. Create a new presentation using a template:

  a. Click the **File** tab to open Backstage view.

  b. Click **New.**

  c. In the *Office.com* section, click the **PowerPoint presentations and slides** icon.

  d. Click the **Medical and healthcare presentations** subcategory folder to look for templates related to nutrition.

  e. Click each template image to see a preview of the template. In this case, click **Health and nutrition presentation with video.**

  f. If you don't find this template by browsing the folders, try using the *Search Office.com for templates* box. Type in: `nutrition`. Press the **Enter** key.

  g. When you find the template, *Health and nutrition presentation with video,* click the **Download** button.

  h. A new presentation opens, containing all the template elements.

3. Save the presentation:

  a. Click the **Save** button on the Quick Access Toolbar.

  b. The *Save As* dialog box appears.

  c. Navigate to the location where you will be saving your completed presentations.

d. Click in the *File name:* box, and type a file name:
   [your initials]PP_SkillReview_0-2

e. Click the **Save** button.

4. Use find and replace:

   a. On the *Home* tab, in the *Editing* group, click the **Replace** button.

   b. In the *Find what:* box, type: **friends**

   c. In the *Replace with:* box, type: **clients**

   d. Click the **Replace All** button. A message should appear noting 3 replacements were made. Click **OK**.

   e. Click the **Close** button to close the *Replace* dialog box.

5. Close and save the presentation, but leave PowerPoint open to continue the exercise:

   a. Click the **File** tab to open Backstage view.

   b. Click the **Close** button.

   c. Click **Save** in the message box to save the changes.

6. Create a new blank presentation:

   a. Click the **File** tab to open Backstage view.

   b. Click **New.**

   c. Under the *Home* section, the *Blank presentation* option is selected by default.

   d. Click the **Create** button beneath the preview of the blank presentation.

   e. Click in the slide. In the title box, click and enter your first and last name.

   f. In the subtitle box, click and type the company name **Home Grown Health**

7. Use PowerPoint Help search:

   a. Click the blue question mark to open PowerPoint Help. In the PowerPoint Help window, in the search box, type the word or phrase you want to look for. In this case, search for help about the *Ribbon.*

   b. Click the **Search** button.

   c. A list of results appears.

   d. Click a result to display the help topic.

   e. Click the back arrow to go back to the results, and choose a different help topic to view. Read several of these help topics looking for useful information about the Ribbon in PowerPoint 2010.

   f. Close the Help window.

8. Use the Mini toolbar:

   a. Select your name and then right-click the selected text. The Mini toolbar displays.

   b. Click the **Font Color** button to make the font color red.

   c. Right-click the selected text again. Click the **Bold** button to make it bold.

9. Use the Ribbon:

   a. Select your name.

   b. On the *Home* tab, in the *Font* group, click the **Increase Font Size** button. Click **Increase Font Size** again.

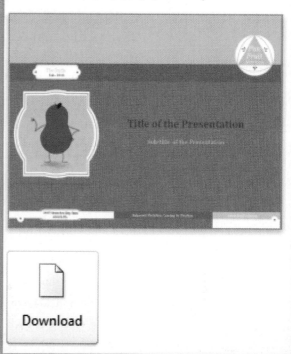

FIGURE PP 0.31

10. Copy your name and the company name to the Office Clipboard:

   a. On the *Home* tab, in the *Clipboard* group, click the Clipboard dialog box launcher.

   b. On your slide, select your name, and click the **Copy** button or use the **Ctrl + C** shortcut. You should see your name on the Clipboard.

   c. Select your company name, and click **Copy.** This too will show on the Clipboard.

11. Open your *[your initials]PP_SkillReview_0-2* presentation:

   a. Click the **File** tab to open Backstage view. Click **Open.**

   b. The *Open* dialog box appears. If necessary, navigate to find the folder location where the presentation you want is stored.

   c. Select the presentation name in the large list box. In this case select *[your initials] PP_SkillReview_0-2.*

   d. Click the **Open** button in the dialog box.

12. Paste from the Clipboard:

   a. If necessary, open the Clipboard: Click the Clipboard dialog box launcher on the *Home* tab.

   b. On the title slide, select the subtitle.

   c. Click your name on the Clipboard to replace the subtitle with your name.

   d. Click **Undo** on the Quick Access Toolbar to try again.

   e. This time, click the arrow at the bottom of the **Paste** button. Choose **Paste Special.**

   f. Scroll down to choose **Unformatted Text.**

   g. Click **OK** to paste the text.

13. Modify the presentation properties:

   a. Click the **File** tab to display Backstage view.

   b. The *Info* tab displays by default.

   c. Click the *Add an author* box and type your name.

   g. Click the *Add a category* box and type **nutrition**

   d. Click the **Home** tab again to return to your presentation.

14. Check spelling:

   a. Click the **Review** Tab.

   b. In the *Proofing* group, click the **Spelling** button.

   c. The first spelling error appears in the *Spelling* dialog box.

   d. The template includes Latin phrases for text placeholders. Choose to ignore all instances of these unknown words.

   e. A message appears to tell you that the spelling check is complete; click **OK.**
   Always proofread your presentations. The *Spell Check* feature is not infallible, especially if you misuse a word yet spell it correctly.

15. View the presentation:

   a. Click the **Slide Show** tab.

   b. In the *Start Slide Show* group, click the **From Beginning** button.

   c. Click the slide to advance the show, and continue clicking to the end of the show.

16. Save the Presentation: Click the **Save** button on the Quick Launch toolbar.

17. Exit PowerPoint and close the presentation:

   a. Click the **File** tab to open Backstage view.

   b. Click the **Exit** button. If prompted, do not save the other file.

In this project you will be taking on the role of a teacher preparing a presentation to use at a parent night for your class of young students.

1. Begin by creating a new blank presentation:

   a. On the title slide enter **Arrowhead Elementary,** your name, **4th grade,** and the date of the parent night, **October 12, 2011**

   b. Use the Ribbon and/or the Mini toolbar to format the text, making it larger or smaller, bold, a different font, and so on, to your taste. Use undo as needed.

   c. Save it as **[your initials] PP_Challenge_0-3_FirstDraft**

   d. Click the **New Slide** button on the *Home* tab of the Ribbon to add a new slide to your presentation.

   e. On the new slide type: **Signed Permission Slips REQUIRED for ALL Field Trips.**

   f. Save and close the first draft presentation file.

2. Create a new presentation using the Office.com template *Back-to-school presentation*. Save it as **[your initials]PP_Challenge_0-3_ ParentNight**. When the message box appears, choose to convert the diagrams in the presentation to shapes.

3. Open *[your initials]PP_Challenge_0-3_ FirstDraft* presentation again.

   a. Use *Copy* and *Paste* commands to copy the name of the text you entered about your presentation into appropriate locations in the presentation created with the template. Experiment with *Paste Special* options to achieve neat and attractive formatting.

   b. Close the first draft presentation.

4. Work in the *[your initials]PP_Challenge_0-3_ParentNight* presentation.

   a. This presentation addresses the student. But you want to use it to address the parents. So use find and replace to replace the word *you* with the words **your child** throughout the presentation, where appropriate.

   b. Use Help to look up: **Add text to a slide.**

   c. On each slide, add or replace text to complete the presentation and customize it to tell about you and your class. Attempt to modify the *My Family* slide, if you like, or delete it, if you prefer.

   d. Check the spelling.

   e. Enter your own name and **parent's night** in the appropriate file properties fields.

5. Save the presentation.

6. Exit PowerPoint.

Back-to-school presentation
Provided by: Microsoft Corporation
Download size: 168KB
Rating: ★★★★☆ (3623 Votes)

Download

FIGURE PP 0.32

In this project you will be creating a teamwork presentation for use with a community group. You will start by creating your own blank presentation and building the presentation from scratch. Then you will decide to try using a template to speed your progress. You will copy what you created yourself into the template-generated presentation and make other changes to customize the presentation to your needs.

1. Begin by creating a new blank presentation.

2. On the title slide, enter **Oak River HOA,** your name, and the date of the presentation.

3. Save it as
   [your initials]PP_Challenge_0-4_FirstDraftTeamwork

   a. Use the Ribbon and/or the Mini toolbar to format the text, making it larger or smaller, bold, a different font, and so forth, to your taste. Use undo as needed.

   b. Save and close the first draft presentation file.

4. Create a new presentation using the *Teamwork Presentation* template from Office.com. Use the same template as shown in Figure PP 0.33. Save it as
   [your initials]PP_Challenge_0-4_Teamwork

Teamwork presentation

Provided by: Microsoft Corporation

Download size: 428KB

Rating: ★★★★☆ (362 Votes)

Teamwork Presentation
Company Name

Download

FIGURE PP 0.33

5. Open your *[your initials]PP_Challenge_0-4_ FirstDraftTeamwork* presentation.

   a. Use *Copy* and *Paste* commands to copy the name of the text you entered about your presentation into the presentation created with the template. Experiment with *Paste Special* options to achieve neat and attractive formatting.

   b. Close the first draft presentation.

6. Work in the *[your initials]PP_Challenge_0-4_Teamwork* presentation.

   a. Use find and replace to replace the word *teamwork* with the phrase **working well together** throughout the presentation. On each slide, add or replace text to customize and complete the presentation.

   b. Use Help to look up: **check spelling**

   c. Check the spelling in the presentation.

   d. Enter your own name and **Oak River HOA** in the appropriate file properties fields.

   e. Save the presentation.

7. Exit PowerPoint.

on your own

In this project you will be preparing a patient education training presentation for staff in a health care organization.

1. Begin by creating a new blank presentation.

   a. On the title slide enter the name of your organization, your name, and the date of the presentation.

   b. Save it as **[your initials]PP_OnYourOwn_0-5_FirstDraft**

   c. Use the Ribbon and/or the Mini toolbar to format the text, making it larger or smaller, bold, a different font, and so forth, to your taste. Use undo as needed.

   d. Save and close the first draft presentation file.

2. Create a new presentation using the *Medical presentation on patient education* template from Office.com. Use the same template as shown in Figure PP 0.34. Save it as `[your initials]PP_OnYourOwn_0-5_PatientEducation`. When the message box appears, choose to convert the diagrams in the presentation to shapes.

3. Open *[your initials]PP_OnYourOwn_0-5_ FirstDraft* presentation.

   a. Use copy and paste to copy the name of the text you entered about your presentation into the presentation created with the template. Experiment with *Paste Special* options to achieve neat and attractive formatting.

   b. Close the first draft presentation.

4. Work in the *[your initials]PP_OnYourOwn_0-5_Patient Education* presentation.

   a. Use find and replace to replace the word *sample* with the word **example** throughout the presentation.

   b. On each slide, add or replace text to complete the presentation and customize it.

   c. Check the spelling.

   d. Enter your own name and your organization name in the appropriate file properties fields.

   e. Save the presentation.

5. In PowerPoint Help look up: `Copy and paste your slides.`

6. Again, create a new presentation using a template. This time choose the template *young plant image slide.*

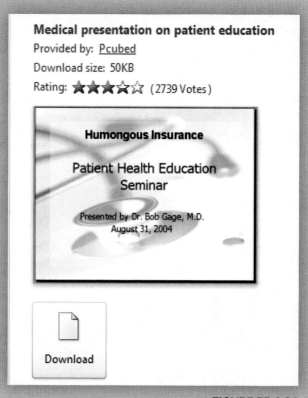

Medical presentation on patient education
Provided by: Pcubed
Download size: 50KB
Rating: ★★★☆ (2739 Votes)

Humongous Insurance

Patient Health Education
Seminar

Presented by Dr. Bob Gage, M.D.
August 31, 2004

Download

FIGURE PP 0.34

7. Cut and paste the plant slide to an appropriate location in the *[your initials] PP_OnYourOwn_0-5_PatientEducation* presentation. You plan to use this slide to discuss the need to nurture each patient's development.

8. Save the *[your initials]PP_OnYourOwn_0-5_PatientEducation* presentation.

9. Exit PowerPoint.

fix it

For this project you will take on the role of a student. You are working with a group to make a presentation for your history class for Black History Month. Your teammate used a template to begin a PowerPoint presentation. He has asked you to complete and perfect the presentation prior to the next group meeting.

1. Open the provided file: *Black History Month.pptx*. Save it as `[your initials]PP_FixIt_0-6`

2. Adjust the text size throughout the presentation, and change the font and color for optimal readability.

3. Make any corrections or additions you see fit.

4. Proofread and check the spelling.

5. Enter your name in the file properties.

6. Use find and replace to replace *Project* with **Presentation**

7. You think the presentation is a bit canned and predictable; you want to add some variety and images. Use PowerPoint Help to look up how to create a presentation from a template and how to copy a slide from one presentation another.

8. Use the content slides templates to generate at least two image and/or quote slides, and then copy and paste them into your group's presentation.

9. Save your group's presentation.

10. Exit PowerPoint.

powerpoint 2010

chapter 1

Getting Started with PowerPoint 2010

In this chapter, you will learn the following skills:

> Use the different view options

> Add slides and sections

> Change slide layouts and add transitions

> Work with the slide master and insert headers and footers

> Add notes for the speaker to use

Skill **1.1**   Introduction to PowerPoint 2010

Skill **1.2**   Understanding Views

Skill **1.3**   Using the Slides Tab

Skill **1.4**   Using the Outline Tab

Skill **1.5**   Adding Slides to Presentations

Skill **1.6**   Adding Sections to Presentations

Skill **1.7**   Changing Slide Layouts

Skill **1.8**   Applying Slide Transitions

Skill **1.9**   Working with the Slide Master

Skill **1.10** Inserting Headers and Footers

Skill **1.11** Adding and Printing Notes

skills

introduction

In this chapter you learn the skills necessary to navigate through and edit a basic PowerPoint 2010 presentation.

1.1 Introduction to PowerPoint 2010

Whether used for a sales pitch or as a teaching tool, a multimedia presentation incorporating graphics, animation, sound, and video is much more compelling than paper handouts or a "talking head" lecture. Microsoft Office PowerPoint 2010 enables you to create robust multimedia presentations. A presentation is made up of a series of slides. Each slide contains content, including text, graphics, audio, and video. You can then manipulate that content by adding transitions, animations, and graphic effects. Before diving in and creating a presentation, you should familiarize yourself with some of PowerPoint's basic features.

When you first start PowerPoint, you will notice the presentation window is divided into three areas:

Slides and Outline Tabs—Display all the slides in the presentation. The *Outline* tab displays only the text content of slides. The *Slides* tab displays thumbnail images of slides.

Slide Pane—Area where you can modify slides, including adding and formatting text, images, SmartArt, tables, charts, and media.

Notes Pane—Area where you can type notes about the current slide displayed in the *Slide* pane. The text you type in the *Notes* pane will not appear when you play your

presentation. These notes can be printed as handouts for your audience or can be used by you during your presentation.

Each slide contains **placeholders** for you to add content to, including

Title—Use to display the title of the presentation or the title for the slide.

Subtitle—Use to display the subtitle of the presentation.

Text—Use to add text to a slide. Be sure to keep your points brief, and use bulleted lists to emphasize text.

SmartArt—Use to add a SmartArt diagram to a slide. SmartArt displays lists in a more graphic format, including, processes, cycles, hierarchical diagrams, and matrices.

Graphic—Add clip art, photographs, or other images to slides.

Charts and Tables—Organize information in a chart or table to give your audience a clear picture of your data.

Media Clips—Add sound and video to your presentation.

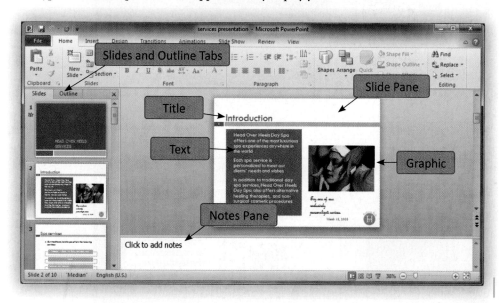

FIGURE PP 1.1

Presentations can be simple or complex, but they all follow some basic steps.

1. **Plan your presentation**—Decide what you want to include and in what order you want to present the information.

2. **Create your slides**—You can create slides from sophisticated templates, or start with blank slides and add formatting and effects to give your presentation a unique look.

3. **Review and rehearse**—Always check your slides for errors. You can also use special effects to add sizzle to your presentation.

4. **Practice**—Practicing your presentation will give you confidence when it comes time to give your presentation in front of an audience.

1.2 Understanding Views

PowerPoint has four main ways to view your presentation: Normal view, Slide Sorter view, Reading view, and Slide Show view. **Normal view** is the view where you will typically create and edit your content. **Slide Sorter view** displays thumbnail pictures of the slides in your presentation and is useful in rearranging the order of slides in a presentation. **Reading view** allows you to run your presentation within the PowerPoint application window. **Slide Show view** displays your slides full screen and allows you to see your presentation the way your audience will.

The easiest way to switch between views is to click one of the view buttons located at the right side of the status bar, near the zoom slider.

Click the **Normal view** button to add or edit content.

Click the **Slide Sorter view** button to view thumbnails of your presentation.

Click the **Reading view** button to view your presentation within the current PowerPoint window.

Click the **Slide Show view** button to view your presentation at full screen as your audience will. To exit Slide Show view, press the Esc key on the keyboard.

FIGURE PP 1.2

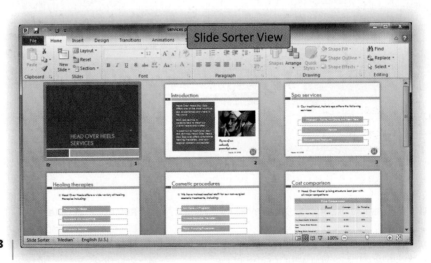

FIGURE PP 1.3

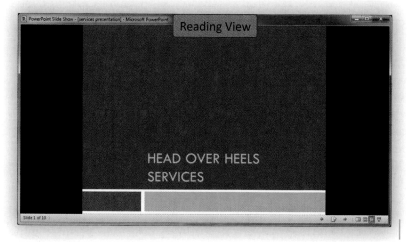

FIGURE PP 1.4

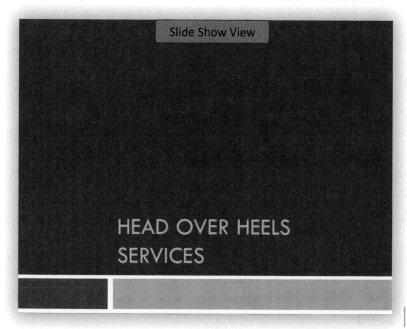

FIGURE PP 1.5

tips & tricks

When you first open a presentation, PowerPoint will display your slides so they fit in the Slide pane. When working in Normal view and Slide Sorter view, you may find you want to change the number of slides displayed onscreen. The **Zoom Bar** (located at the bottom of the PowerPoint window) allows you to change how your slides are displayed in the *Slide* pane. Use the Zoom Bar to magnify your slides to check alignment of text and graphics or to see how your slides will appear when you play your presentation.

try **this**

> To switch views, you can also click the **View** tab and click a view button in the *Presentation Views* group.

> To switch to Slide Show view, you can also click the **Slide Show** tab and click a button in the *Start Slide Show* group.

tell me **more**

In addition to the four main views, PowerPoint also includes the following:

Notes Page view—Allows you to add notes for each slide in your presentation. Each slide appears on its own screen with a large text area for your notes about the slide. The text you type in Notes Page view will not appear when you are playing your presentation. However, you can choose to print your notes along with your slides to hand out to your audience.

Master views—Includes Slide Master view, Handout Master view, and Notes Master view. The master views contain universal settings for the presentation. If you want to make changes that will affect the entire presentation, you should use the master view.

1.3 Using the Slides Tab

The Normal view in PowerPoint includes the *Outline* tab and the *Slides* tab to help you navigate between and work with slides. The **Slides tab** displays thumbnails of all your slides. Use the *Slides* tab to quickly navigate between slides, rearrange the slide order, and review and edit content. In order to make changes to a specific slide, it must first be displayed in the *Slide* pane.

To navigate to a slide using the *Slides* tab:

1. Verify that the **Slides** tab is displayed.
2. Click the thumbnail of the slide you want to display.
3. The slide appears in the *Slide* pane ready for editing.

To edit text on a slide:

1. Click the placeholder with the text you want to change.
2. Click and drag across the text to select it.
3. Type the new text for the placeholder.
4. Click outside the placeholder to deselect it.

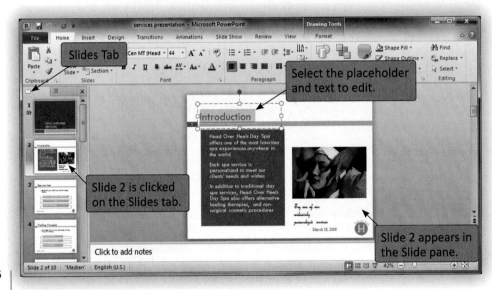

FIGURE PP 1.6

1.4 Using the Outline Tab

When working on a presentation it's easy to focus on the graphic elements of your slides. Adding graphics, transitions, and animations may seem important, but the foundation of an effective presentation is a focused message. When working with text on slides, it is a good idea to keep the amount of text on each slide balanced and to concentrate on one clear message per slide. The Outline tab displays the text from your slides in outline view, allowing you to concentrate on the text aspect of your slides without being distracted by the graphic elements. Use the *Outline* tab to enter and edit your text directly in the outline.

To use the *Outline* tab:

1. Click the tab labeled **Outline.**
2. Click in the text you want to change.
3. Type the new text for the slide.
4. Click the tab labeled **Slides.**
5. View the text you added in the slide's design.

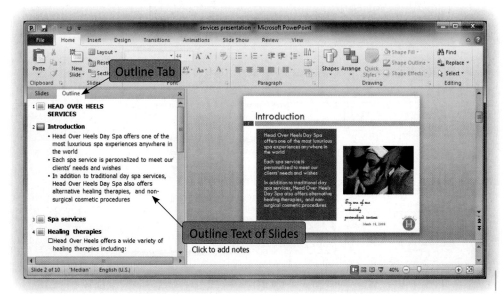

FIGURE PP 1.7

tips & tricks

If your slides include a large amount of text, you can make the *Outline* tab wider to make it easier to write and edit your content. To change the width of the *Outline* tab, place your cursor over the right edge of the pane. When the cursor changes to the resize cursor, click and drag the mouse to the right to make the pane wider or to the left to make the pane narrower.

tell me more

When the *Slides* or *Outline* tab is displayed, the *Slide* pane is sized to display the current slide in its entirety. If you resize either tab, the slide will be resized to fit in the newly sized *Slide* pane. By default, the *Outline* tab is wider than the *Slides* tab to accommodate the slides' text.

1.5 Adding Slides to Presentations

A presentation consists of several slides filled with text and graphics. If you start with a template, your presentation will already include several slides ready to add content. But what if you need to add more information to your presentation? How do you add more slides? PowerPoint makes it easy.

To add a slide to a presentation:

1. On the *Home* tab, in the *Slides* group, click the **New Slide** button arrow.

2. Select a slide layout from the *New Slide* gallery.

3. Add your content to the slide.

4. Continue adding and modifying slides until your presentation is complete.

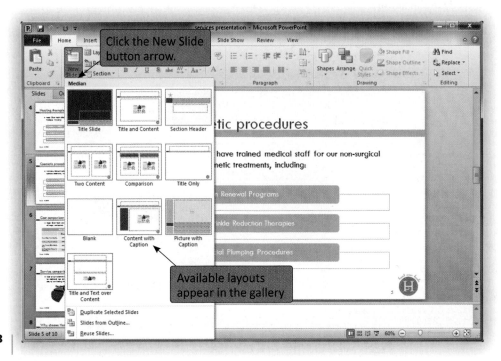

FIGURE PP 1.8

tips & tricks

When you add slides through the *New Slide* gallery, each slide layout includes design elements from the presentation's theme. This helps in creating a consistent look and feel for the entire presentation. If you switch themes, the look of the new slide layouts will change to match that theme.

tell me **more**

There are a number of slide layouts for you to choose from including title only slides, blank slides, title and content slides, side by side content slides, picture with caption slides, and content with caption slides.

try **this**

To add a slide to a presentation, you can also:

> Click the top half of the **New Slide** button.

> Press Ctrl + M on the keyboard.

Note: When you use either of these methods, the new slide added to the presentation will use the same layout as the last slide you added.

1.6 Adding Sections to Presentations

As you work on a presentation and add more slides, you may find it difficult to find a specific slide using the *Slides* tab. Scrolling through 20, 30, or even 40 thumbnails to find the content you are looking for is not a very efficient way to work. PowerPoint 2010 includes the ability to add **sections** to your presentation. You can use sections to create smaller groups of slides within your presentation to help you better organize your work. After you have added sections to your presentation, you can then hide and show the slides' thumbnails by expanding and collapsing the sections.

To add a section to a presentation:

1. On the *Slides* tab, click the thumbnail of the first slide for the section you want to create.
2. On the *Home* tab, in the *Slides* group, click the **Sections** button and select **Add Section.**
3. PowerPoint creates a new section.
4. To collapse the section and hide its slides, click the triangle next to the section name. To expand the section and show the slides, click the triangle again.

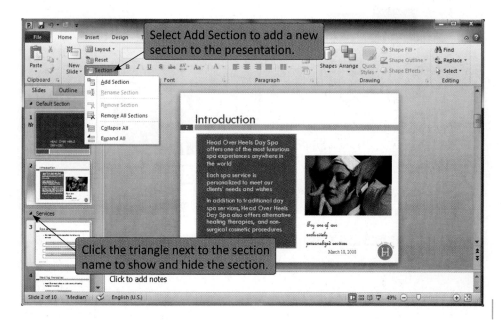

Select Add Section to add a new section to the presentation.

Click the triangle next to the section name to show and hide the section.

FIGURE PP 1.9

tips & tricks

If you have accidentally added a section, you can remove it by clicking the **Sections** button and select **Remove Section.** To quickly remove all the sections from your presentation, click **Remove All Sections** on the menu.

The **Expand All** command shows all the sections and slides in the presentation. The **Collapse All** command hides all the sections and slides in the presentation.

tell me more

When you first add a section to a presentation, it is given the name *Untitled Section.* To rename a section, first select the section to rename. Click the **Section** button and select **Rename Section.** In the *Rename Section* dialog box, type the name for the section and click **Rename.**

try this

› To add a section, you can also right-click a thumbnail on the *Slides* tab and select **Add Section.**

› You can also expand and collapse sections by double-clicking the section name.

1.7 Changing Slide Layouts

After you have created your presentation, you can modify the information displayed on an individual slide. If you add or delete elements, you may want to change the layout of the slide to accommodate the new content. PowerPoint comes with a number of slide layouts for you to use. Choose the one that best suits the content for each slide.

To change the slide layout:

1. Select the slide you want to change.
2. On the *Home* tab, in the *Slides* group, click the **Slide Layout** button.
3. Select a slide layout from the *Slide Layout* gallery.

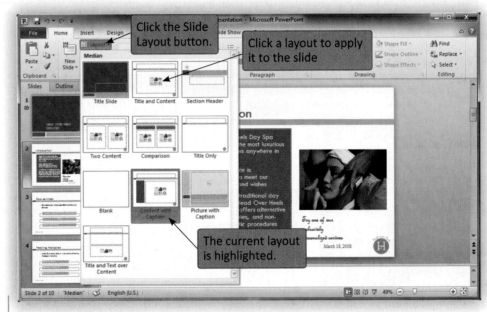

FIGURE PP 1.10

tips & tricks

Once you have selected a new slide layout, you can move and resize placeholders to fit your content. If you have made a number of changes and decide that you want to undo your changes, you can revert the slide to its original design. Click the **Reset** button on the *Home* tab in the *Slides* group to return the slide layout to its default layout.

tell me **more**

One way to share slide layouts with others is through a **Slide Library**. A Slide Library contains slides that have been uploaded to a server for others to view and use in their presentations. When you use a slide from a Slide Library in your presentation, the slide maintains a link to the original slide in the library. If the original slide is modified in any way, you will be notified of the change when you open the presentation. You can choose to update the slide, add the changed slide to your presentation, or keep the slide as it currently appears in the presentation. Using Slide Libraries for creating presentations can help ensure that presentation designs are consistent and up-to-date across large organizations.

try **this**

To change the layout of a slide, you can also right-click any area of the *Slide* pane without a placeholder, point to **Layout,** and select a slide layout.

1.8 Applying Slide Transitions

A **transition** is an effect that occurs when one slide leaves the screen and another one appears. Transitions add movement to your presentation and can keep audiences interested, but remember that overusing transitions can be distracting. Add transitions only where they will improve your presentation.

To apply transitions to a slide:

1. Select the slide to which you want to add the transition.
2. Click the **Transitions** tab.
3. In the *Transition to This Slide* group, click the **More** button and select a transition to apply to the slide.

4. PowerPoint automatically previews the transition for you.
5. Click the **Preview** button to play the transition again.
6. To add a sound effect to a slide, click the arrow next to the *Sound:* box.
7. To add the same transition to all the slides of a presentation, select the slide with the transition you want to apply, and click the **Apply to All** button.

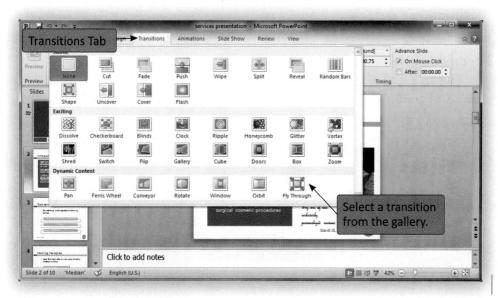

FIGURE PP 1.11

tips & tricks

When you select a transition, PowerPoint applies the default settings for that transition to the slide. You can customize the settings for a transition to create the exact effect you want:

> Click the **Effect Options** button to view the different options for the transition. When you select an option, PowerPoint will automatically play a preview of the new transition.

> Enter a time in seconds in the *Duration:* box or click the up or down arrows to adjust how quickly or slowly the transition happens. Click the **Preview** button to view the new transition speed.

tell me **more**

PowerPoint offers a number of transitions for you to choose from. There are simple fades and dissolves, any number of directional wipes (including shapes and rotations), pushes and covers, stripes and bars, and random transitions. When choosing transitions for your presentation, it is important to keep in mind who your audience will be. If you are presenting in a formal business environment, you will probably want to use more subtle transitions, such as fades and dissolves. If your audience expects more "sizzle" in the presentation, then you may want to choose a complex wipe, such as the Newsflash transition.

try **this**

To apply a transition, you can also click a transition in the *Transition to This Slide* group without opening the *Transitions* gallery.

1.9 Working with the Slide Master

Think of a **slide master** as a slide template that is used throughout your presentation to create a consistent look and feel. Slide masters make it easy to create a standard look throughout an entire presentation by controlling layouts and design elements, such as backgrounds and themes, at the presentation level rather than at the slide level. When you use a slide master to create slides in your presentation, you only need to modify the slide master in Slide Master view to make changes to all the slides in the presentation.

To switch to Slide Master view:

1. Click the **View** tab.
2. In the *Master Views* group, click the **Slide Master** button.
3. PowerPoint switches to Slide Master view. Here you can add more slide masters or new layouts to the existing slide master. You can also modify the slide master or individual layouts within the slide master.
4. Click the **Close Master View** button to return to Normal view.

When you are in Slide Master view, you will notice the second tab on the Ribbon is no longer the *Home* tab, but rather the *Slide Master* tab. The *Slide Master* tab contains the commands for working with the slide master. Specifically, the *Edit Master* group gives you access to the following commands:

Insert Slide Master—Presentations can have more than one slide master. To add another slide master, switch to Slide Master view. On the *Slide Master* tab, click the **Insert Slide Master** button.

Insert Layout—Each slide master contains several layouts that appear in the *New Slide* gallery in Normal view. Click the **Insert Layout** button to add a layout to the master.

Delete Slide—Click the **Delete Slide** button to remove a slide master or layout from the presentation.

Preserve—Click the **Preserve** button to change a master so that it will always be part of the presentation, even if it is not being used. When a master is preserved, a pushpin icon appears next to the slide.

FIGURE PP 1.12

---

tips & tricks

If you want to use the design of your slide master in several presentations, save the slide master as a template (.potx file). Presentations you create using the template will be based on the slide master you saved.

try **this**

To close Slide Master view and return to Normal view, you can also:

> Click the **View** tab. In the *Presentations Views* group, click the **Normal View** button.
> Click the **Normal View** button on the status bar.

tell me **more**

In addition to slide masters, you can create handout masters and notes masters for your presentation. **Handout masters** control how the slides of your presentation look when printed. **Notes masters** control the look of your notes when printed along with the slides. From the Handout Master view and the Notes Master view you can choose to display the header, footer, date, and page number on your printed handouts. You can also change the background of the printed page or add images to the printouts that do not appear in the presentation.

1.10 Inserting Headers and Footers

Headers and **footers** are text that appear on every slide or handout. Typically, headers appear at the top of a handout and footers appear at the bottom. Slides only display footers. Use footers when you want to display the same text on every slide, such as the name of your company. When you add footers to the slide master, they are automatically added to every slide in the presentation.

To add text to the footer of all the slides in a presentation:

1. Verify that the slide master is selected.
2. Click the **Insert** tab.
3. In the *Text* group, click the **Header & Footer** button.
4. On the *Slide* tab of the *Header and Footer* dialog box, select the **Footer** check box.
5. Type the text for the footer in the *Footer* text box.
6. Click the **Apply** button to add the footer to the slide master.

Note: In order to change the footer for the slides associated with a slide master, you must use the *Header and Footer* dialog box. Adding text to the footer box directly on the slide master will not change the footer for the layouts associated with that slide master.

If you want a certain layout to use a different footer, first select the layout you want to change before opening the *Header and Footer* dialog box. When you change the footer, be sure to click the **Apply** button, not the **Apply to All** button.

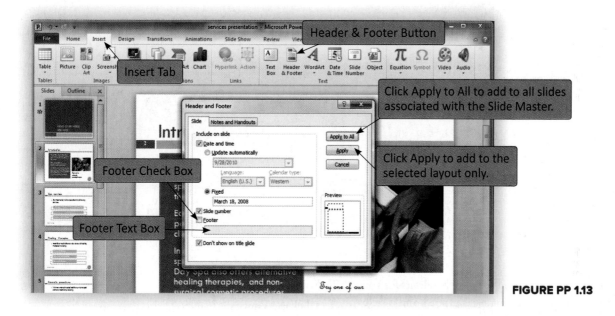

FIGURE PP 1.13

tips & tricks

> To display the date and time on slides, select the **Date and time** check box from the *Slide* tab in the *Header and Footer* dialog box. Click the **Update automatically** radio button to have the date update every time you give the presentation. Click the **Fixed** radio button to have the same date appear every time you present.

> To display the slide number on slides, select the **Slide number** check box.

> If you do not want your footer to display on the title slide of the presentation, select the **Don't show on title slide** check box.

tell me **more**

Notes pages and handouts use different footers than slides. To create a header or footer for your printouts, click the **Notes and Handouts** tab in the *Header and Footer* dialog box. From this tab you can add a header for the printed page, in addition to changing the date and time and footer. You can control whether or not the header, footer, date, or page numbers appear on the printed page from the Handout Master view.

try **this**

To change the header for all slides and layouts, you can also click the **Apply to All** button in the *Header and Footer* dialog box.

1.11 Adding and Printing Notes

Speaker notes are hidden notes you can add to slides. They do not appear as part of the presentation. Speaker notes can be used to help remind you to go to a certain slide in the presentation or to mention a specific detail that may not be included on the slide.

To add speaker notes to slides:

1. Verify you are in Normal view.

2. Click in the *Notes* pane. This is pane at the bottom of the screen with the text *Click to add notes.*

3. Type your note for the slide.

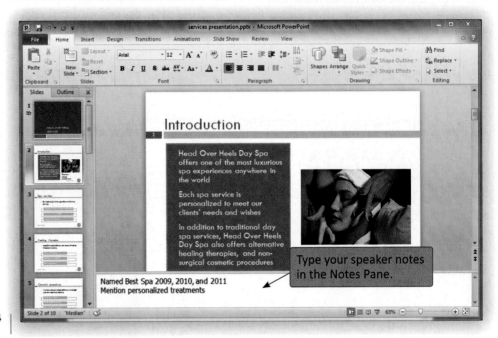

Type your speaker notes in the Notes Pane.

FIGURE PP 1.14

Speaker notes can also be used to create handouts for your audience. You can then print your speaker notes and distribute them to your audience. The Notes view allows you to view how your speaker notes will look when printed. In Notes view, the image of the slide appears at the top of the screen and the speaker notes appear directly below the slide. You can add and format text in Notes view, but you cannot edit the content of the slides.

To switch to Notes view:

1. Click the **View** tab.

2. In the *Presentation Views* group, click the **Notes Page** button.

3. PowerPoint displays your presentation in Notes view.

4. Select the speaker notes text and format the text as you want it to appear when printed.

from the perspective of . . .

TEACHER

Presentations enable me to provide handouts for my students, quickly cover lecture material, and give a professional, visual experience to keep their attention. I can even use presentation software to keep track of my notes by slide as I teach my class.

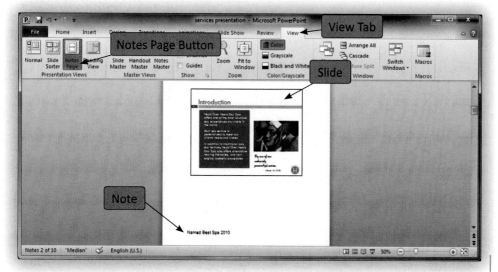

To print your speaker notes:

1. Click the **File** tab.
2. Click the **Print** tab in the Backstage view.
3. Click the first option under *Slides:*.
4. Under *Print Layout*, click **Notes Pages.**
5. Click the **Print** button.

tips & tricks

In PowerPoint 2010 you can use two monitors to display your presentation. When you use two monitors, your audience will see your presentation in Slide Show view, while you will see the presentation in Presenter view. Presenter view allows you to see your notes while you are giving your presentation, making it easier to refer to any notes you have added to slides.

tell me **more**

The **Notes master view** allows you to control how your printed notes pages will look. The Notes master includes placeholders for the header, date, footer, and page number, in addition to a slide image placeholder and a body placeholder. In the body placeholder, you can format the text (changing the font, font size, and other options) of the notes you have entered in the *Notes* pane of the presentation

try **this**

To display the *Print* tab in the Backstage view, you can also press Ctrl + P on the keyboard.

projects

Skill Review **1.1**

In this review, you will use the skills learned in Chapter 1 to edit an existing presentation.

1. Open an existing presentation:

   a. Open Microsoft PowerPoint 2010.

   b. On the *File* tab, click **Open.**

   c. In the *Open* dialog box, navigate to the location of your PowerPoint 2010 student files.

   d. Find *Ch1_Review1_Design_Basics.pptx* and double-click the file to open it.

   e. On the *File* tab, click the **Save As** option.

   f. Change the file name to `[your initials]PP_SkillReview_1-1`, then click **OK.**

2. Use the different view options:

   a. On the *View* tab, in the *Presentation Views* group, click **Slide Sorter** for an overall understanding of the presentation structure.

   b. On the *View* tab, in the *Presentation Views* group, click **Reading** to view the presentation before edits.

   c. On the status bar, click the **Normal view** button to add or edit content.

3. Add slides and sections:

   a. Add a slide:

      (1) On the *Slides* tab, click the thumbnail of **Slide 3.**

      (2) On the *Home* tab, in the *Slides* group, click the **New Slide** button arrow.

      (3) Select the **Title and Content** slide layout from the *New Slide* gallery.

      (4) Click the **Title** placeholder and type: `Define your audience (Who?)`

      (5) Click the **Text** placeholder and type: `What is the reason for the presentation?`

      (6) Press the **Enter** key, then the **Tab** key on your keyboard, then type: `Goal`

      (7) Press the **Enter** key, then the **Tab** key on your keyboard, then type: `Objectives`

   b. Add sections to a presentation:

      (1) On the *Slides* tab, click the thumbnail of **Slide 2.**

      (2) On the *Home* tab, in the *Slides* group, click the **Sections** button and select **Add Section.**

      (3) On the *Home* tab, in the *Slides* group, click the **Sections** button and select **Rename Section.**

      (4) Type: `Plan`

      (5) On the *Slides* tab, click the thumbnail of **Slide 6,** right-click, and select **Add Section.**

      (6) On the *Untitled Section* label, right-click, and select **Rename Section.**

      (7) Type: `Create and Present`

4. Change slide layouts and add transitions:

  a. Change the slide layout:

    (1) On the *Slides* tab, click the thumbnail of **Slide 5.**

    (2) On the *Home* tab, in the *Slides* group, click the **Slide Layout** button.

    (3) Select **Two Content** from the *Slide Layout* gallery.

    (4) Select all of the items in the left text box.

    (5) On the *Home* tab, in the *Paragraph* group, click the **Bullets** button.

    (6) Select the last four items in the left text box (beginning with *Make it easy to follow*), right-click, and select **Cut.**

    (7) Click in the right text box, right-click, and select **Paste.**

  b. Apply transitions to a slide:

    (1) On the *View* tab, in the *Presentation Views* group, click **Slide Sorter.**

    (2) Click the thumbnail of **Slide 1.**

    (3) Click the **Transitions** tab.

    (4) In the *Transition to This Slide* group, click the **Fade** button.

    (5) Click the **Plan** section bar.

    (6) On the *Transitions* tab, in the *Transition to This Slide* group, click the **More** drop-down arrow, then click the **Shape** button.

    (7) Click the **Create and Present** section bar.

    (8) On the *Transitions* tab, in the *Transition to This Slide* group, click the **More** drop-down arrow, then click the **Clock** button.

5. Work with the slide master and insert footers:

  a. Work with the slide master:

    (1) Click the **View** tab.

    (2) In the *Master Views* group, click the **Slide Master** button.

    (3) Click the **Title and Content** slide master.

    (4) Click the **Content** text box.

    (5) On the *Home* tab in the *Font* group, click the **Increase Font Size** button twice.

    (6) On the *Slide Master* tab, in the *Close* group, click the **Close Master View** button to return to Normal view.

  b. Add text to the footer of all the slides in a presentation:

    (1) Click the **View** tab.

    (2) In the *Master Views* group, click the **Slide Master** button.

    (3) Click the **Title and Content** slide master.

    (4) Click the **Insert** tab.

    (5) In the *Text* group, click the **Header & Footer** button.

    (6) On the *Slide* tab of the *Header and Footer* dialog box, select the **Footer** check box.

    (7) In the *Footer* text box, type: `PowerPoint Design Basics`

    (8) Click the **Apply to All** button to add the footer to the slide master.

    (9) On the *Slide Master* tab, in the *Close* group, click the **Close Master View** button to return to Normal view.

6. Add notes for the speaker to use:

a. Add speaker notes to slides:

(1) Verify you are in Normal view.

(2) In the *Slide* pane, click on **Slide 4** (*Define your audience*).

(3) Click in the *Notes* pane below the slide.

(4) Type: `Explain that this matters when making a decision on the information included and the design and/or theme`

b. Switch to Notes view:

(1) Click the **View** tab.

(2) In the *Presentation Views* group, click the **Notes Page** button.

(3) PowerPoint displays your presentation in Notes view.

7. Save the file and close the presentation.

a. On the *File* tab, click **Save.**

b. On the *File* tab, click **Close.**

Skill Review **1.2**

In this review, you will use the skills learned in Chapter 1 to edit an existing presentation.

1. Open an existing presentation:

a. Open Microsoft PowerPoint 2010.

b. On the *File* tab, click **Open.**

c. In the *Open* dialog box, navigate to the location of your PowerPoint 2010 student files.

d. Find *Ch1_Review2_Learning_Styles.pptx* and double-click the file to open it.

e. On the *File* tab, click the **Save As** option.

f. Change the file name to **[your initials] PP_SkillReview_1-2,** then click **OK.**

2. Use the different view options:

a. On the *View* tab, in the *Presentation Views* group, click **Slide Sorter** for an overall understanding of the presentation structure.

b. On the *View* tab, in the *Presentation Views* group, click **Reading** to view the presentation before edits.

c. On the status bar, click the **Normal view** button to add or edit content.

3. Add slides and sections:

a. Add a slide:

(1) On the *Slides* tab, click the thumbnail of **Slide 6.**

(2) On the *Home* tab, in the *Slides* group, click the **New Slide** button arrow.

(3) Select the **Title and Content** slide layout from the *New Slide* gallery.

(4) Click the **Title** placeholder and type: `What Is Your Learning Style?`

(5) Click the **Text** placeholder and type: `My Learning Style Is:`

(6) Press the **Enter** key, then the **Tab** key on your keyboard, and then type one of the following based on your learning style: `Visual, Auditory,` or `Tactile/ Kinesthetic`

b. Add sections to a presentation:

    (1) On the *Slides* tab, click the thumbnail of **Slide 3.**

    (2) On the *Home* tab, in the *Slides* group, click the **Sections** button and select **Add Section.**

    (3) On the *Home* tab, in the *Slides* group, click the **Sections** button and select **Rename Section.**

    (4) Type: `Style Types`

    (5) On the *Slides* tab, click the thumbnail of **Slide 6,** right-click, and select **Add Section.**

    (6) On the *Untitled Section* label, right-click, and select **Rename Section.**

    (7) Type: `Why It Matters`

4. Change slide layouts and add transitions:

a. Change the slide layout:

    (1) On the *Slides* tab, click the thumbnail of **Slide 4.**

    (2) On the *Home* tab, in the *Slides* group, click the **Slide Layout** button.

    (3) Select **Two Content** from the *Slide Layout* gallery.

    (4) Select the second bullet and sub-bullets (beginning with *Increase Learning by*) in the left text box, right-click, and select **Cut.**

    (5) Click in the right text box, right-click, and select **Paste.**

    (6) On the *Slides* tab, click the thumbnail of **Slide 5.**

    (7) On the *Home* tab, in the *Slides* group, click the **Slide Layout** button.

    (8) Select **Two Content** from the *Slide Layout* gallery.

    (9) Select the second bullet and sub-bullets (beginning with *Increase Learning by*) in the left text box, right-click, and select **Cut.**

    (10) Click in the right text box, right-click, and select **Paste.**

b. Apply transitions to a slide:

    (1) On the *View* tab, in the *Presentation Views* group, click **Slide Sorter.**

    (2) Click the thumbnail of **Slide 2.**

    (3) Click the **Transitions** tab.

    (4) In the *Transition to This Slide* group, click the **Fade** button.

    (5) Click the **Style Types** section bar.

    (6) On the *Transitions* tab, in the *Transition to This Slide* group, click the **More** drop-down arrow, then click the **Gallery** button.

    (7) Click the **Why It Matters** section bar.

    (8) On the *Transitions* tab, in the *Transition to This Slide* group, click the **More** drop-down arrow, then click the **Doors** button.

5. Work with the slide master and insert footers:

a. Work with the slide master

    (1) Click the **View** tab.

    (2) In the *Master Views* group, click the **Slide Master** button.

    (3) Click the **Title and Content** slide master.

    (4) Click the *Content* text box.

    (5) On the *Home* tab in the *Font* group, click the **Increase Font Size** button twice.

    (6) Click the **Two Content** slide master.

(7) Click the left *Content* text box.

(8) On the *Home* tab in the *Font* group, click the **Increase Font Size** button twice.

(9) Click the right *Content* text box.

(10) On the *Home* tab in the *Font* group, click the **Increase Font Size** button twice.

(11) On the *Slide Master* tab, in the *Close* group, click the **Close Master View** button to return to Normal view.

b. Add text to the footer of all the slides in a presentation:

(1) Click the **View** tab.

(2) In the *Master Views* group, click the **Slide Master** button.

(3) Click the **Title and Content** slide master.

(4) Click the **Insert** tab.

(5) In the *Text* group, click the **Header & Footer** button.

(6) On the *Slide* tab of the *Header and Footer* dialog box, select the **Footer** check box.

(7) In the *Footer* text box, type: My Learning Styles

(8) Check the **Don't show on title slide** check box if it is not already checked.

(9) Click the **Apply to All** button to add the footer to the slide masters.

(10) On the *Slide Master* tab, in the *Close* group, click the **Close Master View** button to return to Normal view.

6. Add notes for the speaker to use

a. Add speaker notes to slides:

(1) Verify you are in Normal view.

(2) In the *Slide* pane, click on **Slide 7** (*What is your learning style?*).

(3) Click in the *Notes* pane below the slide.

(4) Type: Explain how you determined your learning style and what changes you will make in your study habits, if any.

b. Switch to Notes view:

(1) Click the **View** tab.

(2) In the *Presentation Views* group, click the **Notes Page** button.

(3) PowerPoint displays your presentation in Notes view.

7. Save the file and close the presentation.

a. On the *File* tab, click **Save.**

b. On the *File* tab, click **Close.**

challenge yourself **1**

In this challenge, you will use the skills learned in Chapter 1 to create a Fitness Plan presentation.

1. Create a new presentation:

a. Open Microsoft PowerPoint 2010.

b. Create a new presentation using the *Austin* theme.

c. Save the file as *[your initials]*PP_Challenge_1-3.

d. Use the **Normal view** button to add or edit content.

2. Add slides and sections:

   a. Create slides using **Title** for the first slide and **Title and Content** layouts for the others to include the following:

SLIDE	TITLE TEXT	CONTENT TEXT
Title Slide	My Fitness Plan	Subtitle: Your Name
Slide 2	Diet	Food log More fruits/vegetables Fewer carbs Portion awareness
Slide 3	Exercise	Walk each day Park farther away Take the stairs Include aerobic activity
Slide 4	Rest	Regular bedtime Early start Take a nap when possible ☺
Slide 5	Relaxation	Find a new hobby Go hiking Vacation Read a book Time for "me" "Catch up" with a friend
Slide 6	Family/Personal Time	Schedule "date night" Manicure/pedicure/massage Quiet time
Slide 7	My Goal	*(Type in your fitness goal)*

   b. Add sections to a presentation including:

      (1) **Diet & Exercise** (Slides 2 and 3)

      (2) **Rest/Relaxation/Family** (Slides 4 through 6)

      (3) **My Goal** (Slide 7)

3. Change slide layouts and add transitions:

   a. Change Slide 5 to *Two Content* layout with three bullets each.

   b. Apply four transition types to the presentation: one for Slide 1 and one for each of the three sections.

4. Work with the slide master and insert footers:

   a. Using the slide master, increase the font size for all but the title slide.

   b. Add a footer with the presentation name. Ensure the footer displays on all but the title slide.

5. Add notes for the speaker to use

   a. Add speaker notes to the last slide to explain why you selected this fitness goal.

6. Save the file and close the presentation.

   a. Save and close your file.

challenge yourself 2

You are a member of a small group of friends involved in a wine tasting. In this challenge, you will use the skills learned in Chapter 1 to create a Wine Tasting presentation for your Wine Club.

1. Create a new presentation:

   a. Open Microsoft PowerPoint 2010.

   b. Create a new presentation using a theme of your choice.

   c. Save the file as *[your initials]*`PP_Challenge_1-4`.

   d. Use the **Normal view** button to add or edit content.

2. Add slides and sections:

   a. Create slides using **Title** for the first slide and **Title and Content** layouts for the others to include the following:

SLIDE	TITLE TEXT	CONTENT TEXT
Title Slide	Wine Tasting Basics	Subtitle: Your Name
Slide 2	Varietals: A Sampling of Whites	**Sauvignon Blanc (SO-vin-yon BLAHNK)** Light, crisp acidity and will often contain several fruit components. (Try New Zealand wines for a light citrus) **Chardonnay (shar-dun-NAY)** Full, golden and velvety with hints of fruit, nuts, butter, oak, spice or vanilla and have medium to high acidity. (Try both Oak and Steel Drum) **Riesling (REES-ling)** A bit sweeter and light
Slide 3	Varietals: A Sampling of Reds	**Cabernet Sauvignon (cab-er-NAY SO-vin-yon)** Dark purple or ruby in color, medium to full bodied with intense aromas and flavors Merlot (mur-LO) Low acidity and mellow softness with rich flavors of blackberry, plum and cherry **Pinot Noir (PEE-no NWA)** Light to moderate body with deliciously varied aromas and flavors
Slide 4	The Process	Look at color and clarity Swirl, then smell Taste Attack (alcohol content, tannin levels, acidity, and residual sugar) Evolution (flavor on your tongue/palate) The Finish (lingering taste) Select your favorites
Slide 5	Enjoy	Bring a buddy or a group Relax and enjoy the experience
Slide 6	Be Safe	Know your limits Identify a Designated Driver (or take a cab/tour bus)

b. Add sections to a presentation including:

    (1) **Varietals** (Slides 2 and 3)

    (2) **The Process** (Slides 4 through 6)

3. Change slide layouts and add transitions:

    a. Change slide 4 to *Two Content* layout.

    b. Apply three transition types to the presentation: one for Slide 1 and one for each of the two sections.

4. Work with the slide master and insert footers:

    a. Using the slide master, increase the font size for all but the title slide.

    b. Add a footer with the presentation name. Ensure the footer displays on all but the title slide.

5. Add notes for the speaker to use

    a. Add speaker notes to slide 5 to explain it is why your favorite wine and why you like it.

6. Save the file and close the presentation.

    a. Save and close your file.

on your own

You have just graduated from college and are ready to begin your new career. You would like to provide prospective employers with a PowerPoint résumé to "move beyond" the standard word-processed résumé.

1. Create a PowerPoint résumé that includes the following information:

    a. Contact Info (For this assignment you can include only your name and e-mail address.)

    b. Career Objective

    c. Key Skills

    d. Education

    e. Experience (Don't forget volunteer work.)

2. Add sections for each category.

3. Use multiple slide layouts and transitions.

4. Include your name in a footer for all slides except the title slide.

5. Add notes for the speaker to use.

6. Save your file as *[your initials]* `PP_OnYourOwn_1-5.`

fix it

You have been assigned the task of fixing an existing presentation based on the skills learned in Chapter 1.

1. Using Microsoft Office, open *Ch1_Fixit_Saving_Money.pptx.*

2. Save the file as *[your initials]* `PP_FixIt_1-6.`

3. Change the theme to **BlackTie.**

4. Add three sections: **Getting Started, Decrease Spending,** and **Increase Income**

5. Change the slide layout for the *Decrease Spending* slide to **Two Content.**

6. Add transitions.

7. Use the slide master to add bullets to the content slides.

8. Add a footer with the file name to all slides except the title slide.

9. Add a note with more suggestions for decreased spending.

chapter 2

Adding Content to Slides

In this chapter, you will learn the following skills:

> Work with text within slides including adding text, formatting lists, and using outlines

> Organize text with WordArt, the content placeholder, and tables

> Add interest through charts, SmartArt, and shapes with text

> Add graphics including clip art images, screenshots, and pictures

> Add media to slides including sounds and movies

Skill **2.1** Adding Text to Slides

Skill **2.2** Adding Bulleted and Numbered Lists

Skill **2.3** Opening a Word Outline as a Presentation

Skill **2.4** Adding WordArt to Slides

Skill **2.5** Understand the Content Placeholder

Skill **2.6** Creating Tables in Presentations

Skill **2.7** Adding Charts to Slides

Skill **2.8** Adding SmartArt to Slides

Skill **2.9** Adding Shapes to Slides

Skill **2.10** Adding Text to Shapes

Skill **2.11** Adding Clip Art Images to Slides

Skill **2.12** Adding Screenshots to Slides

Skill **2.13** Adding Pictures to Slides

Skill **2.14** Adding Sounds to Slides

Skill **2.15** Adding Movies to Slides

skills

introduction

In this chapter you learn the skills necessary to edit and add content to a PowerPoint 2010 presentation.

2.1 Adding Text to Slides

A good presentation consists of a balance of text and graphics. It is important to remember to keep text brief. Short, clear points convey your message to your audience better than rambling paragraphs of text. You can add text to slides by using text placeholders and text boxes. **Text placeholders** are predefined areas in slide layouts where you enter text. **Text boxes** are boxes that you add to the slide layout to enter text where you want it.

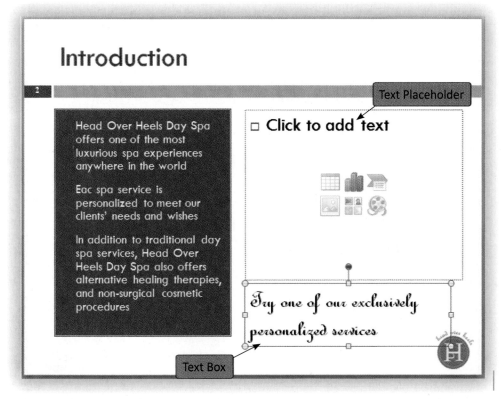

FIGURE PP 2.1

To add text to a text placeholder, click inside the text placeholder and type the text you want to add. Click outside the placeholder to deselect it.

To add a text box:

1. Click the **Insert** tab.

2. In the *Text* group, click the **Text Box** button.

3. Click on the slide where you want the text to appear.

4. Type your text.

5. Click outside the text box to deselect it.

FIGURE PP 2.2

tips & tricks

Text in a placeholder can be edited on the *Outline* tab or in the slide, but text you enter in a text box can only be edited on the slide.

try this

To enter text in a placeholder, you can also type the text on the *Outline* tab.

tell me more

Text placeholders are a part of the slide layout and cannot be added directly to a slide. You can only add text placeholders to slide layouts in Slide Master view. To add a text placeholder, first switch to Slide Master view. On the *Slide Master* tab, click the **Insert Placeholder** button and select **Text**. As you can see from the *Insert Placeholder* menu, you can add placeholders for pictures, charts, tables, SmartArt, media, and clip art, as well as text.

2.2 Adding Bulleted and Numbered Lists

Use bulleted and numbered lists to organize your information into brief points. **Bulleted lists** are used to organize information that does not have to be displayed in a particular order, such as features of a product. **Numbered lists** are used to organize information that must be presented in a certain order, such as step-by-step instructions.

Healing therapies

Head Over Heels offers a wide variety of healing therapies including: **Bulleted List**

- Therapeutic Massage
- Acupressure and Acupuncture
- Chiropractic Services

Why choose Head Over Heels?

Numbered List

1. 5 star rating from Best Spas
2. Personalized services and maintenance plans
3. Dedicated, friendly staff to meet your every need
4. Wide range of services
5. Relaxing, luxurious surroundings

FIGURE PP 2.3

To add a bulleted list to a slide:

1. Select the text you want to display in a list.

2. On the *Home* tab, in the *Paragraph* group, click the arrow next to the **Bullets** button.

3. Select a bullet style from the gallery.

To add a numbered list to a slide:

1. Select the text you want to display in a list.

2. On the *Home* tab, in the *Paragraph* group, click the arrow next to the **Numbering** button.

3. Select a numbering style from the gallery.

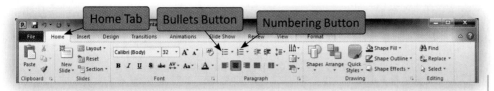

FIGURE PP 2.4

tips & tricks

Sometimes you will want to include subpoints in your bulleted and numbered lists. When a list includes point and subpoints, it is called a **multilevel list**. In PowerPoint, you can create a multilevel list by demoting and promoting points in lists. To move a point down a level in a list, click the **Increase Indent** button. To move a point up a level in a list, click the **Decrease Indent** button.

tell me **more**

The *Bullets and Numbering* dialog box allows you to modify the look of your lists. Click the **Bulleted** tab to change the style, size, and color of the bulleted list. Click the **Numbered** tab to change the type and color of the numbers or to change the starting point of the list. To open the *Bullets and Numbering* dialog box, click **Bullets and Numbering . . .** located below the *Bullets* gallery and the *Numbering* gallery.

try **this**

To add a bulleted list:

> Right-click the selected text, point to **Bullets,** and select a style from the submenu.

> Right-click the selected text. On the Mini toolbar, click the arrow next to the **Bullets** button and select a style.

To add a numbered list:

> Right-click the selected text, point to **Numbering,** and select a style from the submenu.

To apply the most recently used bullet or numbering style to a list, click the **Bullets** or **Numbering** button in the *Paragraph* group.

2.3 Opening a Word Outline as a Presentation

When organizing the content for a presentation, you may find it helpful to write your text in a Word document and then import it into PowerPoint. Use heading styles in the Word document to ensure that the content will convert to a presentation in a uniform manner. Each Heading 1 style becomes the title on the slide, and each Heading 2 style becomes the main text on the slide. After you have saved the Word document, you can then import the content, creating the base slides for your presentation.

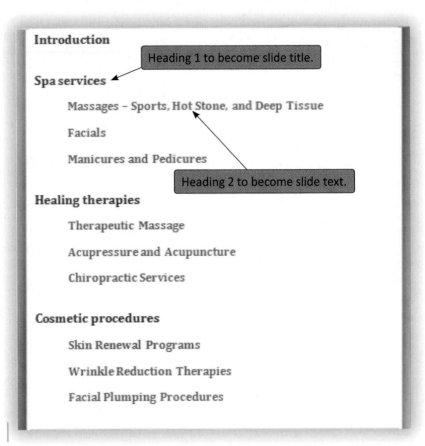

FIGURE PP 2.5

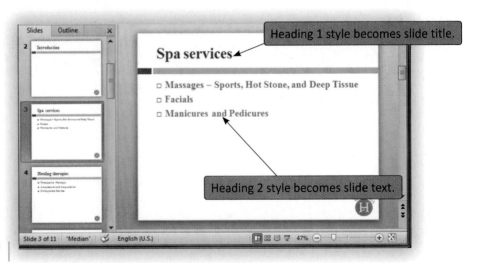

FIGURE PP 2.6

To insert slides from a Word outline:

1. Click in the presentation where you want to insert the slides.

2. On the *Home* tab, in the *Slides* group, click the arrow below the **New Slide** button and select **Slides from Outline . . .**

3. In the *Insert Outline* dialog box, select the file you want to insert.

4. Click the **Insert** button.

5. The slides are added to the presentation based on the heading styles in the Word document.

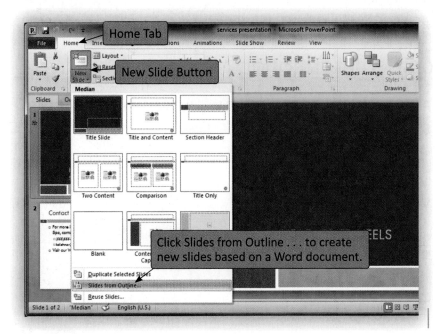

FIGURE PP 2.7

tips & tricks

When you insert an outline, all the slides will use the default slide design. Click the **Layout** button on the *Home* tab to change the layout of a slide. Click the **Design** tab to make any changes to a slide's design.

tell me **more**

You can import many file formats from Word, including Word documents (both .docx and .doc), plain text (.txt), rich text format (.rtf), and HTML (.htm).

2.4 Adding WordArt to Slides

Sometimes you'll want to call attention to text that you add to a slide. You can format the text by using character effects, or if you want the text to really stand out, you can use **WordArt.**

WordArt Quick Styles are predefined graphic styles you apply to text. These styles include a combination of color, fills, outlines, and effects.

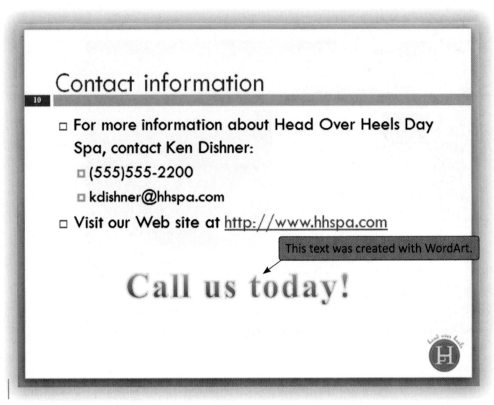

FIGURE PP 2.8

To add WordArt to slides:

1. Click the **Insert** tab.

2. In the *Text* group, click the **WordArt** button and select a Quick Style from the gallery.

3. Replace the text "Your Text Here" with the text for your slide.

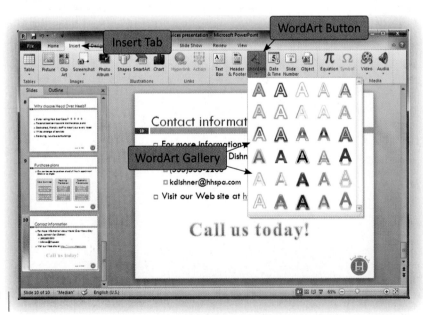

FIGURE PP 2.9

from the perspective of . . .

DENTAL HYGIENIST

In my profession as a dental hygienist, I created a fun presentation showing good oral hygiene habits. Using presentation software, I was able to add clip art, music, and cartoons. My young patients love it.

After you have added WordArt to your document, you can modify it just as you would any other text. Use the *Font* box and *Font Size* box on the *Home* tab to change the font or font size of WordArt.

In previous versions of Microsoft Office, WordArt came with a predefined set of graphic styles that could be formatted, but on a very limited basis. Beginning with Power-Point 2007, WordArt was changed to allow a wide range of stylization. When you add WordArt to a slide, the *Drawing Tools Format* contextual tab appears. In the *WordArt Styles* group you can apply Quick Styles to your Word-Art, or modify it further by changing the text fill, text outline, and text effects.

tips & tricks

Be sure to limit the use of WordArt to a small amount of text. Overuse of WordArt can be distracting to your audience.

tell me more

You can change the look of WordArt using the commands in the *Transform* gallery. You can choose to display the text along a path or to distort the letters, creating a warped effect. To transform WordArt, first click the **Format** tab under *Drawing Tools*. In the *WordArt Styles* group, click the **Text Effects** button. Point to **Transform** and select an option from the gallery.

2.5 Understanding the Content Placeholder

A good presentation contains a balance of text, graphics, charts, and other subject matter. The **content placeholder** is a special type of placeholder that gives you a quick way to add a variety of material to your presentations. In PowerPoint, you can add several types of content to your slides through the content placeholder:

To add content to a slide through the content placeholder:

1. Click the icon of the type of content you want to add.
2. The associated dialog box or task pane appears.
3. Add the content in the same manner as if you accessed the command from the Ribbon.

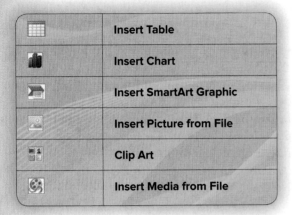

	Insert Table
	Insert Chart
	Insert SmartArt Graphic
	Insert Picture from File
	Clip Art
	Insert Media from File

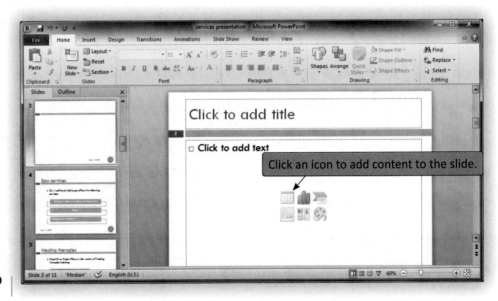

FIGURE PP 2.10

tips & tricks

When you add slides to a presentation, you can choose slides that are preformatted with content placeholders. Some slide layouts contain one content placeholder, but other layouts include multiple content placeholders, allowing you to add more than one content type to a slide.

2.6 Creating Tables in Presentations

When you have a large amount of data on one slide, you will want to organize the data so it is easier for your audience to understand. A **table** helps you organize information for effective display. Tables are organized by rows, which display horizontally, and columns, which display vertically. The intersection of a row and a column is referred to as a **cell**. Tables can be used to display everything from dates in a calendar to sales numbers to product inventory.

To add a table to a slide:

1. Click the **Insert** tab.
2. Click the **Table** button.
3. Select the number of cells you want by moving the cursor across and down the squares.
4. When the description at the top of the menu displays the number of rows and columns you want, click the mouse.
5. The table is inserted into your presentation.

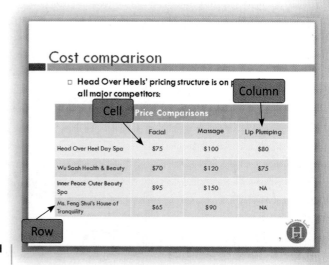

FIGURE PP 2.11

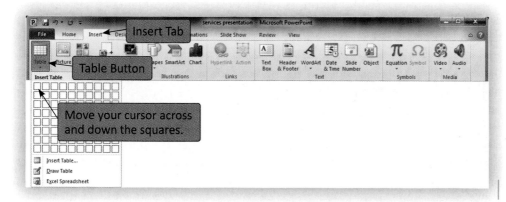

FIGURE PP 2.12

tell me **more**

When you add a table to a slide, the *Table Tools* contextual tabs display. These tabs contain commands for working with tables. From the *Design* tab, you can modify the rows and columns, apply table styles and effects, and change the table's borders. From the *Layout* tab, you can delete and add rows and columns, change the alignment of text in cells, change the size of cells, and change the size of the table.

try **this**

To add a table from the *Insert Table* dialog box:

> Click the **Table** button and select **Insert Table . . .**
> Click the **Insert Table** icon in the content placeholder.

In the *Insert Table* dialog box, enter the number of rows and columns for your table. Click **OK** to add the table to the slide.

2.7 Adding Charts to Slides

When creating a PowerPoint presentation, you will want to display your data in the most visual way possible. One way to display data graphically is by using charts. A **chart** takes the information you have entered in a spreadsheet and converts it to a visual representation. In PowerPoint, you can create a wide variety of charts including bar charts (both stack and 3-D), pie charts, column charts, scatter charts, and line charts.

To add a chart to a presentation:

1. Click the **Insert** tab.
2. In the *Illustrations* group, click the **Insert Chart** button.
3. In the *Insert Chart* dialog box, click a chart type category to display that category in the right pane.
4. Click a chart type in the right pane to select it.
5. Click **OK** to add the chart to the slide.

FIGURE PP 2.13

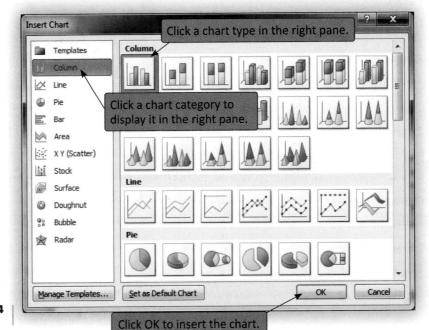

FIGURE PP 2.14

tips & tricks

If you typically use one type of chart for your presentations, you can set that chart type as the default chart type. In the *Insert Chart* dialog box, select the chart type you want to set as the default. Next, click the **Set as Default Chart** button. Now when you open the *Insert Chart* dialog box, that chart type will automatically be selected and you won't need to search through the different chart types to find the one you want to use.

tell me **more**

When you add a chart to a presentation, PowerPoint will automatically launch Microsoft Excel, with sample data for your chart entered for you. Just replace the sample data with your own data, close Excel, and return to PowerPoint to see your finished chart.

try **this**

To open the *Insert Chart* dialog box, you can also click the **Insert Chart** icon in the content placeholder on the slide.

2.8 Adding SmartArt to Slides

SmartArt is a way to take your ideas and make them visual. Where presentations used to have plain bulleted and ordered lists, now they can have SmartArt. SmartArt images are visual diagrams containing graphic elements with text boxes in which you enter information. Using SmartArt not only makes your presentation look better but helps convey the information in a more meaningful way.

There are eight categories of SmartArt for you to choose from:

List—Use to list items that ***do not*** need to be in a particular order.

Process—Use to list items that ***do*** need to be in a particular order.

Cycle—Use for a process that repeats over and over again.

Hierarchy—Use to show branching, in either a decision tree or an organization chart.

Relationship—Use to show relationships between items.

Matrix—Use to show how an item fits into the whole.

Pyramid—Use to illustrate how things relate to each other with the largest item being on the bottom and the smallest item being on the top.

Picture—Use to show a series of pictures along with text in the diagram.

To insert a SmartArt diagram:

1. Click the **Insert** tab.
2. In the *Illustrations* group, click the **Insert SmartArt Graphic** button.
3. In the *Choose a SmartArt Graphic* dialog box, click a SmartArt graphic type.
4. Click **OK**.
5. The SmartArt diagram is added to the slide.

FIGURE PP 2.15

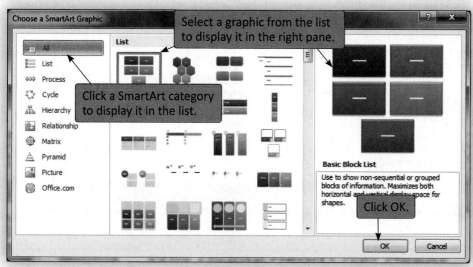

FIGURE PP 2.16

tips & tricks

When choosing a SmartArt diagram, it is important that the diagram type suits your content. In the *Choose a SmartArt Graphic* dialog box, click a SmartArt type to display a preview of the SmartArt. The preview displays not only what the diagram will look like, but also includes a description of the best uses for the diagram type.

tell me **more**

You can also convert existing text into SmartArt:

1. Select the text you want to convert.
2. On the *Home* tab, in the *Paragraph* group, click the **Convert to SmartArt Graphic** button and select a SmartArt style to apply to the text.

try **this**

To insert a SmartArt diagram, you can also click the **SmartArt** icon in a content placeholder.

skill **2.8**   Adding SmartArt to Slides   PP-35

2.9 Adding Shapes to Slides

A **shape** is a drawing object that you can quickly add to your presentation. The PowerPoint *Shapes* gallery gives you access to a number of prebuilt shapes to add to your presentation.

There are a number of types of shapes that you can add to slides, including

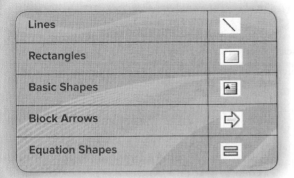

Lines	
Rectangles	
Basic Shapes	
Block Arrows	
Equation Shapes	

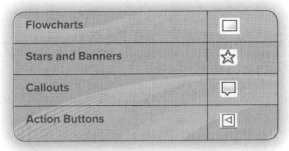

Flowcharts	
Stars and Banners	
Callouts	
Action Buttons	

To add a shape to a slide:

1. Click the **Insert** tab.
2. In the *Illustrations* group, click the **Shapes** button and select an option from the *Shapes* gallery.
3. The cursor changes to a crosshair ✛.
4. Click anywhere on the document to add the shape.

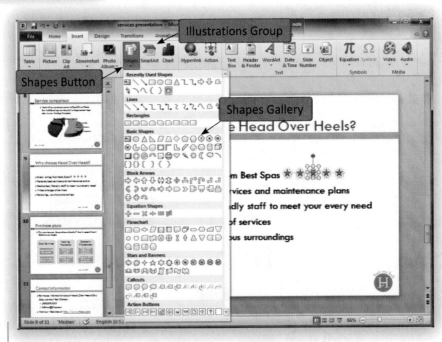

FIGURE PP 2.17

---

tips & tricks

Once you have added a shape to a document, there are a number of ways you can work with it:

> To resize a graphic: click a resize handle (⊕ or ⊝) and drag toward the center of the image to make it smaller or away from the center of the image to make it larger.

> To rotate a graphic: click the rotate handle ⟳ and drag your mouse to the right to rotate the image clockwise or to the left to rotate the image counterclockwise.

> To move a graphic: point to the graphic and when the cursor changes to the move cursor ✛, click and drag the image to the new location.

tell me more

When you insert a shape into a presentation, the *Format* tab under *Drawing Tools* displays. This tab is called a contextual tab because it only displays when a drawing object is the active element. The *Format* tab contains tools to change the look of the shape, such as shape styles, effects, and placement on the page.

try this

To add a shape, you can also click the **Shapes** button in the *Drawing* group on the *Home* tab.

2.10 Adding Text to Shapes

One way to bring attention to text on a slide is to include it as part of a shape. A shape will draw your audience's focus to whatever text you add to it. When you add a shape to a slide, the shape behaves as a text box. All you need to do to add text to the shape is begin typing. You can also go back and add text to shapes that you previously added to a slide.

To add text to an existing shape:

1. Select the shape you want to add text to.
2. Type the text you want to add to the shape.
3. Click outside the shape.

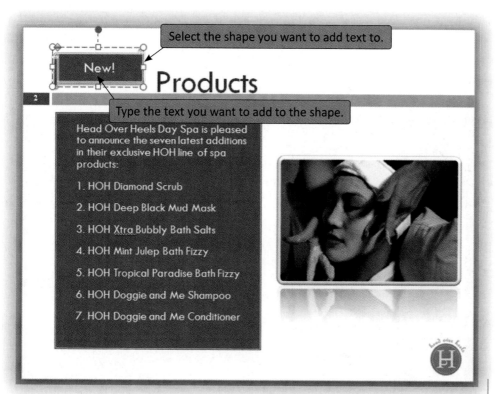

FIGURE PP 2.18

tips & tricks

When adding text to shapes, be sure not to use this design element too often. If every slide in your presentation has a shape with text, your presentation can seem too busy and the emphasis of the text is lost.

tell me more

Just as with any text box, you can add complex formatting to the text you add to a shape. You can apply bold, italic, and other character formatting to the shape's text. You can also change the font size and color. If you really want to make the text stand out, you can apply the WordArt formatting styles to add shadows, 3-D rotation, glows, and reflections to the text.

try this

To add text to a shape, right-click the shape and select **Edit Text.** The cursor appears in the shape ready for you to add your text.

2.11 Adding Clip Art Images to Slides

PowerPoint's **clip art** feature allows you to insert clips into your presentation. These clips include images, photographs, scanned material, animations, sound, and video. By default, PowerPoint inserts these clips as embedded objects, meaning they become part of the presentation (changing the source file will not change them in the new document). The *Clip Art* task pane allows you to search for different kinds of clips from many different sources.

To add clip art to a slide:

1. Click the **Insert** tab.
2. In the *Images* group, click the **Clip Art** button.
3. The *Clip Art* task pane appears.
4. Type a word or phrase describing the clip you want to add in the *Search for:* box.
5. Click the **Go** button.
6. Click the clip you want to add it to the slide.

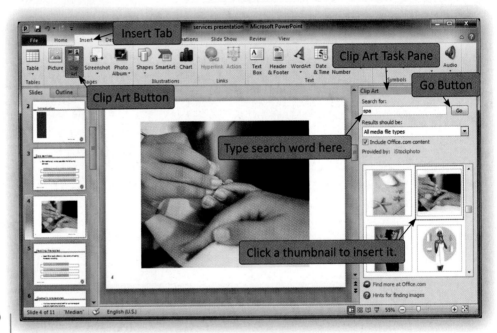

FIGURE PP 2.19

tips & tricks

You can narrow your search by media type, only searching for illustrations or photographs or videos or audio clips. Click the **Results should be:** arrow and click the check box in front of a media type to include or exclude those types of files from your search. Click the **All media types** check box to select and deselect all types at once.

tell me **more**

Microsoft's Web site for Office content, *Office.com*, contains more clips for you to use in your documents. If you are connected to the Internet, click the **Include Office.com content** check box to include content from the Web site in your search results.

try **this**

To display the *Clip Art* pane, you can also click the **Clip Art** icon in the content placeholder.

To insert an image from the *Clip Art* task pane, you can also point to the image and click the arrow that appears. A menu of options displays. Click **Insert** on the menu to add the clip to your document.

2.12 Adding Screenshots to Slides

A **screenshot** captures the image on the computer screen (such as an application's interface or a Web page) and creates an image that can then be used just as any other drawing or picture. With previous versions of PowerPoint, you had to use another application to create the screenshot and then insert the image through PowerPoint. In PowerPoint 2010, you can now use the *Insert Screenshot* command to capture and insert screenshots into presentations all from within the PowerPoint interface.

To add a screenshot to a presentation:

1. Click the **Insert** tab.
2. In the *Images* group, click the **Screenshot** button.
3. The *Available Windows* section displays a thumbnail image of each of the currently open windows.
4. Click a thumbnail to add the screenshot of that window to the presentation.

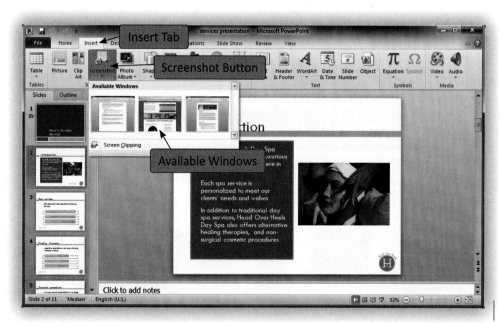

FIGURE PP 2.20

tips & tricks

The *Screenshot* gallery displays thumbnails of all the currently open windows. But what if you want to take a screenshot of only part of a window, or a screenshot of the entire desktop? You can use the *Screen Clipping* tool to take a screenshot of any part of the computer screen.

tell me **more**

After you have inserted a screenshot into a presentation, the *Format* tab under the *Picture Tools* contextual tab displays. This tab is called a contextual tab because it only displays when a drawing object is the active element. The *Format* tab contains tools to change the look of the image, such as color correction, artistic effects, and picture styles.

2.13 Adding Pictures to Slides

Sometimes adding a photograph or an illustration to a slide will convey a message better than text alone. Use the *Insert Picture* dialog box to insert pictures that you created in another program or downloaded from your smart phone or digital camera into your presentation.

To insert an image from a file:

1. Click the **Insert** tab.

2. In the *Images* group, click the **Insert Picture from File** button.

3. The *Insert Picture* dialog box opens.

4. Navigate to the file location, select the file, and click **Insert.**

FIGURE PP 2.21

FIGURE PP 2.22

tips & tricks

By default, PowerPoint inserts pictures as embedded objects, meaning they become part of the new document. Changing the source file will not change or affect the newly inserted image.

tell me **more**

You can create photograph slide shows including captions using PowerPoint's **Photo Album** feature. On the *Insert* tab, in the *Images* group, click the **Photo Album** button. Use the *Photo Album* dialog box to add photos, create captions, and modify the layout. Click the **Create** button to create the photo album as a new presentation.

try **this**

To open the *Insert Picture* dialog box, you can also click the **Insert Picture from File** icon ⬚ in the content placeholder.

2.14 Adding Sounds to Slides

Sound files, such as music or sound effects, can enhance your slides, making them more engaging to your audience. You can add sounds to your presentation from the Clip Organizer, from files you have downloaded from the Internet, or from files you've recorded yourself.

To insert a sound:

1. Click the **Insert** tab.
2. In the *Media* group, click the **Insert Audio** button.
3. In the *Insert Audio* dialog box, browse to find the file you want and click the sound file to select it.
4. Click **Insert** to add the sound file into your presentation.

FIGURE PP 2.23

FIGURE PP 2.24

tips & tricks

When you add a sound to a slide, a sound icon is added to the slide. When you run your presentation, this icon will display as part of the slide, and a play bar will display when you rest your pointer over it. To hide the icon, click the **Playback** tab under *Audio Tools*. In the *Audio Options* group, click the **Hide During Show** check box.

try this

To open the *Insert Audio* dialog box, you can also click the arrow next to the **Insert Audio** button and select **Audio from File . . .**

tell me more

When you add a sound to a slide, the *Audio Tools* contextual tabs display. These tabs contain commands for working with sound objects in PowerPoint. The *Format* tab allows you to change the look of the sound icon in the presentation, including applying artistic effects and Quick Styles to the icon. The *Playback* tab provides tools for editing the audio file within PowerPoint. From the *Playback* tab, you can change the slide show volume, fade the audio in and out, loop the sound, and preview the sound.

2.15 Adding Movies to Slides

A movie is a multimedia clip that includes moving images and sounds. If you already have digital movies ready to go, you can add them directly into your presentation. If you don't have digital movies, PowerPoint comes with preset sound and animation files to add to your presentation.

To insert a movie:

1. Click the **Insert** tab.
2. In the *Media* group, click the **Insert Video** button.

3. In the *Insert Video* dialog box, browse to find the file you want and click the movie file to select it.
4. Click **Insert** to add the movie file into your presentation.

FIGURE PP 2.25

FIGURE 2.26

tell me **more**

Some of the movie formats that PowerPoint supports include

> **Windows video file format (.avi)**

> **Windows media video format (.wmv)**

> **MPEG format (.mpeg or .mpg)**

> **MP4 video format (.mp4)**

> **QuickTime movie format (.mov)**

try **this**

To open the *Insert Movie* dialog box, you can also

> Click the **Insert Video** button arrow and select **Video from File . . .**

> Click the **Insert Media Clip** icon [ ] in the content placeholder.

Skill Review **2.1**

In this review, you will use the skills learned in Chapter 2 to edit an existing presentation.

1. Open an existing presentation:

a. Open Microsoft PowerPoint 2010.

b. On the *File* tab, click **Open.**

c. In the *Open* dialog box, navigate to the location of your PowerPoint 2010 student files.

d. Find *Ch2_Review1_HealthFair.pptx* and double-click the file to open it.

e. On the *File* tab, click the **Save As** option.

f. Change the file name to **[your initials] PP_SkillReview_2-1,** then click **OK.**

2. Work with text within slides including adding text, formatting lists, and using outlines:

a. Add a text box:

(1) Click the **Insert** tab.

(2) In the *Text* group, click the **Text Box** button.

(3) Click on **Slide 1,** in the top center of the right panel.

(4) Type: January 24, 2011

(5) Click outside the text box to deselect it.

b. Add a numbered list to a slide:

(1) On **Slide 2,** click in the text box placeholder.

(2) On the *Home* tab, click the arrow next to the **Numbering** button.

(3) Select the **1., 2., 3.** style from the gallery.

(4) Type: Increase Health Awareness, then press **Enter.**

(5) Type: Include Activities for All Ages, then press **Enter.**

(6) Type: Motivate Participants to Make Positive Health Choices.

c. Add a bulleted list to a slide:

(1) On **Slide 3,** click the edge of the **content text box** to select it.

(2) On the *Home* tab, click the arrow next to the **Bullets** button.

(3) Select the **Checkmark Bullets** style from the gallery.

d. Insert slides from a Word outline:

(1) In the *Slide* pane, click between **Slide 3** and **Slide 4.**

(2) On the *Home* tab, in the *Slides* group, click the **New Slide** button arrow and select **Slides from Outline . . .**

(3) In the *Insert Outline* dialog box, select the *Ch2_Review1_Target_Outline.docx* file.

(4) Click the **Insert** button.

3. Organize text with WordArt, *Content* placeholder, and tables:

a. Add WordArt to slides:

(1) Click on **Slide 5.**

(2) Click the **Insert** tab.

(3) In the *Text* group, click the **WordArt** button and select the **Fill–Olive Green, Accent 3, Outline–Text 2** Quick Style (last style in the first row) from the gallery.

(4) Replace the text **"Your Text Here"** with `Activities`.

(5) Select the **WordArt box** and drag it until it's centered across the top of the slide.

b. Use the *Content* placeholder to create a table and add a table to a slide:

(1) On **Slide 5,** click the **Insert Table** icon in the *Content* placeholder.

(2) In the *Insert Table* dialog box, use the arrow, to enter **3** columns and **4** rows. Click **OK.**

(3) The table is inserted into your presentation.

(4) On the *Table Tools Design* tab, in the *Table Styles* group, click the **More** button. In the gallery, select **Medium Style 2–Accent 3.**

(5) Add the following text:

ACTIVITY	TOPIC	TARGET AUDIENCE
Glo-Germ Demo	Hand Washing	ALL
You Booze, You Cruise, You Lose	Driver/Passenger	T, A
Bicycle Rodeo	Bicycle/Pedestrian Safety	C, T

4. Add interest through charts, SmartArt, and shapes with text:

a. Add a chart:

(1) Add a new slide.

(2) In the *Title* placeholder, type: `Attendance`

(3) Click in the *Content* placeholder.

(4) Click the **Insert** tab.

(5) In the *Illustrations* group, click the **Chart** button.

(6) In the *Insert Chart* dialog box, click the **Column** category to display that category in the right pane.

(7) Click the **Clustered Cylinder** type in the right pane to select it.

(8) Click **OK** to add the chart to the slide.

(9) Change the text in the *Chart in Microsoft PowerPoint Excel* pop-up from:

	Series 1	Series 2	Series 3
Category 1	4.3	2.4	2
Category 2	2.5	4.4	2
Category 3	3.5	1.8	3
Category 4	4.5	2.8	5

to:

	2010	2011	2012
Children	85	130	145
Teens	70	60	85
Adults	90	95	110

    (10) Close the Excel window.

  b. Use *SmartArt* objects:

    (1) Add a new slide

    (2) Delete the *Title* placeholder.

    (3) In the *Content* placeholder, click the **Insert SmartArt Graphic** button.

    (4) In the *Choose a SmartArt Graphic* dialog box, click the **Relationship** category.

    (5) Click the **Funnel** icon in the right pane.

    (6) Click **OK.**

    (7) The SmartArt diagram has been added to the slide.

    (8) In the *Type your text here* pane, type (one per line):

       Activities

       Demos

       Giveaways

       Fun

    (9) Close the *Type your text here* pane.

  c. Add shapes with text:

    (1) Click above the Funnel SmartArt.

    (2) Click the **Insert** tab.

    (3) In the *Illustrations* group, click the **Shapes** button.

    (4) In the *Stars and Banners* category, click the **Horizontal Scroll** shape in the gallery. Click above the Funnel SmartArt to add the shape to the slide.

    (5) Type: Join Us.

5. Add graphics including clip art images and pictures:

  a. Add *clip art* images:

    (1) Click on **Slide 4.**

    (2) Click the **Insert** tab.

    (3) In the *Images* group, click the **Clip Art** button.

    (4) In the *Clip Art* pane, type: Target in the *Search for:* box.

    (5) Click the **Go** button.

    (6) Click the clip of your choice to add it to the slide.

  b. Add a picture from a file:

    (1) Click on **Slide 6.**

    (2) Click the **Insert** tab.

    (3) In the *Images* group, click the **Picture** button.

    (4) The *Insert Picture* dialog box opens.

    (5) Navigate to the data files folder, select the *bikes.jpg* file, and click **Insert.**

    (6) Click and drag the *bikes* picture to align below the *bicycle rodeo* text.

6. Add media to slides including sounds and movies:

a. Add sound:

(1) Click on **Slide 7.**

(2) Click the **Insert** tab.

(3) In the *Media* group, click the **Insert Audio** button.

(4) The *Insert Audio* dialog box opens.

(5) Navigate to the data files folder, select the *applause.mp3* sound file.

(6) Click **Insert** to insert the sound file into your presentation.

(7) Click the **Audio Tools Playback** tab.

(8) In the *Audio Options* group, click the **Start** drop-down list, select **Automatically,** and select the **Hide During Show** check box.

b. Insert a movie:

(1) Click on **Slide 6.**

(2) Click the **Insert** tab.

(3) In the *Media* group, click the **Insert Video** button.

(4) The *Insert Video* dialog box opens.

(5) Navigate to the data files folder, select the *activities.wmv* video file.

(6) Click **Insert** to insert the video file into your presentation.

(7) Select the movie clip and drag it below the table.

7. View the presentation:

(1) On the *View* tab, in the *Presentation Views* group, click **Slide Sorter** for an overall understanding of the presentation structure.

(2) On the status bar, click the **Normal** button to add or edit content.

(3) Save the file.

Skill Review 2.2

In this review, you will use the skills learned in Chapter 2 to edit an existing presentation.

1. Open an existing presentation:

a. Open Microsoft PowerPoint 2010.

b. On the *File* tab, click **Open.**

c. In the *Open* dialog box, navigate to the location of your PowerPoint 2010 student files.

d. Find *Ch2_Review2_IdentityTheft.pptx* and double-click the file to open it.

e. On the *File* tab, click the **Save As** option.

f. Change the file name to **[your initials]PP_SkillReview_2-2,** and then click **OK.**

2. Work with text within slides including adding text, formatting lists, and using outlines:

a. Add a text box:

(1) Click the **Insert** tab.

(2) In the *Text* group, click the **Text Box** button.

(3) Click on **Slide 1,** in the center, below the line.

(4) Type: The Basics

(5) Click outside the text box to deselect it.

b. Add a numbered list to a slide:

    (1) On **Slide 2,** click in the text box placeholder.

    (2) On the *Home* tab, click the arrow next to the **Numbering** button.

    (3) Select the **1., 2., 3.** style from the gallery.

    (4) Type: `Prevent`, then press **Enter.**

    (5) Type: `Perceive`, then press **Enter.**

    (6) Type: `Protect`, then press **Enter.**

c. Add a bulleted list to a slide:

    (1) On **Slide 3,** click the edge of the **content text box** to select it.

    (2) On the *Home* tab, click the arrow next to the **Bullets** button.

    (3) Select the **Hollow Square** bullet style from the gallery.

d. Insert slides from a Word outline:

    (1) In the *Slide* pane, click between **Slide 3** and **Slide 4.**

    (2) On the *Home* tab, in the *Slides* group, click the **New Slide** button arrow and select **Slides from Outline . . .**

    (3) In the *Insert Outline* dialog box, select the *Ch2_Review2_Target_Outline.docx* file.

    (4) Click the **Insert** button.

    (5) On the *Target Audience Key* slide (4), select *Title* placeholder and the *Content* placeholder.

    (6) On the *Home* tab, in the *Font* group, click the **Font Color** drop-down arrow and select **White, Text 1.**

3. Organize text with WordArt, *Content* placeholder, and tables:

a. Add *WordArt* to slides:

    (1) Click on **Slide 5.**

    (2) Click the **Insert** tab.

    (3) In the *Text* group, click the **WordArt** button and select the **Fill–White, Drop Shadow** (third style in the first row) from the gallery.

    (4) Replace the text **"Your Text Here"** with `The Basics`

    (5) Select the **WordArt box** and drag it until it's centered across the top of the slide.

b. Use the *Content* placeholder to create a table and add a table to a slide:

    (1) On **Slide 5,** click the **Insert Table** icon in the *Content* placeholder.

    (2) In the *Insert Table* dialog box, use the drop-down arrows to select **3** columns and **4** rows. Click **OK.**

    (3) The table is inserted into your presentation.

    (4) On the *Table Tools Design* tab, in the *Table Styles* group, click the **More** button. In the gallery, select **Medium Style 2.**

    (5) Add the following text:

PREVENT	PERCEIVE	PULL THROUGH
Protect your Social Security number	Learn the signs of identity theft	Take the steps to recover
Be careful when using the Internet	Monitor your information	Freeze credit and set Fraud Alert
Treat your mail and trash carefully	Obtain and review free credit report	Prove you are a victim

(6) Select the last three rows.

(7) On the *Home* tab, in the *Font* group, click the **Font Color** arrow, and select **Black, Background 1.**

4. Add interest through charts, SmartArt, and shapes with text:

a. Add a chart:

(1) Add a new slide after **Slide 5.**

(2) In the *Title* placeholder, type: FTC Top 10 Consumer Fraud Complaint Categories

(3) Click in the *Content* placeholder.

(4) Click the **Insert** tab.

(5) In the *Illustrations* group, click the **Chart** button.

(6) In the *Insert Chart* dialog box, click the **Pie** category to display that category in the right pane.

(7) Click the **Pie in 3-D** type in the right pane to select it.

(8) Click **OK** to add the chart to the slide.

(9) Change the text in the *Chart in Microsoft PowerPoint Excel* pop-up from:

	Sales
1st Qtr	8.2
2nd Qtr	3.2
3rd Qtr	1.4
4th Qtr	1.2

to:

	%
Identity Theft	37
Internet Auctions	12
Foreign Money Offers	8
Shop-at-Home/Catalog Sales	7
Prizes/Sweepstakes and Lotteries	7
Internet Services and Computer Complaints	5
Business Opportunities and Work-at-Home Plans	2
Advance-Fee Loans and Credit Protection	2
Telephone Services	2
Other	17

(10) When you are finished, close the Excel window.

(11) Click the *Legend* text box in the chart to select it.

(12) On the *Home* tab, in the *Font* group, change the font size to **10.5.**

(13) Select the *Chart Title* text box and press **Delete.**

(14) Right-click the chart to display the shortcut menu; then select **Add Data Labels.**

b. Use *SmartArt* objects:

    (1) Add a new slide.

    (2) Delete the *Title* placeholder.

    (3) In the *Content* placeholder, click the **Insert SmartArt Graphic** button.

    (4) In the *Choose a SmartArt Graphic* dialog box, click the **Relationship** category.

    (5) Click the **Basic Venn** icon in the right pane.

    (6) Click **OK.**

    (7) The SmartArt diagram has been added to the slide.

    (8) In the *Type your text here* pane, type (one per line):

        `Prevent`

        `Perceive`

        `Pull Through`

    (9) Close the *Type your text here* pane.

c. Add shapes with text:

    (1) Click the **Insert** tab.

    (2) In the *Illustrations* group, click the **Shapes** button.

    (3) In the *Stars and Banners* category, click the **Horizontal Scroll** shape in the gallery to add it to the slide.

    (4) Type: `Remember`

5. Add graphics including clip art images and pictures:

a. Add *clip art* images:

    (1) On **Slide 4,** click to the right of the bulleted list.

    (2) Click the **Insert** tab.

    (3) In the *Images* group, click the **Clip Art** button.

    (4) In the *Clip Art* pane, type: `Target` in the *Search for:* box.

    (5) Click the **Go** button.

    (6) Click the clip of your choice to add it to the slide.

b. Add a *screenshot*:

    (1) Open your Internet browser and go to http://www.ftc.gov/bcp/edu/microsites/ idtheft/consumers/filing-a-report.html

    (2) Maximize your *[your initials]PP_SkillReview_2-2.pptx* file.

    (3) Select the **Filing a Complaint** slide.

    (4) Click the **Insert** tab.

    (5) In the *Images* group, click the **Screenshot** drop-down arrow and select the browser window with the FTC site.

    (6) A screenshot of the Web page will display on your slide.

    (7) If necessary, select the *screenshot* and resize and center it under the table.

c. Add a picture from a file:

    (1) Click the **Objectives** slide.

    (2) Click the **Insert** tab.

    (3) In the *Images* group, click the **Picture** button.

    (4) The *Insert Picture* dialog box opens.

    (5) Navigate to the data files folder, select the *thief.png* file, and click **Insert.**

    (6) Click and drag the *thief* picture to center it on the page.

6. View the presentation:

    a. On the *View* tab, in the *Presentation Views* group, click **Slide Sorter** for an overall understanding of the presentation structure.

    b. On the status bar, click the **Normal** button to add or edit content.

    c. Save the file.

challenge yourself 1

In this challenge, you will use the skills learned in Chapter 2 to create a team orientation presentation.

1. Create a new presentation:

    a. Open Microsoft PowerPoint 2010.

    b. Create a new presentation using the *Perspective* theme.

    c. Save the file as *[your initials]*`PP_Challenge_2-3`.

    d. Use the **Normal view** button to add or edit content.

2. Work with text within slides including adding text, formatting lists, and using outlines:

    a. Add text:

      (1) Type the title: `Team Orientation`

      (2) Add the subtitle: `The Basics`

    b. Add lists to slides:

      (1) Add a slide titled `Welcome & Introduction`

      (2) Create a *numbered* list including the following items:

        `1.Welcome`

        `2.Team objectives`

        `3.Member introduction`

      (3) Add a slide entitled `Topics`

      (4) Create a *bulleted* list using the **Checkmark Bullets** style from the gallery. Include the following items:

        • `Professional attitude`

        • `Quality work`

        • `Active participant`

        • `Provide constructive feedback`

    c. Insert slides from a Word outline:

      (1) Add a new *Slide from Outline*, using the *Ch2_Chall1_Outline.docx* file.

      (2) Change the *Title* text color to **Orange, Text 2** and the bullet text to **White, Text 1**.

3. Organize text with WordArt, *Content* placeholder, and tables:

    a. Add a new slide using the *Title and Content* layout.

    b. Replace the title with WordArt with the text: SMART. Use the style **Fill–White Drop Shadow** (third style in the first row) from the gallery.

    c. Select the **WordArt** box and drag it until it's centered across the top of the slide.

    d. Add a table using the *Content* placeholder with **2** columns and **6** rows with the **Medium Style, Accent 2**.

e. Add the following text:

GUIDELINE	TO BE EFFECTIVE
Specific	Is it clear?
Measurable	Can it be measured effectively?
Attainable	Can it be completed?
Relevant	Does it apply here?
Time Bound	When will it be completed?

4. Add interest through charts, SmartArt, and shapes with text:

    a. Add a chart:

        (1) Add a new slide titled Time Commitment

        (2) Add a chart using the **Pie in 3-D** type.

        (3) Include the following information:

        Preparation   **30%**

        Communication **40%**

        Reporting   **20%**

        Publishing   **10%**

        (4) Add data labels to the chart.

    b. Use SmartArt objects:

        (1) Add a new slide using the **Blank** layout.

        (2) Insert a **SmartArt** graphic using the **Basic Cycle.**

        (3) In the *Type your text here* pane, type (one per line), then resize the graphic if necessary.

        (4) Add a **Horizontal Scroll** shape above the SmartArt graphic with the text SMART Review

5. Add graphics including *clip art* images, screenshots, and pictures:

    a. On **Slide 4,** add a **Target** clip art to the right of the bulleted list.

    b. Add a new slide at the end of the presentation. Use the *Title and Content* layout.

    c. Title the slide: Teamwork Activities

    d. Open your Internet browser and go to: http://www.teampedia.net/

    e. Use the **Screenshot** command to add a screenshot of the Teampedia site to the *Content* placeholder.

    f. Click **Slide 5.**

    g. Navigate to the data files folder and insert the *whistle.jpg* picture.

    h. Click and drag the *whistle* picture to align it to the left of the *Title* text on the page, resizing if needed.

6. Add media to slides including sounds and movies:

    a. Click the **Time Commitment** slide.

    b. Navigate to the data files folder and insert the *time.mp3* audio file. Adjust options to hide it and run automatically.

    c. Click the **Topics** slide.

    d. Navigate to the data files folder and insert the *team.wmv* video file.

    e. Select the video and drag it to center it after the bullets.

    f. View the presentation, edit as needed, and then save the file.

challenge yourself 2

You are a member of group that is tasked with planning a class reunion. In this challenge, you will use the skills learned in Chapter 2 to create a presentation for your group members.

1. Create a new presentation:

    a. Open Microsoft PowerPoint 2010.

    b. Create a new presentation using the *Oriel* theme.

    c. Save the file as *[your initials]*`PP_Challenge_2-4`.

    d. Use the **Normal view** button to add or edit content.

2. Work with text within slides including adding text, formatting lists, and using outlines:

    a. Add text:

        (1) Type the title: `Class Reunion: 10th`

        (2) Add the *name of your high school* as the subtitle.

    b. Add lists to slides:

        (1) Add a slide titled `Welcome & Introduction`

        (2) Create a *numbered* list including the following items:

```
1.Welcome
2.Planning committee
3.Initial meeting objectives
4.Theme discussion
5.Task assignment
6.Action plan
```

        (3) Add a slide titled `Planning Committee`

        (4) Create a *bulleted* list using the **Hollow Square Bullets** style from the gallery. Include the following items:

- `Jane March`
- `Rob Walker`
- `John Patterson`
- `Michelle Johnson`
- `Mateo Ruiz`

    c. Insert slides from a Word outline:

        (1) Add a new *Slide from Outline*, using the *Ch2_Chall2_Obj_Outline.docx* file.

        (2) Select the **Music, Food,** and **Decorations** bullets and indent them.

3. Organize text with WordArt, *Content* placeholder, and tables:

   a. Add a new slide using the *Title and Content* layout.

   b. Replace the title with a WordArt centered across the top of the slide with the text: Initial Tasks. Use the style **Fill–Orange, Transparent Accent 1, Outline–Accent1** from the gallery. It is the first style in the second row of the gallery.

   c. Add a table using the *Content* placeholder with **3** columns and **10** rows with the **Medium Style, Accent 1.**

   d. Add the following text:

TASK	ASSIGNED	DUE
Select date	All	Today
Select theme	All	Today
Location options	Jon & Sally	2nd Mtg
Menu options	Jon & Sally	2nd Mtg
Music options	Nikki & Preston	2nd Mtg
Decoration options	Stacy	2nd Mtg
Class list	Chance	2nd Mtg
Budget final	Alyssa	3rd Mtg
Invitations	Lalia	3rd Mtg

4. Add interest through charts, SmartArt, and shapes with text:

   a. Add a chart:

     (1) Add a new slide entitled Budget

     (2) Add a *chart* using the **Pie in 3-D** type.

     (3) Include the following information:

        Venue   30%

        Decorations 20%

        Music   10%

        Food   30%

        Invitations 10%

     (4) Add data labels to the chart.

   b. Use *SmartArt* objects:

     (1) Add a new slide using the **Blank** layout.

     (2) Insert a **SmartArt** graphic using the **Radial Venn.** It is located in the *Relationship* category in the *Choose a SmartArt Graphic* dialog box.

     (3) Type the following; then resize the graphic if necessary.

Theme (*center text line*)
Decorations
Music
Food
Invitations

 (4) Add a **Horizontal Scroll** shape above the SmartArt graphic with the text Theme
   Based

5. Add graphics including clip art images, screenshots, and pictures:

 a. On **Slide 4,** add a **Target** clip art to the right of the bulleted list.

 b. Add a new slide at the end of the presentation. Use the *Title and Content* layout.

 c. Title the slide: Our School

 d. Open your Internet browser and go to your high school's Web page.

 e. Use the **Screenshot** command to add a screenshot of the Web page to the *Content* placeholder.

 f. Click the **Initial Tasks** slide.

 g. Navigate to the data files folder and insert the *whistle.jpg* picture.

 h. Click and drag the *whistle* picture to align it left of the *Title* text on the page, resizing if needed.

6. Add media to slides including sounds and movies.

 a. Click the **Theme Based** slide.

 b. Navigate to the data files folder and insert the *theme.mp3* audio file. Adjust options to hide it and run automatically.

 c. Click the **Planning Committee** slide.

 d. Navigate to the data files folder and insert the *reunion.wmv* video file.

 e. Select the video and drag it to center it after the bullets.

7. View the presentation, edit as needed, and then save the file.

on your own

You have decided to begin an online business and need to create a preliminary business plan to share with prospective lenders

1. Create a PowerPoint business plan that includes the following information:

 a. Prospective company name.

 b. Contact info (for this assignment you can include only your name and e-mail address).

 c. List of three objectives for your business (numbered list).

 d. Key employee positions (bulleted list).

 e. Use a Word outline to create a list of products (include the file with your PowerPoint file).

 f. Include a table with at least three items or services and their prices.

 g. Add a summary budget chart.

 h. Use SmartArt to create a diagram to illustrate relationships among your services/products.

 i. Add a clip art image.

 j. Include a screenshot of a Web page relating to your products/services.

 k. Add a sound clip and a video clip to your presentation.

 l. Save the file as *[your initials]*PP_OnYourOwn_2-5.

You have been assigned the task of fixing an existing presentation based on the skills learned in Chapter 2.

1. Using Microsoft Office, open *Ch2_Fixit_Careers.pptx*.

2. Save the file as **[your initials]PP_FixIt_2-6.**

3. Use a text box to add your name and the date to the *Title* slide.

4. Change the text to bullets on the *Desired Skills* slide.

5. Add a slide between slides 3 and 4. Include a table with two columns having the titles below and a list of at least three items under each:

   a. **My Interests**

   b. **Possible Careers**

6. Add a new slide with a chart with each of the careers you listed and the possibility percentage that you will select that career. (For example, teaching, 60%; computer repair, 10%; Web design, 30%). Add data labels and a slide title.

7. Add a SmartArt to illustrate the relationship(s) between your careers.

8. Add the *No Symbol* shape over the text *If it's not broken, don't fix it* on the last slide.

9. Add graphics including clip art images, screenshots, and pictures.

10. Add media to slides including sounds and movies.

11. Save the file.

chapter 3

Formatting Presentations

In this chapter, you will learn the following skills:

> Change themes and theme effects

> Apply Quick Styles to text boxes, tables, and shapes, and adjust the layout of SmartArt

> Show the ruler and gridlines, and change placeholder size

> Edit image alignment, grouping, rotating, and sizing

> Apply animation effects

Skill **3.1** Changing the Presentation Theme

Skill **3.2** Changing the Color Theme

Skill **3.3** Changing the Theme Effects

Skill **3.4** Changing the Slide Background

Skill **3.5** Changing Fonts

Skill **3.6** Changing the Look of Text Boxes

Skill **3.7** Applying Quick Styles to Text Boxes

Skill **3.8** Applying Quick Styles to Tables

Skill **3.9** Using the Shape Styles Gallery

Skill **3.10** Changing the Layout of SmartArt

Skill **3.11** Using the Picture Styles Gallery

Skill **3.12** Showing the Ruler and Gridlines

Skill **3.13** Changing the Size of Images

Skill **3.14** Changing the Size of a Placeholder

Skill **3.15** Aligning, Grouping, and Rotating Images

Skill **3.16** Applying Animation Effects

Skill **3.17** Modifying Animations

skills

introduction

In this chapter you learn the skills necessary to edit and format a PowerPoint 2010 presentation using themes, Quick Styles, text boxes, and animation effects. By incorporating pictures, animation, color, and backgrounds, you can create a very professional-looking presentation.

3.1 Changing the Presentation Theme

A **theme** is a group of formatting options that you apply to a presentation. Themes include font, color, and effect styles that are applied to specific elements of a presentation. In PowerPoint, themes also include background styles. When you apply a theme, all the slides in the presentation are affected.

To apply a theme to the presentation:

1. Click the **Design** tab.
2. In the *Themes* group, click the **More** button.
3. Select an option in the *Themes* gallery.
4. All the slides in your presentation now use the new theme.

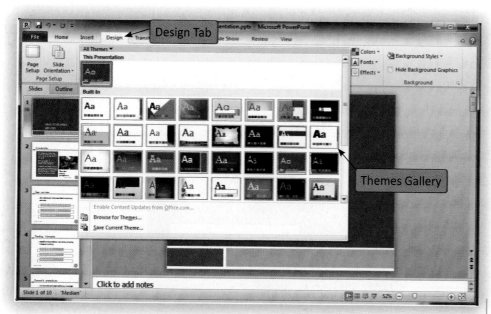

FIGURE PP 3.1

tell me **more**

Although themes are designed to make it easy for you to create a cohesive look for presentations, you may find that the themes available in the Microsoft Office applications are close to what you want but not quite right for your presentation. To create your own version of a theme, all you need to do is change the theme's color, font, or effect styles. When you modify an existing theme, you can save it as your own custom theme. The file will be saved with the .thmx file extension. The theme will be saved in the *Document Themes* folder and will be available from Excel, Word, and Outlook as well as PowerPoint.

try **this**

To apply a theme, you can also click a theme on the Ribbon without opening the gallery.

You can also change the theme of a presentation from Slide Master view. On the *Slide Master* tab, in the *Edit Themes* group, click the **Themes** button, and select a theme.

3.2 Changing the Color Theme

When creating a presentation, it is important to choose colors that work well together. Poor color choices can detract from the message you are trying to convey in your presentation. If the colors you choose are too muted, your presentation may seem dull. If the colors you choose are too harsh and clash with each other, your presentation may seem busy and unfocused.

PowerPoint 2010 includes a number of color themes for you to choose from. A color theme is a set of colors that complement each other and are designed to work well in a presentation. A color theme will change the color of backgrounds, placeholders, text, tables, charts, SmartArt, and drawing objects in a presentation. When you apply a theme to a presentation, this includes a color theme, which includes default theme colors for presentation elements. You can change the color theme without affecting the other components of the theme.

To apply a color theme to a slide master:

1. Click the **Design** tab.
2. In the *Themes* group, click the **Theme Colors** button.
3. Select a color theme from the list that appears.

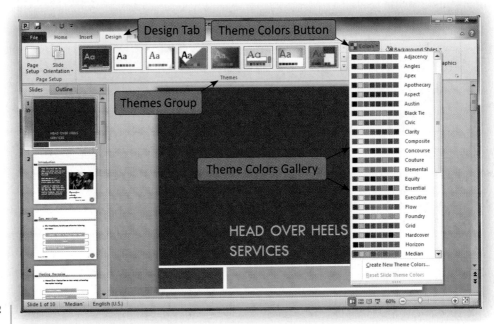

FIGURE PP 3.2

tips & tricks

You can create a new color theme, selecting your own colors for text and accents. To create a custom color theme, click the **Theme Colors** button and select **Create New Theme Colors . . .** Change the theme colors and give the theme a name.

tell me **more**

When you change the color theme for a presentation, the color options for presentation elements will change. The theme colors will appear in the *Font Color* menu, as well as in the *Table Styles* and *Shape Styles* galleries. Choose your colors from these preset theme colors to ensure your document has a consistent color design.

try **this**

You can also change the color theme of a presentation from Slide Master view. On the *Slide Master* tab, in the *Edit Themes* group, click the **Theme Colors** button, and select a color theme.

3.3 Changing the Theme Effects

In PowerPoint 2010, you can add graphic effects to drawing objects and text. These graphic effects give you the ability to create dynamic images without the help of a professional designer. You can create sophisticated fills for objects and control the shape outline for objects, including the color, weight, and line style.

Using these new effects can be overwhelming at first. How do you know which effects go well together? A part of a presentation's theme is the **theme effects**. The theme effects consist of line and fill effects that you apply to objects on your slides, giving you a starting point to create sophisticated images in your presentations.

To apply theme effects to the presentation:

1. Click the **Design** tab.
2. In the *Themes* group, click the **Theme Effects** button.
3. Select a theme effect from the gallery that appears.

FIGURE PP 3.3

tell me **more**

Theme effects are the same in the following Microsoft Office 2010 applications: Word, Excel, PowerPoint, and Outlook. These applications include 40 prebuilt theme effect combinations for you to choose from. Unlike theme fonts and theme colors, you cannot create your own theme effects in the Microsoft Office 2010 applications.

try **this**

You can also change the theme effects of a presentation from Slide Master view. On the *Slide Master* tab, in the *Edit Themes* group, click the **Theme Effects** button, and select an option.

3.4 Changing the Slide Background

A **background** is the graphic element that fills a slide. Backgrounds can be solid colors, textures, or even images. Each theme in PowerPoint provides a variety of background styles from which to choose. Background styles acquire their colors from the presentation's theme and range in color from light to dark. The background styles for themes also include different background textures, depending on the theme you choose. When you apply a theme to a presentation the default background styles will be applied to your slides. To change just the background of all the slides in a presentation (and not other theme elements such as fonts), you should change the background style for the presentation.

To change the background style:

1. Click the **Design** tab.
2. In the *Background* group, click the **Background Styles** button.
3. Select an option from the *Background Styles* gallery.

FIGURE PP 3.4

3.5 Changing Fonts

A **font**, or typeface, refers to a set of characters of a certain design. The font is the shape of the character or number as it appears on-screen. You can change the look of text by changing the font, the font size, or the font color.

To change the font:

1. Select the text to be changed.
2. On the *Home* tab, in the *Font* group, click the arrow next to the **Font** box.
3. Scroll the list to find the new font.
4. Click the font name.

To change the size of the text:

1. Select the text to be changed.
2. On the *Home* tab, in the *Font* group, click the arrow next to the **Font Size** box.

3. Scroll the list to find the new font size.
4. Click the size you want.

To change the color of the text:

1. Select the text to be changed.
2. On the *Home* tab, in the *Font* group, click the arrow next to the **Font Color** button.
3. Click the color you want.

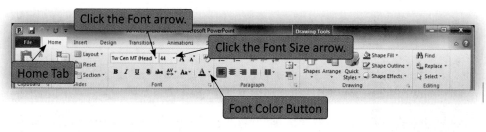

FIGURE PP 3.5

tips & tricks

Using different fonts, font sizes, and font colors can enhance your presentation, giving it a distinctive appearance. However, when you create a presentation it is best to limit the number of fonts, font sizes, and font colors you use. Using multiple fonts and effects in one presentation can give it a disorganized and unprofessional appearance.

tell me more

PowerPoint offers many fonts. Serif fonts, such as Cambria and Times New Roman, have an embellishment at the end of each stroke. They are used for notes pages, printed pages, and body text. Sans serif fonts, such as Calibri and Arial, do not have an embellishment at the end of each stroke. They are typically used for titles and subtitles in on-screen presentations since they have a clean look.

try this

To change the font, right-click the text, click the arrow next to the **Font** box on the Mini toolbar, and select an option.

To change the font size, right-click the text, click the arrow next to the **Font Size** box on the Mini toolbar, and select an option.

To change the font color, right-click the text, click the arrow next to the **Font Color** button on the Mini toolbar, and select an option.

3.6 Changing the Look of Text Boxes

Text boxes are content containers that allow you to place text anywhere on a slide. When you first add a text box to a slide, the text box uses the default font from the theme and has no background or border. If you want the text in a text box to stand out on a slide, you can customize the look of the text box by applying fill, outline, and shape effects.

To change the look of a text box:

1. Select the text box you want to change.
2. Click the **Format** tab under *Drawing Tools*.
3. To change the fill effects on a text box:
   a. In the *Shape Styles* group, click the **Shape Fill** button.
   b. Select an option from the color palette.
4. To change the shape outline of a text box:
   a. In the *Shape Styles* group, click the **Shape Outline** button.
   b. Select an option from the color palette.
   c. Point to **Weight** and select a thickness option for the outline.
   d. Point to **Dashes** and select a dash style for the outline.
5. To change the shape effects on a text box:
   a. In the *Shape Styles* group, click the **Shape Effects** button.
   b. Point to **Presets** and select a predetermined combination of shape effects.
   c. Point to any other options on the menu to choose from a variety of shadow, reflection, glow, soft edges, bevel, and 3-D rotation effects.

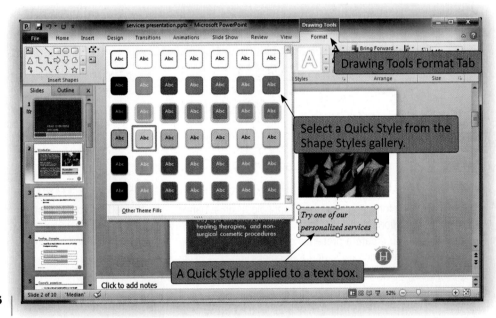

FIGURE PP 3.6

---

tips & tricks

You can resize text boxes just as you would resize any image in PowerPoint. First, point to one of the resize handles on the text box. When the mouse changes to the resize cursor, click and drag the mouse toward the center of the image to make it smaller, or drag the mouse away from the center of the image to make it larger. When the image is the size you want, release the mouse button.

tell me **more**

If you want to further adjust the visual effects of a text box, you can use the *Format Shape* dialog box. The *Format Shape* dialog box allows you to finely tune the graphic look of a shape by changing its fill, line color and style, shadow, and 3-D format. To open the *Format Shape* dialog box, click the dialog launcher in the *Shape Styles* group on the *Drawing Tools Format* tab. Click an effect category on the left to display the controls for the effect in the area on the right.

3.7 Applying Quick Styles to Text Boxes

Quick Styles are a combination of formatting that give elements of your presentation a more polished, graphical look without a lot of work. Quick Styles can be applied to text boxes and include a combination of borders, shadows, reflections, and picture shapes, such as rounded corners or skewed perspective. Instead of applying each of these formatting elements one at a time, you can apply a combination of elements at one time using a preset Quick Style.

To apply a Quick Style to a text box:

1. Select the text box you want to apply the Quick Style to.
2. Click the **Format** tab under *Drawing Tools*.
3. In the *Shape Styles* group, click the **More** button.
4. In the *Shape Styles* gallery, click a Quick Style to apply it to the text box.

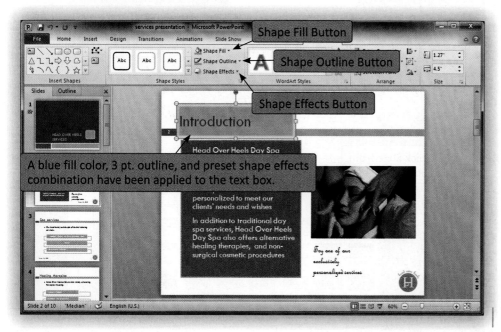

FIGURE PP 3.7

tips & tricks

You can further modify the look of text boxes by using the *Shading*, *Borders*, and *Effects* buttons in the *Shape Styles* group.

tell me **more**

When you insert a text box into a presentation, the *Format* tab under *Drawing Tools* displays. This tab is called a contextual tab because it only displays when a text box is the active element. The *Format* tab contains tools to change the look of the text box, such as shape styles, WordArt styles, sizing, and arrangement options.

try **this**

The *Shape Styles* group on the Ribbon displays the latest Quick Styles you have used. If you want to apply a recently used Quick Style, you can click the option directly from the Ribbon without opening the *Shape Styles* gallery.

3.8 Applying Quick Styles to Tables

Just as you can apply complex formatting to text boxes using Quick Styles for shapes, you can also apply complex formatting to tables using Quick Styles for tables. With Quick Styles for tables, you can apply the borders and shading for a table with one command, giving your table a professional, sophisticated look without a lot of work.

To apply a Quick Style to a table:

1. Click the **Design** tab under *Table Tools*.
2. In the *Table Styles* group, click the **More** button.
3. In the *Table Styles* gallery, click a Quick Style to apply it to the table.

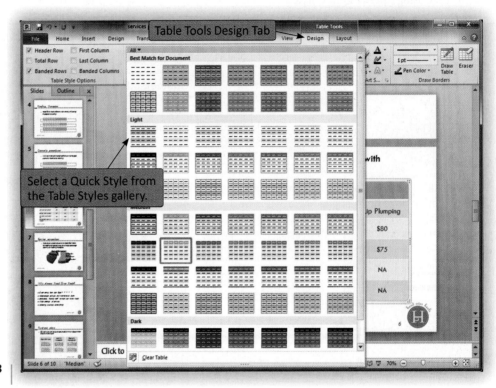

FIGURE PP 3.8

tips & tricks

To remove all formatting from the table, click the **Clear Table** button at the bottom of the *Table Quick Styles* gallery.

You can further modify the look of tables by using the *Shading*, *Borders*, and *Effects* buttons in the *Table Styles* group.

tell me **more**

When you insert a table into a presentation, the *Design* and *Layout* tabs under *Table Tools* display. These tabs are called contextual tabs because they only display when a table is the active element. The *Design* tab contains tools to change the look of the table, such as Quick Styles, Word Art, and borders. The *Layout* tab contains tools for changing the structure of a table, including adding and removing rows and columns, resizing the table, and changing the alignment of text.

try **this**

The *Table Styles* group on the Ribbon displays the latest Quick Styles set you chose. If you want to apply a recently used Quick Style, you can click the option directly from the Ribbon without opening the *Table Styles* gallery.

3.9 Using the Shape Styles Gallery

Once you have added a basic shape to a slide, you can apply complex formatting and styles to the shape. You can change the fill or outline color using one of the colors from your presentation's theme. You can also change the shape effects, applying shadows, reflections, glows, and 3-D effects to the shape. But the easiest way to format a shape is to apply a Quick Style. The *Shape Styles* gallery includes a number of Quick Styles, making it easy for you to apply complex formatting to shapes.

To apply a Quick Style to a shape:

1. Click the **Format** tab under *Drawing Tools*.
2. In the *Shape Styles* group, click the **More** button.
3. In the *Shape Styles* gallery, click a Quick Style to apply it to the shape.

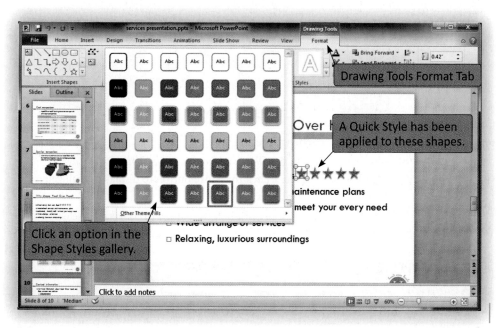

FIGURE PP 3.9

tips & tricks

To change a shape, click the **Edit Shape** button, point to **Change Shape,** and select an option.

You can further modify the look of shapes by using the *Shading*, *Borders*, and *Effects* buttons in the *Shape Styles* group.

tell me **more**

Once you have mastered applying the prebuilt shape styles to shapes, you can try further refining those styles using the *Format Shape* dialog box. The *Format Shape* dialog box allows you to finely tune the graphic look of a shape by changing its fill, line color and style, shadow, and 3-D format. To open the *Format Shape* dialog box, click the dialog launcher in the *Shape Styles* group on the *Format* tab under *Drawing Tools*.

try **this**

The *Shape Styles* group on the Ribbon displays the latest Quick Styles you have used. If you want to apply a recently used Quick Style, you can click the option directly from the Ribbon without opening the *Shape Styles* gallery.

3.10 Changing the Layout of SmartArt

SmartArt diagrams are designed to display specific types of data in a visual manner. Each SmartArt diagram includes a default layout for you to add data to. But what if your information does not fit the default layout? Or what if you want to add shapes under other shapes? You can use the *SmartArt Tools* contextual tab to add shapes and promote and demote shapes in SmartArt diagrams.

To change the layout of a SmartArt diagram:

1. On the *Design* tab under *Table Tools,* in the *Create Graphic* group, click the **Add Shape** button and select an option for adding a shape.

2. Click the **Demote Selection** button to move the new shape down one level in the diagram organization.

3. Click the **Promote Selection** button to move the new shape up one level in the diagram organization.

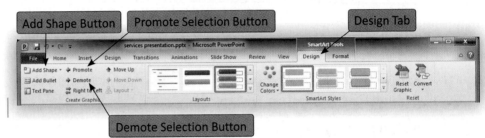

FIGURE PP 3.10

After you have added a SmartArt diagram to your slide, you may find a different layout would convey your information better. For example, you may have initially chosen a list diagram, but then later realized a cycle diagram is more appropriate for your information. You can change the diagram layout rather than re-creating the entire diagram over again.

To change the diagram type:

1. On the *Design* tab under *Table Tools,* in the *Layouts* gallery, click the **More** button to display the full gallery of layouts.

2. Click an option in the gallery to convert the selected SmartArt diagram into the new layout.

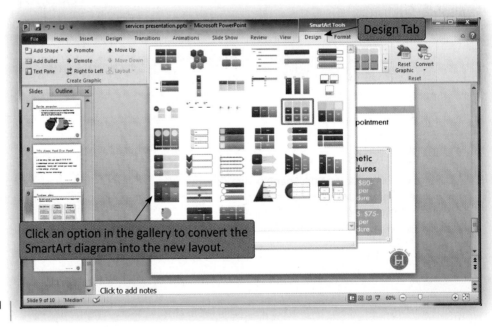

FIGURE PP 3.11

tips & tricks

By default SmartArt diagrams display information from left to right, as you would read text on a page. If you want to change the direction of information in the diagram, click the **Right to Left** button in the *Create Graphic* group. The diagram now flows from the right side of the slide to the left side.

try this

You can add more shapes to a SmartArt diagram by right-clicking the shape in the diagram, pointing to **Add Shape**, and selecting an option.

3.11 Using the Picture Styles Gallery

When creating a presentation, you want to grab the audience's attention. What makes one presentation stand out from another isn't necessarily the content of the slides, but the graphics used to convey that content. PowerPoint comes with a number of picture Quick Styles you can apply to images, instantly giving them a more sophisticated look. Picture Quick Styles include a combination of graphic effects, such as borders, shadows, 3-D rotation, and reflections.

To apply a picture Quick Style to an image:

1. Click the **Format** tab under *Picture Tools*.
2. In the *Picture Styles* group, click the **More** button ⬇.
3. In the *Picture Styles* gallery, click a Quick Style to apply it to the shape.

Click an option in the gallery to apply the Quick Style to the picture.

FIGURE PP 3.12

tips & tricks

You can further modify the look of pictures by using the *Picture Border* and *Picture Effects* buttons in the *Picture Styles* group.

tell me more

When you insert a picture into a presentation, the *Format* tab under *Picture Tools* displays. This tab is called a contextual tab because it only displays when a picture is the active element. The *Format* tab contains tools to change the look of a picture, such as applying artistic effects, changing the color, and cropping the image.

try this

The *Picture Styles* group on the Ribbon displays the latest Quick Styles you have used. If you want to apply a recently used Quick Style, you can click the option directly from the Ribbon without opening the *Picture Styles* gallery.

3.12 Showing the Ruler and Gridlines

When you are designing slides in your presentation, aligning placeholders and graphics can be the difference between a polished presentation and one that looks thrown together. Use PowerPoint's rulers and gridlines as visual tools to check the placement of text and graphics on your slides. The ruler allows you to control the placement of text in placeholders, including tabs and indents. **Gridlines** are a series of dotted vertical and horizontal lines that divide the slide into small boxes, giving you visual markers for aligning placeholders and graphics.

To display gridlines in PowerPoint:

1. Click the **View** tab.
2. In the *Show* group, click the **Gridlines** check box to select it.

To display the ruler in PowerPoint:

1. Click the **View** tab.
2. In the *Show* group, click the **Ruler** check box to select it.

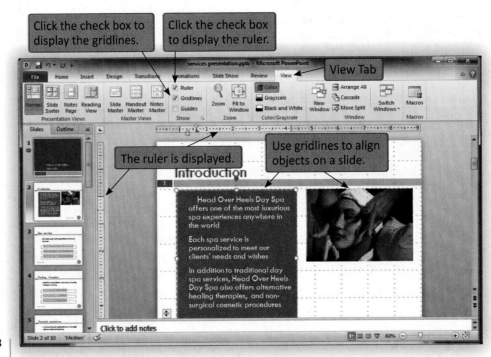

FIGURE PP 3.13

---

tips & tricks

You can modify the look and behavior of gridlines in the *Grid and Guides* dialog box. To open the *Grid and Guides* dialog box, click the dialog launcher in the *Show* group. Select the **Snap objects to grid** option to force objects to line up along an intersection in the grid when you insert or move them. For more precise layout, change the spacing in the grid to a smaller number.

tell me **more**

The grid and ruler are only visible when you are working on the presentation. They do not appear when you show the presentation in Slide Show view or when you print handouts.

try **this**

To display gridlines, you can also:

1. Click the **Format** tab under *Picture Tools*.
2. In the *Arrange* group, click the **Align** button and select **View Gridlines.**

3.13 Changing the Size of Images

When you first add an image to a slide, more than likely it is not the size you want. It will either be too small or too large. In PowerPoint, you can resize images using the resize handles that appear at the corners and sides of an image when it is selected.

To resize an image using the drag method:

1. Point to one of the resize handles ⬚ on the image.

2. When the mouse changes to the resize cursor ⬈ , click and drag the mouse:

   › Drag the mouse toward the center of the image to make it smaller.

   › Drag the mouse away from the center of the image to make it larger.

3. When the image is the size you want, release the mouse button.

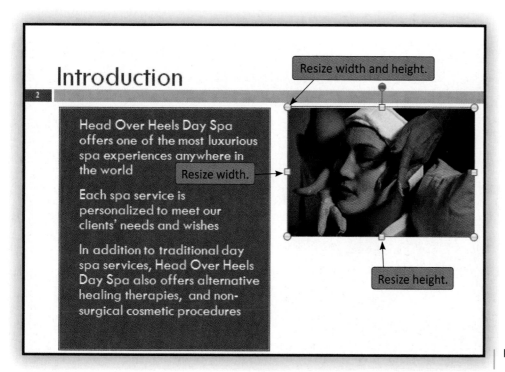

FIGURE PP 3.14

tips & tricks

When using one of the corner resize handles, press ⇧Shift on the keyboard as you drag the mouse to constrain the aspect ratio of the image. Constraining the aspect ratio resizes the width by the same percentage as the height. This prevents the image from becoming distorted.

tell me **more**

When an image is selected, you will see two types of resize handles:

⬚ Appears in the middle of one of the sides of the image. This allows you to resize the width or the height, but not both at the same time.

◯ Appears at the four corners of the image. This allows you to change the width and height of the image at the same time.

try **this**

You can also resize an image by entering the width and height of the image in the **Width:** and **Height:** boxes in the *Size* group on the *Format* tab under *Picture Tools*.

3.14 Changing the Size of a Placeholder

A **placeholder** is a container on a slide that holds text or other content, such as a table, chart, or image. Placeholders are outlined with a dotted line that does not display in the presentation when it is running. You can use the same steps for changing the size of an image to change the size of a placeholder.

To change the size of a placeholder:

1. Point to one of the resize handles ⬍ on the placeholder.

2. When the mouse changes to the resize cursor ⬈, click and drag the mouse:

   > Drag the mouse toward the center of the placeholder to make it smaller.

   > Drag the mouse away from the center of the placeholder to make it larger.

3. When the placeholder is the size you want, release the mouse button.

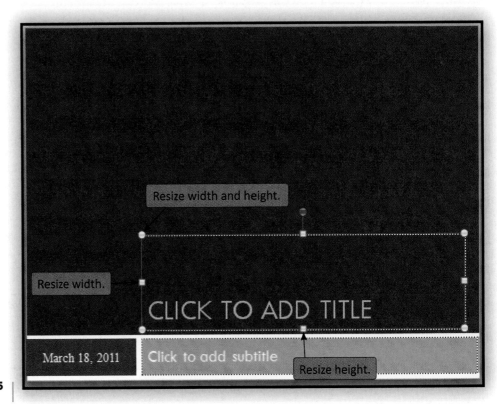

FIGURE PP 3.15

---

tips & tricks

When using one of the corner resize handles ⬖, press ⬆Shift on the keyboard as you drag the mouse to constrain the aspect ratio of the image and prevent the image from becoming distorted.

tell me **more**

You can only add placeholders from Slide Master view. To add a placeholder to a layout, click the **View** tab. In *Master Views* group, click the **Slide Master** button. PowerPoint switches to Slide Master view. In the *Master Layout* group, click the **Insert Placeholder** button and select an option.

try **this**

You can also resize a placeholder by entering the width and height of the placeholder in the **Width:** and **Height:** boxes in the *Size* group on the *Format* tab under *Picture Tools*.

3.15 Aligning, Grouping, and Rotating Images

When designing a presentation, it is important to place your graphics so that they will have the most impact on your audience. Any graphics that appear in a straight line should be aligned, to ensure that they are precisely placed. On the other hand, you may want to rotate one graphic to make it stand out on the slide. You can also select multiple images on a slide and group them together, thus turning multiple objects into a single object that you can easily move, rotate, or resize as one.

To align graphics on a slide:

1. Click the **Format** tab under *Picture Tools*.
2. In the *Arrange* group, click the **Align** button and select an option:
   > The **Align Left, Align Center,** and **Align Right** commands align graphics along an invisible vertical line.
   > The **Align Top, Align Middle,** and **Align Bottom** commands align graphics along an invisible horizontal line.
   > Click the **Align to Slide** option to align graphics along the edges and center of the slide, rather than relative to each other.
   > The **Distribute Horizontally** and **Distribute Vertically** options evenly space the graphics on the slide. In order to use these options, the **Align to Slide** option must be active.

To rotate graphics on a slide:

1. Click the **Format** tab under *Picture Tools*.
2. In the *Arrange* group, click the **Rotate** button and select an option:
   > **Rotate Left 90°**—rotates the graphic 90 degrees counterclockwise.
   > **Rotate Right 90°**—rotates the graphic 90 degrees clockwise.
   > **Flip Horizontal**—reflects the graphic along the vertical axis.
   > **Flip Vertical**—reflects the graphic along the horizontal axis.

To group graphics on a slide:

1. Select the graphics you want to group as one object.
2. Click the **Format** tab under *Picture Tools*.
3. In the *Arrange* group, click the **Group** button and select an option.

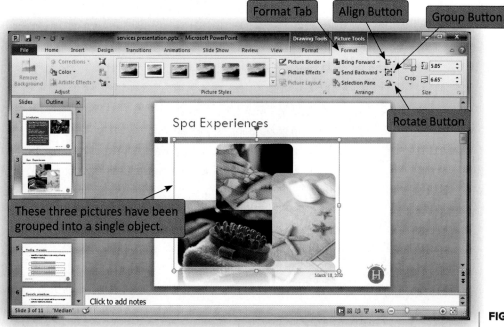

FIGURE PP 3.16

from the perspective of . . .

RETAIL MANAGER

Working in the marketing field, I need to advertise to clients and present at business meetings. With various formatting capabilities such as themes, animations, clip art, and SmartArt, presentation software enables me to quickly create and give professional presentations that incorporate multimedia.

tips & tricks

From the *View* tab you can display gridlines in the *Slide* pane, which is helpful when you have many graphics you want to align. To learn more about this feature, see the topic *Showing the Ruler and Gridlines* in this chapter.

tell me more

Placeholders cannot be grouped. Similarly, objects that have been added to a placeholder cannot be grouped with other objects. In order to group objects, you must add objects to the slide independent of a placeholder.

try this

To group graphics, you can also:

1. Select the graphics you want to group as one object.
2. Right-click the selected graphics, point to *Group*, and select **Group.**

3.16 Applying Animation Effects

Adding **animations** to slides can help emphasize important points and grab your audience's attention. In PowerPoint you can animate individual objects on a slide, including text, images, charts, tables, and SmartArt.

There are four basic types of animation schemes:

Entrance—animates the object coming on to the slide; starts with the object not visible and ends with the object visible. Examples of *Entrance* animations include *Fade In, Split, Fly In,* and *Appear.*

Emphasis—animates the object on the screen. Examples of *Emphasis* animations include *Pulse, Spin, Grow/Shrink,* and *Teeter.*

Exit—animates the object leaving the slide; starts with the object visible and ends with the object not visible.

Examples of *Exit* animations include *Fade, Disappear, Float Out,* and *Wipe.*

Motion Paths—animates the object along an invisible line. Examples of *Motion Path* animations include *Lines, Arcs,* and *Loops.*

To add an animation to an object:

1. Select the object you want to animate.
2. Click the **Animations** tab.
3. In the *Animation* group, click the **More** button.
4. In the *Animation* gallery, click an option to apply it to the object.

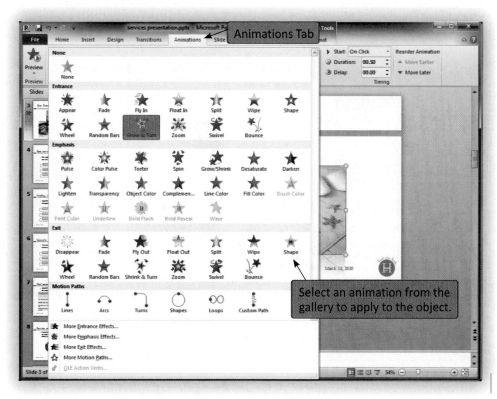

FIGURE PP 3.17

---

tips & tricks

To remove an animation, select **None** in the gallery.

try **this**

To add an animation, you can also select an animation option from the *Advanced Animation* gallery.

3.17 Modifying Animations

Although PowerPoint comes with a number of easy-to-use, prebuilt animations, you may find that you want to further customize those animations to better suit your needs. You can create complex animations by adding additional animations, changing the effect options, and modifying the timing of animations. All these properties can be changed from the *Animations* tab.

To customize an animation:

1. Select the object with the animation you want to modify.
2. Click the **Animations** tab on the Ribbon.
3. Click the **Effects Options** button to change the default behavior of the animation.

4. Click the **Add Animation** button to add more animations to an object, including entrance effects, emphasis effects, exit effects, and motion paths.
5. Click the arrow next to the *Start:* box and select when the animation will play—*On Click, With Previous,* or *After Previous.*
6. Enter a time in the *Duration:* box to control how fast or slow the animation plays. The higher the number, the slower the animation.
7. Enter a time in the *Delay:* box to add a break before the animation plays.

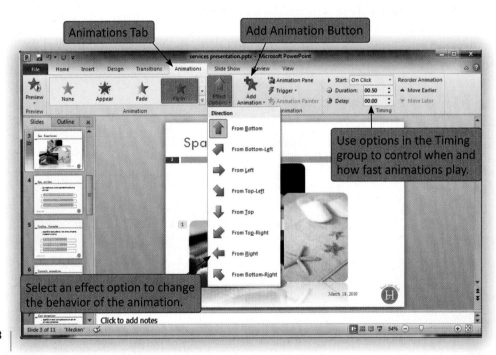

FIGURE PP 3.18

tips & tricks

When you add animations to objects, a number appears next to the object with the animation. This number indicates the order in which the animations will play. To reorder animations, click the **Move Earlier** or **Move Later** buttons in the *Timing* group.

tell me **more**

To see an overview of all the animation effects for a slide, click the **Animation Pane** button. The Animation pane lists each animation for the current slide and the order in which they will play. From the Animation pane, you can modify the behavior of each animation and then preview any changes you make.

Skill Review 3.1

In this review, you will use the skills learned in Chapter 3 to edit an existing presentation.

1. Open an existing presentation:

   a. Open Microsoft PowerPoint 2010.

   b. On the *File* tab, click **Open.**

   c. In the *Open* dialog box, navigate to the location of your PowerPoint 2010 student files.

   d. Find *Ch3_Review1_NewPC.pptx* and double-click the file to open it.

   e. On the *File* tab, click the **Save As** option.

   f. Change the file name to *[your initials]*`PP_SkillReview_3-1,` and then click **OK.**

2. Change themes and theme effects:

   a. Apply a theme to the slide master:

     (1) Verify that you are in Slide Master view and that the slide master is selected.

     (2) On the *Slide Master* tab, in the *Edit Theme* group, click the **Themes** button.

     (3) Click the **Metro** theme in the gallery.

     (4) All the slides in your presentation now use the new theme.

     (5) Close the Slide Master view.

   b. Apply a color theme in Normal view:

     (1) On the *Design* tab, in the *Themes* group, click the **Theme Colors** button.

     (2) Select the **Trek** color theme from the list that appears.

   c. Change the background style:

     (1) On the *Design* tab, in the *Background* group, click the **Background Styles** button.

     (2) Select **Style 8** from the *Background Styles* gallery.

   d. Change the font:

     (1) On **Slide 1,** select the **Title** placeholder.

     (2) On the *Home* tab, click the arrow next to the **Font** box.

     (3) Scroll the list to find **Corbel** and click the font name.

   e. Change the size of the text:

     (1) On the *Home* tab, click the arrow next to the **Font Size** box.

     (2) Scroll the list to find **60,** and then click it.

3. Apply *Quick Styles* to text boxes, tables, and shapes, and adjust the layout of SmartArt:

   a. Apply *Quick Styles* to a text box:

     (1) On **Slide 3,** select the **Title** text box.

     (2) On the *Home* tab, in the *Drawing* group, click the **Quick Styles** button and select **Moderate Effect–Brown, Accent 4** (fifth row, fifth effect).

   b. Change the look of a text box:

     (1) On the *Home* tab, in the *Drawing* group, click the **Shape Effects** button, point to **Bevel,** and select **Cool Slant** (first row, fourth effect).

     (2) On the *Home* tab, in the *Paragraph* group, click the **Center** button.

c. Apply *Quick Styles* to a table:

    (1) On **Slide 3,** select all the cells in the table.

    (2) On the *Table Tools Design* tab, in the *Table Styles* group, click the **More** button and select the **Themed Style 2–Accent 4** (second row, fifth effect) style.

    (3) On the *Home* tab, in the *Font* group, click the **Bold** and **Shadow** buttons.

d. Use the *Shape Styles* gallery:

    (1) On **Slide 3,** select the = shape. Press the **Ctrl** key and select the ≠ shape.

    (2) Click the **Drawing Tools Format** tab.

    (3) In the *Shape Styles* group, click the **More** button and select **Moderate Effect–Brown, Accent 4** (fifth row, fifth effect).

e. Change the layout of SmartArt:

    (1) On **Slide 2,** select the **Process SmartArt** object.

    (2) On the *SmartArt Tools Design* tab, in the *Layouts* group, click the **More** button and select the **Step-Up Process** layout.

    (3) Place your mouse on one of the corners of the SmartArt object. When the mouse changes to the resize cursor, click and drag the mouse to decrease the size of the object.

    (4) Move the SmartArt object to align to the right of the first bullet item.

4. Apply a picture style to an image:

a. On **Slide 1,** select the picture.

b. Click the **Format** tab under *Picture Tools*.

c. In the *Picture Styles* group, click the **More** button and select the **Soft Edge Oval** style.

5. Show the ruler and gridlines, and change placeholder size:

a. Show the ruler and gridlines:

    (1) Display gridlines in PowerPoint:

      (a) Click the **View** tab.

      (b) In the *Show* group, click the **Gridlines** check box to select it.

    (2) Display the ruler in PowerPoint:

      (a) Click the **View** tab.

      (b) In the *Show* group, click the **Ruler** check box to select it.

b. Change the size of a placeholder:

    (1) On **Slide 2,** select the *Title* placeholder.

    (2) Place your mouse on the middle right sizing tool.

    (3) When the mouse changes to the resize cursor, click and drag the mouse to the left to decrease the size of the object until the right side aligns with **1″** on the horizontal ruler.

6. Edit image alignment, grouping, rotating, and sizing:

a. Align, group, and rotate images:

    (1) Align graphics on a slide:

      (a) On **Slide 4,** select the first image. Press the **Ctrl** key and select the second and third images.

      (b) Click the **Format** tab under *Picture Tools*.

      (c) In the *Arrange* group, click the **Align** button and select **Align Bottom**.

(2) Rotate graphics on a slide:

    (a) On **Slide 4,** select the **shopping cart** image.

    (b) In the *Arrange* group, click the **Rotate** button and select **Flip Horizontal.**

(3) Group graphics on a slide:

    (a) On **Slide 4,** select the four graphics.

    (b) In the *Arrange* group, click the **Group** button and select **Group.**

b. Change the size of images:

(1) On **Slide 4,** select the grouped graphic.

(2) Point to one of the resize handles on lower-right side of the image.

(3) When the mouse changes to the resize cursor, press the **Shift** key and drag the mouse until the image equals a height of **1.5** inches.

7. Apply animation effects to an object:

a. On **Slide 2,** select the **Content** placeholder.

b. Click the **Animations** tab.

c. In the *Animation* group, click the **More** button and select **Fly In.**

d. In the *Animation* group, click the **Effect Options** button and select **From Bottom-Left.**

e. View the presentation.

f. Save the presentation.

Skill Review **3.2**

In this review, you will use the skills learned in Chapter 3 to edit an existing presentation.

1. Open an existing presentation:

a. Open Microsoft PowerPoint 2010.

b. On the *File* tab, click **Open.**

c. In the *Open* dialog box, navigate to the location of your PowerPoint 2010 student files.

d. Find *Ch3_Review2_MedPlan.pptx* and double-click the file to open it.

e. On the *File* tab, click the **Save As** option.

f. Change the file name to *[your initials]* PP_SkillReview_3-2, and then click **OK.**

2. Change themes and theme effects:

a. Apply a theme to the slide master:

(1) Verify that you are in Slide Master view and that the slide master is selected.

(2) On the *Slide Master* tab, in the *Edit Theme* group, click the **Themes** button.

(3) Click the **Grid** theme in the gallery.

(4) All the slides in your presentation now use the new theme.

(5) Close the Slide Master view.

b. Apply a color theme in Normal view:

(1) On the *Design* tab, in the *Themes* group, click the **Theme Colors** button.

(2) Select the **Essential** color theme from the list that appears.

    c. Change the background style:

       (1) On the *Design* tab, in the *Background* group, click the **Background Styles** button.

       (2) Select **Style 2** from the *Background Styles* gallery.

    d. Change the font:

       (1) Select **Slide 1.**

       (2) Select the **Title** placeholder.

       (3) On the *Home* tab, in the *Font* group, click the arrow next to the **Font** box.

       (4) Scroll the list to find **Berlin Sans FB** and click the font name.

    e. Change the size of the text:

       (1) On the *Home* tab, in the *Font* group, click the arrow next to the **Font Size** box.

       (2) Scroll the list to find **36,** and then click it.

3. Apply *Quick Styles* to text boxes, tables, and shapes, and adjust the layout of SmartArt:

    a. Apply *Quick Styles* to a text box:

       (1) On **Slide 3,** select the **Title** text box.

       (2) On the *Home* tab, in the *Drawing* group, click the **Quick Styles** button and select **Subtle Effect–Orange, Accent 5** (fourth row, sixth effect).

    b. Change the look of a text box:

       (1) On the *Home* tab, in the *Drawing* group, click the **Shape Effect** button, point to **Soft Edges,** and select **5 Point.**

    c. Apply *Quick Styles* to a table:

       (1) On **Slide 3,** select all cells in the table.

       (2) On the *Table Tools Design* tab, in the *Table Styles* group, click the **More** button and select **Themed Style 1–Accent 5** (the sixth option in the first row).

       (3) Click the edge of the table and move it centered, below the title.

    d. Use the *Shape Styles* gallery:

       (1) On **Slide 3,** select the shape.

       (2) Click the **Drawing Tools Format** tab.

       (3) In the *Shape Styles* group, click the **More** button and select **Intense Effect–Orange, Accent 5** (the sixth option in the last row).

       (4) In the *Shape Styles* group, click the **Shape Fill** button and select **Red, Text 2.**

    e. Change the layout of SmartArt:

       (1) On **Slide 2,** select the **SmartArt** object.

       (2) On the *SmartArt Tools Design* tab, in the *Layouts* group, click the **More** button and select the **Vertical Curved List** layout (the third option in the sixth row).

       (3) Place your mouse on one of the corners of the SmartArt object. When the mouse changes to the resize cursor, click and drag the mouse to increase the size of the object.

       (4) On the *SmartArt Tools Design* tab, in the *SmartArt Styles* group, click the **Change Colors** button and select **Dark 2–Outline.**

       (5) Move the SmartArt object to align to the right of the second bullet item.

4. Apply a picture style to an image:

    a. On **Slide 1,** select the picture.

    b. Click the **Format** tab under *Picture Tools.*

c. In the *Picture Styles* group, click the **More** button and select the **Rotated, White** style.

d. Select the picture and move it, centered near the top of the right panel.

5. Show the ruler and gridlines, and change placeholder size:

a. Show the ruler and gridlines:

(1) Display gridlines in PowerPoint:

    (a) Click the **View** tab.

    (b) In the *Show* group, click the **Gridlines** check box to select it.

(2) Display the ruler in PowerPoint:

    (a) Click the **View** tab.

    (b) In the *Show* group, click the **Ruler** check box to select it.

b. Change the size of a placeholder:

(1) On **Slide 3,** select the **Title** placeholder.

(2) Place your mouse on the middle right sizing tool.

(3) When the mouse changes to the resize cursor, click and drag the mouse to the left to decrease the size of the object until the right side aligns with the 3″ mark on the right side of the horizontal ruler.

(4) Repeat to decrease the size until the left side aligns with the 3″ mark on the left side of the horizontal ruler.

6. Edit image alignment, grouping, rotating, and sizing:

a. Align, group, and rotate images:

(1) Align graphics on a slide:

    (a) On **Slide 4,** select the first image. Press the **Ctrl** key and select the second and third images.

    (b) Click the **Format** tab under *Picture Tools.*

    (c) In the *Arrange* group, click the **Align** button and **Align Middle.**

(2) Rotate graphics on a slide:

    (a) On **Slide 4,** select the right image.

    (b) On the *Picture Tools Format* tab, in the *Arrange* group, click the **Rotate** button and select **Flip Horizontal.**

(3) Group graphics on a slide:

    (a) On **Slide 4,** select the three graphics.

    (b) On the *Picture Tools Format* tab, in the *Arrange* group, click the **Group** button and select **Group.**

b. Change the size of images:

(1) Point to one of the resize handles on lower-right side of the image.

(2) When the mouse changes to the resize cursor, press the **Shift** key and drag the mouse until the image equals a height of **1.6** inches.

7. Apply animation effects to an object:

a. On **Slide 2,** select the **Content** placeholder.

b. Click the **Animations** tab.

c. In the *Animation* group, click the **More** button and select **Wheel** entrance effect.

d. In the *Animation* group, click the **Effect Options** button and select **4 Spokes.**

e. Save the presentation.

challenge yourself 1

In this challenge, you will use the skills learned in Chapter 3 to format a presentation.

1. Open an existing presentation:
   a. Open Microsoft PowerPoint 2010.
   b. Navigate to the location of your PowerPoint 2010 student files.
   c. Open *3_Chall1_Childproof.pptx.*
   d. Save the file as **[your initials]PP_Challenge_3-3.**

2. Change themes and theme effects:
   a. Apply a theme to the slide master:
      (1) From Slide Master view, change the theme to the **Solstice** theme.
      (2) Close the Slide Master view.
   b. Apply a color theme in Normal view:
      (1) From Normal view, change the theme colors for the presentation to use the **Waveform** color theme.
   c. Change the background style:
      (1) Change the background for the presentation to the **Style 2** background style.
   d. Change the font and font size:
      (1) Select the title on **Slide 1.**
      (2) Change the font to **40 point Comic Sans MS.**

3. Apply *Quick Styles* to text boxes, tables, and shapes, and adjust the layout of SmartArt:
   a. Apply *Quick Styles* to a text box and change the look of a text box:
      (1) On **Slide 1,** change the *Title* text box to the **Moderate Effect–Blue, Accent 2** Quick Style.
      (2) Change the shape effect to **Bevel** and select **Cool Slant.**
      (3) Change the shape effect to **3-D Rotation** and select **Isometric Right Up.**
   b. Apply *Quick Styles* to a table.
      (1) On **Slide 3,** select the table.
      (2) Change the table style to **Dark Style–Accent 1.**
      (3) Center the table below the title.
   c. Use the *Shape Styles* gallery:
      (1) On **Slide 3,** change the shape's style to **Light 1 Outline, Colored Fill–Blue, Accent 2.**
      (2) Change the shape's fill to **Blue–Accent 1.**
   d. Changing the layout of SmartArt:
      (1) On **Slide 2,** change the SmartArt object to the **Continuous Cycle** layout.
      (2) Reduce the size of the SmartArt and align it to the right of the bullets.
      (3) Change the color to **Colorful–Accent Colors.**

4. Apply a picture style to an image:
   a. On **Slide 1,** change the picture style to **Bevel Cross.**
   b. Enlarge the picture to a height of 4 inches.

5. Show the ruler and gridlines, and change placeholder size:
   a. Show the ruler and gridlines:
      (1) Display the **Gridlines.**
      (2) Display the **Ruler.**

b. Change the size of a placeholder:

    (1) On **Slide 1,** select the **Title** placeholder.

    (2) Increase the size to encompass the text in one line.

6. Edit image alignment, grouping, rotating, and sizing:

  a. Align, rotate, and group images:

    (1) On **Slide 4,** select all of the images and **Align Middle.**

    (2) Flip the left image horizontally.

    (3) Group the three images.

  b. Change the size of images:

    (1) On **Slide 4,** select the grouped image.

    (2) Enlarge the grouped image to a height of **3** inches.

7. Apply animation effects to an object:

  a. On **Slide 2,** animate the bullets using the **Fly-In from Bottom Left** effect.

  b. View and save the presentation.

challenge yourself 2

In this challenge, you will use the skills learned in Chapter 3 to format a Web design presentation.

1. Open an existing presentation:

  a. Open Microsoft PowerPoint 2010.

  b. Navigate to the location of your PowerPoint 2010 student files.

  c. Open *3_Chall2_WebDesign.pptx.*

  d. Save the file as *[your initials]*`PP_Challenge_3-4.`

2. Change themes and theme effects:

  a. Apply a theme to the slide master:

    (1) Verify that you are in Slide Master view and that the slide master is selected.

    (2) Change the theme to the **Concourse** theme.

    (3) Close the Slide Master view.

  b. Apply a color theme in Normal view:

    (1) From the *Design* tab, change the theme colors for the presentation to use the **Technic** color theme.

  c. Change the background style and font size:

    (1) Change the background for the presentation to the **Style 8** background style.

    (2) Select the title of **Slide 1.**

    (3) Change the font to **54 point Century Gothic.**

3. Apply *Quick Styles* to text boxes, tables, and shapes, and adjust the layout of SmartArt:

  a. Apply *Quick Styles* to a text box and change the look of a text box:

    (1) On **Slide 1,** change the *Title* text box to the **Intense Effect–Aqua, Accent 1** Quick Style.

    (2) Change the shape effect to **Bevel** and select **Aqua 18 pt glow–Accent color 1.**

    (3) Change the shape effect to **3-D Rotation** and select **Off-Axis 1 Right.**

b. Apply *Quick Styles* to a table:

   (1) On **Slide 3,** select the table.

   (2) Change the table style to **Themed Style 2–Accent 1.**

   (3) Center the table on the page.

c. Use the *Shape Styles* gallery:

   (1) On **Slide 3,** change the shape's style to **Intense Effect–Aqua Accent 1.**

   (2) Change the shape's fill to **Gray–80% Background 2.**

d. Change the layout of SmartArt:

   (1) On **Slide 2,** change the SmartArt object to the **Step-Down Process** layout.

   (2) Reduce the size of the SmartArt and center it below the bullets.

   (3) Change the color to **Colorful Range–Accent Colors 3–4.**

4. Apply a picture style to an image:

   a. On **Slide 1,** change the *Picture Style* to **Soft Edge oval.**

   b. Adjust the picture's color to **Aqua–Accent 1 Light.**

5. Show the ruler and gridlines, and change placeholder size:

   a. Show the ruler and gridlines:

      (1) Display the **Gridlines.**

      (2) Display the **Ruler.**

   b. Change the size of a placeholder:

      (1) On **Slide 1,** select the **Title** placeholder.

      (2) Increase the size of the placeholder to fit well on the slide.

6. Edit image alignment, grouping, rotating, and sizing:

   a. Align, rotate, and group images:

      (1) On **Slide 4,** select both of the images and **Align Middle.**

      (2) Flip the right image horizontally.

      (3) Group the images.

   b. Change the size of images:

      (1) On **Slide 4,** select the grouped image.

      (2) Enlarge the grouped image to a height of **2** inches.

7. Apply animation effects to an object:

   a. On **Slide 2,** animate the bullets using the **Fly-In from Bottom Right** effect.

   b. View and save the presentation.

on your own

Today is your first day teaching your class and you need to create an introductory presentation to share with your students.

1. Create a PowerPoint presentation entitled **[your initials] PP_OnYourOwn_3-5** that includes the following information and components:

2. Use the **Hardcover** theme.

3. Add slides.

SLIDE	TITLE	ADDITIONAL INFORMATION
Slide 1	Welcome & Introduction	Insert a Building Block graphic lower-right corner
Slide 2	The Plan	Bullets: › Welcome › Introductions › Course Schedule › Textbooks › Student Responsibilities
Slide 3	Introduction	Insert Table (1 column, 6 rows) First row—blank Rows 2–6 (one item per row): › Your Name › Birth place › Area of study › Favorite (or dream) vacation › Something interesting about you
Slide 4	Student Responsibilities	Bullets › To attend every class › Be in class on time and not leave early › Be prepared › Participate—it's your class—you are responsible for what you learn! › Contact instructor if problems occur › Courtesy and respect › Have fun!
Slide 5	Let's Get Started!	

4. On **Slide 1,** apply the **Beveled-Perspective** picture style.

5. On **Slide 2,** add a **SmartArt** for the bullet items using the **Basic Cycle** layout.

6. Apply the **Polished** SmartArt style.

7. On **Slide 3,** change the table to the **Medium Accent 2–Accent 5** table style.

8. On **Slide 4,** add a **5-point Star** shape in the lower-right corner.

9. Apply **Colored Fill–Dark Red Accent 5** shape style and a **Bevel Circle** shape effect.

10. On **Slide 5,** apply the **Title Slide** layout.

11. Insert two photographs from the *Clip Art* gallery that pertain to your class (i.e., globe and mouse).

12. **Align** the photographs in the middle.

13. **Group** the photographs.

14. Display the **Ruler** and **Gridlines.**

15. On **Slides 2 and 4,** animate the bullets using a **Fly-In from Bottom** animation.

16. View and save the presentation.

fix it

You have been assigned the task of fixing an existing presentation based on the skills learned in Chapter 3.

1. Using PowerPoint 2010, open *Ch3_Fixit_AutoSafety.pptx*.
2. Save the file as *[your initials]*`PP_FixIt_3-6`.
3. Change the *Master Slide Theme* to **Verve.**
4. Change the *Theme Color* to **Module.**
5. On **Slide 1,** apply the **Soft-Edged Oval** picture style.
6. On **Slide 2,** change the SmartArt layout to **Text Cycle.**
7. Apply the **Inset** SmartArt style.
8. On **Slide 3,** change the table to the **Light Style 1–Accent 2** table style.
9. Apply the **Colored Fill–Light Accent 1** shape style and the **Cool Slant** shape effect.
10. On **Slide 4, Align** the photographs in the middle.
11. **Group** the photographs.
12. Display the **Ruler** and **Gridlines.**
13. On **Slide 2,** animate the bullets using a **Fly-In from Bottom-Left** animation.
14. View and save the file.

chapter **4**

Managing and Delivering Presentations

In this chapter, you will learn the following skills:

Skill **4.1** Deleting Slides from Presentations

Skill **4.2** Changing the Order of Slides

Skill **4.3** Copying and Pasting Slides

Skill **4.4** Using the Office Clipboard

Skill **4.5** Defining a Custom Show

Skill **4.6** Hiding Slides

Skill **4.7** Adding Hyperlinks to Slides

Skill **4.8** Adding Comments

Skill **4.9** Rehearsing Timings

Skill **4.10** Starting the Slide Show

Skill **4.11** Using Presentation Tools

Skill **4.12** Printing Presentations

Skill **4.13** Customizing Handout Masters

Skill **4.14** Previewing and Printing Handouts

> Delete, reorder, copy, and paste slides, and use the Office Clipboard

> Define a custom show and hide slides

> Add hyperlinks and comments

> Rehearse timings and use navigation tools

> Print presentations and handouts

skills

introduction

In this chapter, you will acquire the tools to give a professional presentation. Editing skills such as using the Office Clipboard, changing the order of slides, and copying and pasting slides will help you manage your presentation. Once the presentation is final, this chapter will guide you through the actual presentation process including rehearsing timing and creating handouts for your audience.

4.1 Deleting Slides from Presentations

After you have created all the content for your presentation, it is a good idea to carefully review the slides. As you make a final review, you may find that a slide you created is not really necessary, and you want to permanently remove it. You can remove an entire slide of content by deleting it from the *Slides* tab.

To delete a slide:

1. On the *Slides* tab, right-click the slide you want to delete.
2. Click **Delete Slide** on the menu that appears.

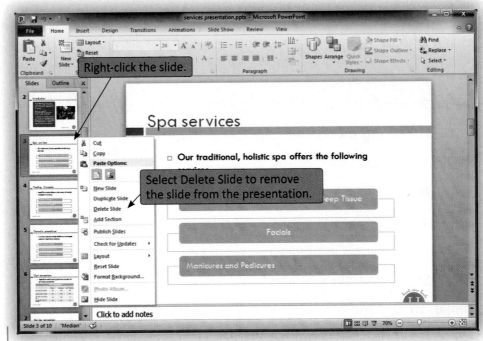

FIGURE PP 4.1

tips & tricks

You can delete multiple slides at once:

1. Click a slide you want to delete and press ⇧Shift on the keyboard.

2. With the *Shift* key still pressed, click another slide. Notice, all the slides between the two slides you clicked have been selected.

3. Right-click any of the selected slides and select **Delete Slide.**

If you want to select slides that are not next to each other, press Ctrl on the keyboard instead of ⇧Shift and click each slide you want to delete. Only the slides you clicked are selected.

try this

To delete a slide, you can also select the slide and press Delete on the keyboard.

4.2 Changing the Order of Slides

One of the most important aspects of a presentation is the flow of the information. It is important that your slides appear in a logical, grouped order for your audience to fully grasp the message you are trying to present. After you have reviewed your presentation, you may find that you want to switch the order of some of your slides. You can change the slide order from the *Slides* tab in Normal view or in Slide Sorter view.

To change the slide order from the *Slides* tab:

1. Select the thumbnail of the slide you want to move.
2. Click and drag until the gray line appears where you want the slide, and then release the mouse button.

The *Slides* tab in Normal view displays the thumbnails of your slides in a vertical pane. Slide Sorter view displays thumbnails of slides in a grid. Slide Sorter view is useful for seeing how your slides work together; you can then move slides around, experimenting with the order.

To change the slide order in Slide Sorter view:

1. Select the thumbnail of the slide you want to move.
2. Click and drag until the gray line appears where you want the slide, and then release the mouse button.

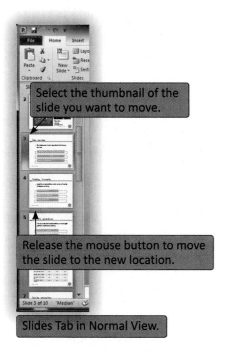

Slides Tab in Normal View.

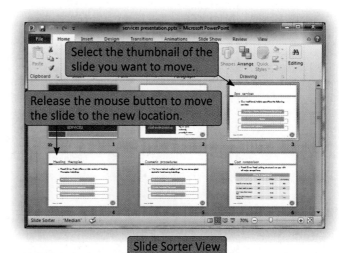

Slide Sorter View

FIGURE PP 4.2

tips & tricks

To select more than one slide to move, select the first slide, then press the ⇧Shift key, and then select the last slide in the set.

tell me **more**

Each slide thumbnail appears with a number next to it indicating its location in the presentation. When you change the order of slides, PowerPoint automatically renumbers the slides for you.

try **this**

To move or copy a slide by dragging, right-click the slide you want to move and drag it to the new location. When you release the mouse button, a menu of options will appear, allowing you to move the slide, copy the slide, or cancel the action.

4.3 Copying and Pasting Slides

You may find when you are creating your presentation that one slide's content and layout is similar to another slide's content and layout that you need to add. Instead of having to re-create all the content for the second slide, you can copy the first slide, paste it into the presentation where you want it to appear, and then change the content you need to change.

To copy and paste slides:

1. Select the slide you want to copy.

2. On the *Home* tab, in the *Clipboard* group, click the **Copy** button.

3. Click the slide that you want to appear before the new slide.

4. Click the **Paste** button.

5. The new slide has been added to the presentation.

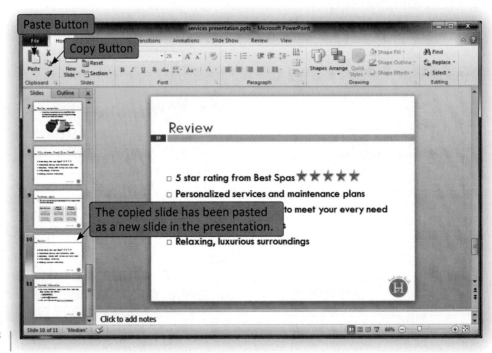

FIGURE PP 4.3

---

tips & tricks

If you want the copy of the slide to appear directly after the slide you are copying, click the arrow next to the *Copy* button and select **Duplicate.**

Click **Cut** in the *Clipboard* group to copy the slide to the Office Clipboard and remove it from its current location in the presentation.

tell me **more**

The *Paste* button now includes a menu of options for pasting slides. You can choose to use the current presentation's theme, keep the formatting for the copied slide, or paste the slide as a picture. If you paste the slide as a picture, it will be inserted as a single image and you will not be able to edit the content.

try **this**

To copy a slide:

> Click the arrow next to the *Copy* button and select **Copy.**

> Press Ctrl + C on the keyboard.

> Right-click the slide and select **Copy.**

To paste a slide:

> Click the arrow below the *Paste* button and select a paste option.

> Press Ctrl + V on the keyboard.

> Right-click the slide and select a paste option.

4.4 Using the Office Clipboard

When you cut or copy items, they are placed on the **Office Clipboard**. A short description or thumbnail of the item represents each item in the task pane, so you know which item you are pasting into your presentation. The Office Clipboard can store up to 24 items for use in the current presentation or any other Office application.

To paste an item from the Office Clipboard into a presentation:

1. Select the item you want to copy.
2. On the *Home* tab, in the *Clipboard* group, click the **Copy** button.
3. Place your cursor where you want to paste the item.
4. On the *Home* tab, in the *Clipboard* group, click the **Clipboard** dialog launcher.
5. The Clipboard task pane appears.
6. Click the item you want to paste.

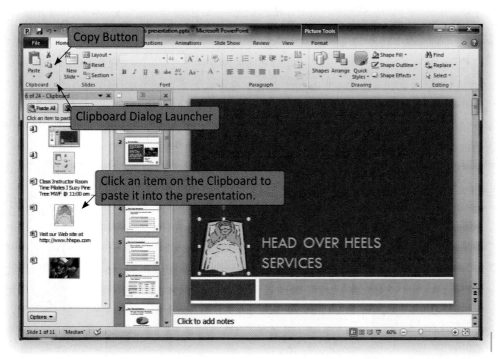

FIGURE PP 4.4

---

tips & tricks

> To remove an item from the Office Clipboard, point to the item, click the arrow that appears, and select **Delete.**

> To add all the items in the Office Clipboard at once, click the **Paste All** button at the top of the task pane.

> To remove all the items from the Office Clipboard at once, click the **Clear All** button at the top of the task pane.

tell me **more**

The Office Clipboard makes it easy to copy and paste items between presentations and between applications. The icons in the Office Clipboard identify the type of document from which each item originated (Word, Excel, Paint, etc.). When you copy an item in one application, such as Excel, the item will appear in the task pane when the Office Clipboard is opened in PowerPoint.

try **this**

To paste an item, you can also point to the item in the Clipboard task pane, click the arrow that appears, and select **Paste.**

4.5 Defining a Custom Show

A **custom slide show** is a slide show that runs inside another presentation. Custom shows give you the ability to customize your presentation for your audience. Instead of creating multiple presentations for different audiences, you can add custom shows to the original presentation and repurpose the presentation for different audiences.

To define a custom slide show:

1. Click the **Slide Show** tab.
2. In the *Start Slide Show* group, click the **Custom Slide Show** button and select **Custom Shows . . .**
3. In the *Custom Shows* dialog box, click the **New . . .** button.
4. In the *Define Custom Show* dialog box, select the slides you want in your custom show.
5. Click the **Add** button.
6. Click the up ⬆ and down ⬇ arrows to reorder your slides.
7. In the *Slide show name:* box, type the name of the custom show.
8. Click **OK** to add the custom show to your presentation.
9. To close the *Custom Shows* dialog box, click the **Close** button.

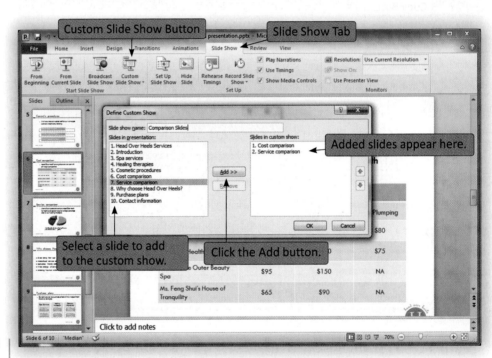

FIGURE PP 4.5

tips & tricks

› To play a custom show, click the **Custom Slide Show** button and select the name of the custom show you want to play. The custom show will open in Slide Show view, allowing you to run through the slides in the custom show.

› In the *Custom Shows* dialog box, click the **Show** button to preview the custom slide show.

tell me **more**

There are two main types of custom slide shows: basic and hyperlinked. Basic custom slide shows display a subset of slides of the main presentation. For example, if you only have 30 minutes to present, but your presentation is 45 minutes long, you could create two custom shows within the same presentation: one with 45 minutes of content and the other with 30 minutes of content. Hyperlinked custom slide shows display slides that are not part of the main presentation. Use hyperlinked custom slide shows for content that you may or may not want to access in the presentation.

4.6 Hiding Slides

When you practice your presentation, you may find that you want to omit certain slides, but that you do not want to delete them from your presentation, in case you need them later. Hiding slides allows you to prevent slides from being seen without permanently removing them.

To hide slides:

1. Select the slide you want to hide.

2. Click the **Slide Show** tab.

3. In the *Set Up* group, click the **Hide Slide** button.

When a slide is hidden, the hidden slide icon **2** appears over the slide number in the *Slide* pane.

To unhide the slide, click the **Hide Slide** button again.

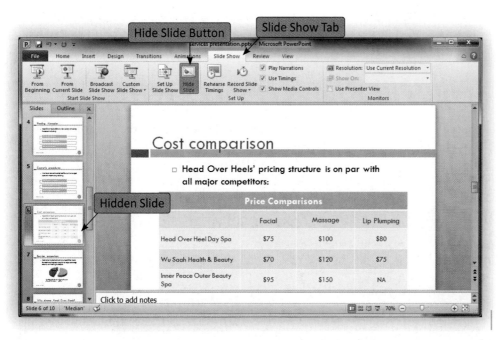

FIGURE PP 4.6

tips & tricks

To unhide a slide during a presentation, right-click any slide, point to **Go to Slide,** and select the slide you want to display. Hidden slides will appear in the list with parentheses around the number. For example, if the third slide in a presentation is hidden, the menu will display the number as (3).

try **this**

To hide a slide, you can also right-click the slide on the *Slides* tab and select **Hide Slide.** To unhide a slide, right-click the slide again and select **Unhide Slide.**

4.7 Adding Hyperlinks to Slides

A **hyperlink** is text or a graphic that when clicked takes you to a new location. You can use hyperlinks to navigate to Web pages, other PowerPoint presentations, custom shows, or any slide in the presentation. When you point to a hyperlink, your mouse cursor turns to a hand, indicating that it is something that can be clicked.

Some hyperlinks include ScreenTips. A **ScreenTip** is a bubble with text that appears when the mouse is placed over

the link. Add a ScreenTip to include a more meaningful description of the hyperlink.

To add a hyperlink from one slide to another slide in the same presentation:

1. Select the text or object you want as the link.
2. Click the **Insert** tab.
3. In the *Links* group, click the **Insert Hyperlink** button.

FIGURE PP 4.7

4. The *Insert Hyperlink* dialog box opens.
5. Under *Link to:* select **Place in This Document.**
6. Select the slide to link to.

7. Type the text for the ScreenTip in the *Text to display:* box.
8. Click **OK** to insert the hyperlink into your presentation.

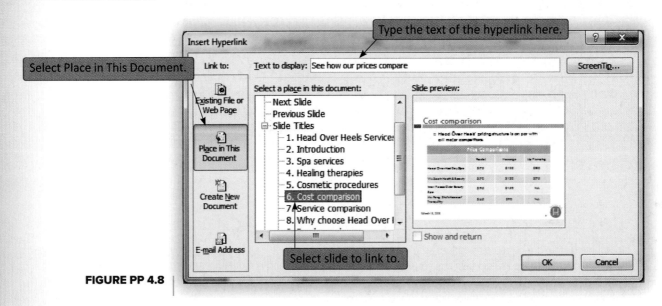

FIGURE PP 4.8

---

tips & tricks

To remove a hyperlink, first select the hyperlink you want to remove. In the *Links* group, click the **Hyperlink** button. In the *Edit Hyperlink* dialog box, click the **Remove Hyperlink** button.

tell me **more**

Text hyperlinks follow the color scheme of the presentation, and change color after they have been clicked.

try **this**

To open the *Insert Hyperlink* dialog box, you can also

> Right-click the object and select **Hyperlink . . .** from the menu.
> Press [Ctrl] + [K] on the keyboard.

4.8 Adding Comments

Comments are small messages you add to slides that are not meant to be a part of the presentation. Comments are useful when you are reviewing a presentation and want to add messages about changes or errors on a slide.

To insert a comment on a slide:

1. Click the **Review** tab.
2. In the *Comments* group, click the **New Comment** button.
3. A balloon appears on the screen with the cursor ready for you to enter your comment.
4. Type your comment.
5. Click outside the comment to minimize it.

6. To view the comment, click the comment's icon on the slide.

If you do not want your comments to display in the *Slide* pane, you can hide the comments in the presentation. On the *Review* tab, in the *Comments* group, click the **Show Markup** button to hide the comments in the presentation. Click the **Show Markup** button again to show the comments. The *Show Markup* button toggles between its normal and active state when clicked. When comments are displayed in a presentation, the *Show Markup* button appears in its active state. When comments are hidden, the *Show Markup* button returns to its normal state.

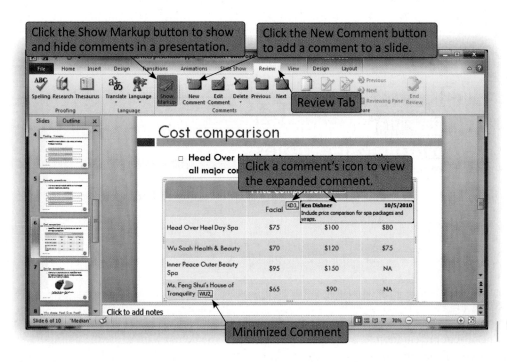

FIGURE PP 4.9

---

tips & tricks

Click the **Delete Comment** button on the Ribbon to delete a comment from the presentation.

tell me **more**

To edit a comment, first display the comment you want to edit. In the *Comments* group, click the **Edit Comment** button. Edit the comment in the balloon and click outside the comment to minimize it.

try **this**

To insert a comment, you can also right-click any comment and select **New Comment** from the menu.

4.9 Rehearsing Timings

Timing is an important part of your presentation. For example, you wouldn't want to be part way through explaining the content of a slide and have your presentation advance before you are ready. Before you give your presentation, it is a good idea to rehearse what you will say and set up the timing for the slide show. Use PowerPoint's Rehearse Timings feature to synchronize your verbal presentation with your slides.

To use PowerPoint's Rehearse Timing feature:

1. Click the **Slide Show** tab.
2. In the *Set Up* group, click the **Rehearse Timings** button.

3. When the first slide appears, begin rehearsing your presentation.
4. Click the **Pause** button if you want to stop the timer.
5. Click the **Next** button to advance to the next slide.
6. Continue rehearsing each slide, clicking the **Next** button to advance the slides, until you reach the end of the presentation.
7. At the end of the presentation, you will be asked if you want to keep the timing as part of your slide show. Click **Yes** to include the timings as part of the presentation.

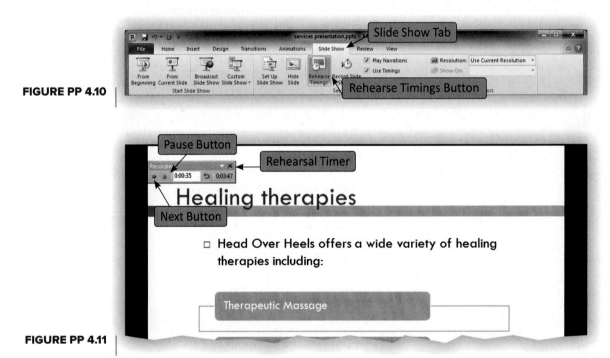

FIGURE PP 4.10

FIGURE PP 4.11

After you have rehearsed the timing of your presentation, you can choose to use the timings or not. If you want to use the timings, select the **Use Rehearsed Timings** check box in the *Set Up* group. If you do not want to use the timings, uncheck the box.

tips & tricks

When you are timing your presentation, be sure to speak slowly and carefully, and to pause slightly before you advance to the next slide.

tell me **more**

PowerPoint also includes the ability to record your own narration for a presentation and then include the narration as part of the presentation. Click the **Record Slide Show** button to record narration along with the timing for slides.

try **this**

You can enter the timing for a slide directly into the *Slide Time* box.

4.10 Starting the Slide Show

You can choose to start your presentation from the beginning, playing it all the way through. But what if you find you don't have as much time as you originally planned to present? You can also choose to start the presentation from any slide in the presentation.

To start a presentation from the beginning:

1. Click the **Slide Show** tab.
2. In the *Start Slide Show* group, click the **From Beginning** button.

To start a presentation from the current slide:

1. Click the **Slide Show** tab.
2. In the *Start Slide Show* group, click the **From Current Slide** button.

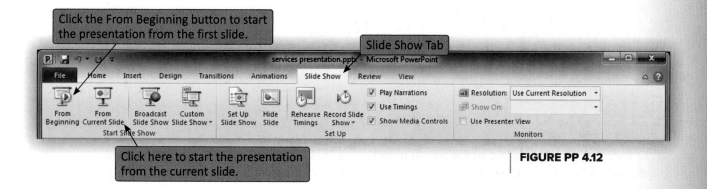

Click the From Beginning button to start the presentation from the first slide.

Slide Show Tab

Click here to start the presentation from the current slide.

FIGURE PP 4.12

tips & tricks

Another way to start a presentation from the beginning is to select the first slide in the presentation and use any of the methods for playing the presentation from the current slide.

try **this**

To start a slide show from the current slide, you can also click the **Slide Show** view button 🖵 on the status bar.

4.11 Using Presentation Tools

Once you have started the slide show, you will need a way to advance through the slides as you talk. You can use the Rehearse Timings feature to automatically advance the slide show for you. However, if you want the freedom to depart from your script, you will want to navigate the slide show yourself. This table lists commands for navigating a presentation in Slide Show view using the mouse and the keyboard:

Slide Show Navigation		
COMMAND	**MOUSE COMMAND**	**KEYBOARD COMMAND**
Next Slide	Left-click on the slide. Right-click and select **Next.**	Press **Enter.** Press the **Spacebar.**
Previous Slide	Right-click and select **Previous.**	Press **Backspace.**
Specific Slide	Right-click, point to **Go to Slide,** and select the slide.	Press the number of the slide and press **Enter.**
Exit the Presentation	Right-click and select **End Show.**	Press **Escape.**

The presentation tools in PowerPoint allow you to write on your slides while you are giving your presentation. You can use the **Pen** tool to underline or circle important points as you discuss them. Use the **Highlighter** tool to add color behind text on slides and emphasize parts of your slides.

To make notations on slides using the presentation tools:

1. In Slide Show view, click the **Pointer Options** button.

2. Select a pointer option **Pen** or **Highlighter.**

3. Click and drag the mouse to write on the slide or highlight part of the slide.

4. Click the **Pointer Options** button and select **Arrow** to return to the arrow pointer.

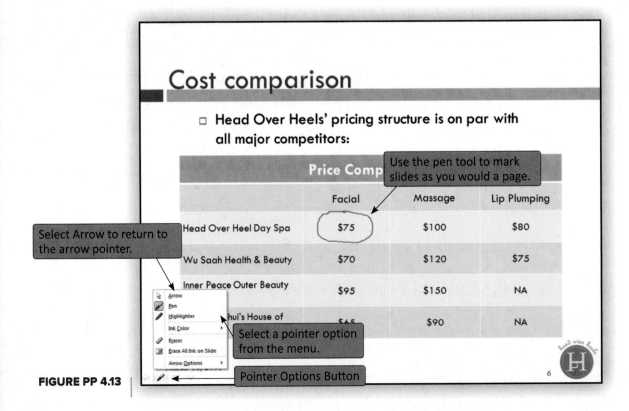

FIGURE PP 4.13

from the perspective of . . .

STUDENT

I was terrified at the idea of presenting in my oral communication class. Using presentation software I integrated tables, pictures, text, video, and sound, all in one presentation. The day I presented, I rocked!

tips & tricks

> If you want to see the last slide you viewed, but it is not part of the slide order, right-click the presentation and select **Last Viewed** on the menu.

> To view a custom show, right-click the presentation, point to **Custom Show,** and select a custom show.

try **this**

You can also use the *Slide Show* toolbar, located in the lower-left corner of the slide, to navigate through a presentation.

> Click the **Next** button to navigate to the next slide in the presentation.

> Click the **Previous** button to navigate to the previous slide in the presentation.

> Click the **Slide Show Menu** button for access to more powerful navigation commands, such as navigating to a specific slide.

4.12 Printing Presentations

Printing has changed significantly in PowerPoint 2010. Previous versions of PowerPoint relied on *Print Preview* for setting printing options. In PowerPoint 2010, the *Print* tab in Backstage view provides access to all of the printing options for presentations. From the *Print* tab in Backstage view, you can adjust your settings to print the slides in color, grayscale, or black and white. You can also adjust other elements of the slide, such as the header and footer.

To preview and print a presentation:

1. Click the **File** tab to open Backstage view.

2. Click the **Print** tab.

3. Verify that the correct printer name is displayed in the *Printer* section.

4. In the *Settings* section, the last button displays the color options for printing the presentation. By default, *Color* is selected. To change the print selection, click the button, and then click an option: **Color, Grayscale,** or **Pure Black and White.**

5. Click the **Print** button to print.

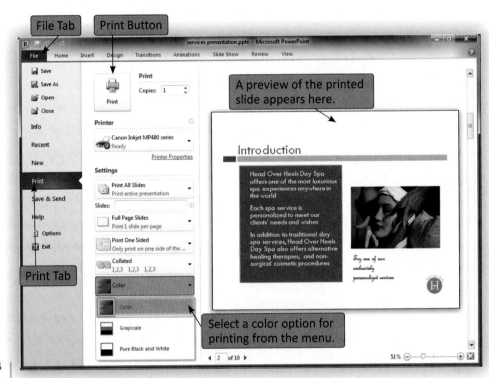

FIGURE PP 4.14

4.13 Customizing Handout Masters

The **Handout Master** view allows you to modify how the printed version of your presentation will look. When you open the presentation in Handout Master view, you will see a preview of the printed page with dotted placeholders for the slides, header, footer, page number, and date.

To open Handout Master view:

1. Click the **View** tab.
2. In the *Master Views* group, click the **Handout Master** button.

FIGURE PP 4.15

You can show and hide placeholders in Handout Master view. When you hide a placeholder, it no longer appears in the Handout Master view. To show and hide a placeholder, on the *Handout Master* tab, in the *Placeholders* group, click the placeholder's check box.

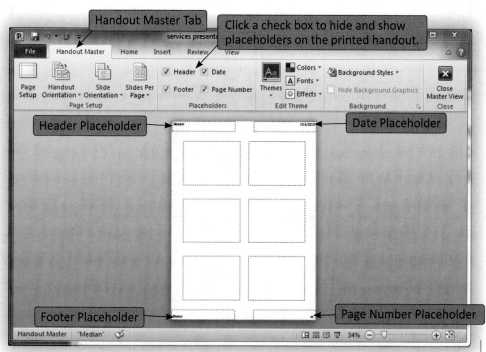

FIGURE PP 4.16

Placeholders you can hide and show include

Header—appears in the upper-left corner of the page and displays the text you entered for the header in the *Header and Footer* dialog box.

Date—appears in the upper-right corner of the page and displays the date.

Footer—appears in the lower-left corner of the page and displays the text you entered for the footer.

Page Number—appears in the lower-right corner of the page and displays the current number of the printed page (not the slide number).

4.14 Previewing and Printing Handouts

In addition to printing slides, PowerPoint also gives you the ability to print handouts, notes, and an outline of the presentation. A **handout** is a printout of your presentation with anywhere from one to nine slides per page and with areas for taking notes. The **Notes Pages** option will print a copy of the slide with its associated note, if there is one. Select **Outline View** when you want to print a text outline of your presentation. As with printing presentations, printing of handouts, notes pages, and outlines are all done from the *Print* tab in Backstage view.

To preview and print outlines, handouts, and notes:

1. Click the **File** tab to open Backstage view.
2. Click the **Print** tab.
3. Verify that the correct printer name is displayed in the *Printer* section.
4. In the *Settings* section, the second button displays the page options for printing the presentation. By default, *Full Page Slides* is selected. To change the print selection, click the button and then select an option.
5. Click the **Print** button to print.

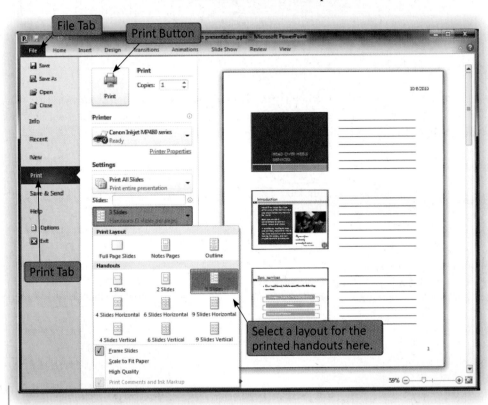

FIGURE PP 4.17

tips & tricks

The *Handouts (3 Slides)* layout includes lines next to the slide image. This layout is useful if you want to print your presentation for your audience and include an area where they can easily write notes to correspond with each slide.

try this

To open the *Print* tab in Backstage view, you can use the keyboard shortcut Ctrl + P.

tell me more

From the *Page Options* button, you can also adjust the following settings:

Scale to Fit Paper—resizes the slides to fit the paper size.

Frame Slides—draws a thin border around the slides for the printed version.

High Quality—prints slides in a higher resolution, allowing for more detailed images and effects.

Print Comments and Ink Markup—allows you to include comments and ink markup in your printed presentation.

projects

Skill Review **4.1**

In this review, you will use the skills learned in Chapter 4 to manage and deliver an existing presentation.

1. Open an existing presentation:
   a. Open Microsoft PowerPoint 2010.
   b. On the *File* tab, click **Open.**
   c. In the *Open* dialog box, navigate to the location of your PowerPoint 2010 student files.
   d. Find *Ch4_Review1_Menu.pptx* and double-click the file to open it.
   e. On the *File* tab, click the **Save As** option.
   f. Change the file name to **[your initials]PP_SkillReview_4-1,** and then click **OK.**

2. Delete, reorder, copy, and paste slides, and use the Office Clipboard.
   a. Delete and reorder slides:
      (1) Right-click **Slide 6** on the *Slides* tab.
      (2) Select **Delete Slide.**
      (3) Click the **Undo** button to redisplay the slide.
   b. Reorder slides from the *Slides* tab:
      (1) Select the thumbnail of **Slide 7.**
      (2) Click and drag until the gray line appears above **Slide 6,** and then release the mouse button.
   c. Use the Office Clipboard to copy and paste slides:
      (1) Select the thumbnail of **Slide 7.**
      (2) On the *Home* tab, in the *Clipboard* group, click the **Copy** button.
      (3) Click between the thumbnails of **Slide 1** and **Slide 2.**
      (4) On the *Home* tab, in the *Clipboard* group, click the **Paste** button.

3. Define a custom show:
   a. Click the **Slide Show** tab.
   b. In the *Start Slide Show* group, click the **Custom Slide Show** button and select **Custom Shows . . .**
   c. Click the **New . . .** button.
   d. In the *Define Custom Show* dialog box, select **Slides 1, 3, 4, 5, 6, 7,** and **8.**
   e. Click the **Add** button.
   f. In the *Slide show name:* box, type **Basic**
   g. Click **OK** to add the custom show to your presentation.
   h. To close the *Custom Shows* dialog box, click the **Close** button.

4. Add hyperlinks and comments.
   a. Add a hyperlink from one slide to another slide in the same presentation:
      (1) On **Slide 3,** select the **Food Log** text.
      (2) Click the **Insert** tab.

(3) In the *Links* group, click the **Insert Hyperlink** button.

(4) The *Insert Hyperlink* dialog box opens.

(5) Under *Link to:* select **Place in This Document**.

(6) Select **Slide 4** to link to.

(7) Click **OK** to insert the hyperlink into your worksheet.

b. Add comments:

(1) On **Slide 3,** select the **Fewer carbs** text; then click the **Review** tab.

(2) In the *Comments* group, click the **New Comment** button.

(3) A balloon appears on the screen with the cursor ready for you to enter your comment.

(4) Type: Bad carbs - choose healthy carbs

(5) Click outside the comment to hide it.

5. Rehearse timings and use navigation tools.

a. Use PowerPoint's Rehearse Timing feature:

(1) Click the **Slide Show** tab.

(2) In the *Set Up* group, click the **Rehearse Timings** button.

(3) When the first slide appears, begin rehearsing your presentation.

(4) Click the **Pause** button if you want to stop the timer.

(5) Click the **Next** button to advance to the next slide.

(6) Continue rehearsing each slide, clicking the **Next** button to advance the slides, until you reach the end of the presentation.

(7) At the end of the presentation, you will be asked if you want to keep the timing as part of your slide show. Click **No.**

b. Start a presentation from the beginning:

(1) Click the **Slide Show** tab.

(2) In the *Start Slide Show* group, click the **From Beginning** button.

(3) Exit the presentation by pressing the [Esc] key on the keyboard.

c. Start a presentation from the current slide:

(1) Click the **Slide Show** tab.

(2) In the *Start Slide Show* group, click the **From Current Slide** button.

d. Navigate through the presentation using the keyboard:

(1) To advance to the next slide: press [←Enter] or the **Spacebar.**

(2) To go to the previous slide: press [←Backspace].

(3) To jump to a specific slide: type the number of the slide and press [←Enter].

(4) To exit the presentation: press [Esc].

e. Navigate through your presentation using only the mouse:

(1) To advance to the next slide: click the mouse or right-click and select **Next.**

(2) To go to the previous slide: right-click and select **Previous.**

(3) To jump to a specific slide: right-click, point to **Go to Slide,** and select the name of the slide.

(4) To exit the presentation: right-click and select **End Show.**

6. Print presentations and handouts:

a. Print the presentation:

(1) Click the **File** tab to open Backstage view; then click the **Print** tab.

(2) In the *Settings* section, click the **Color** button and select **Grayscale** to change the color option for the presentation.

(3) Click the **Print** button to print your slides.

b. Customize *Handout Masters:*

(1) Click the **View** tab.

(2) In the *Master Views* group, click the **Handout Master** button.

(3) In the *Placeholders* group, click the **Date** check box to remove the date from the printed handout.

c. Preview and print outlines, handouts, and notes:

(1) Click the **File** tab to open Backstage view; then click the **Print** tab.

(2) In the *Settings* section, click the second button, and select **Outline.**

(3) Click the **Print** button and print your handouts.

(4) Save the presentation.

Skill Review **4.2**

In this review, you will use the skills learned in Chapter 4 to manage and deliver an existing presentation.

1. Open an existing presentation:

a. Open Microsoft PowerPoint 2010.

b. On the *File* tab, click **Open.**

c. In the *Open* dialog box, navigate to the location of your PowerPoint 2010 student files.

d. Find *Ch4_Review2_EmergingTech.pptx* and double-click the file to open it.

e. On the *File* tab, click the **Save As** option.

f. Change the file name to **[your initials]PP_SkillReview_4-2,** and then click **OK.**

2. Delete, reorder, copy, and paste slides, and use the Office Clipboard.

a. Delete a slide:

(1) Right-click **Slide 6** on the *Slides* tab.

(2) Select **Delete Slide.**

(3) Click the **Undo** button to redisplay the slide.

b. Reorder slides from the *Slides* tab:

(1) Select the thumbnail of **Slide 7.**

(2) Click and drag until the gray line appears above *Slide 6*, and then release the mouse button.

c. Use the Office Clipboard to copy and paste slides:

(1) Select the thumbnail of **Slide 7.**

(2) On the *Home* tab, in the *Clipboard* group, click the **Copy** button.

(3) Click between the thumbnails of **Slide 1** and **Slide 2.**

(4) On the *Home* tab, in the *Clipboard* group, click the **Paste** button.

3. Define a custom show and hide slides.

a. Define a custom show:

(1) Click the **Slide Show** tab.

(2) In the *Start Slide Show* group, click the **Custom Slide Show** button and select **Custom Shows . . .**

(3) Click the **New . . .** button.

(4) In the *Define Custom Show* dialog box, select **Slides 1, 3, 4, 5, 6, 7,** and **8.**

(5) Click the **Add** button.

(6) In the *Slide show name:* box, type `Basic`

(7) Click **OK** to add the custom show to your presentation.

(8) To close the *Custom Shows* dialog box, click the **Close** button.

b. Hide slides:

(1) Right-click **Slide 2** on the *Slides tab*.

(2) Select **Hide Slide.**

4. Add hyperlinks and comments.

a. Add a hyperlink from one slide to another slide in the same presentation:

(1) On **Slide 5,** select the **Communication** text.

(2) Click the **Insert** tab.

(3) In the *Links* group, click the **Insert Hyperlink** button.

(4) The *Insert Hyperlink* dialog box opens.

(5) Under *Link to:* select **Place in This Document.**

(6) Select **Slide 6** to link to.

(7) Click **OK** to insert the hyperlink into your worksheet.

b. Add comments:

(1) On **Slide 4,** select the **IPad** and **IPod** bullet points; then click the **Review** tab.

(2) In the *Comments* group, click the **New Comment** button.

(3) A balloon appears on the screen with the cursor ready for you to enter your comment.

(4) Type: `Change bullets to iPad and iPod`

(5) Click outside the comment to hide it.

5. Rehearse timings and use navigation tools.

a. Use PowerPoint's Rehearse Timing feature:

(1) Click the **Slide Show** tab.

(2) In the *Set Up* group, click the **Rehearse Timings** button.

(3) When the first slide appears, begin rehearsing your presentation.

(4) Click the **Pause** button if you want to stop the timer.

(5) Click the **Next** button to advance to the next slide.

(6) Continue rehearsing each slide, clicking the **Next** button to advance the slides, until you reach the end of the presentation.

(7) At the end of the presentation, you will be asked if you want to keep the timing as part of your slide show. Click **No.**

b. Start a presentation from the beginning:

(1) Click the **Slide Show** tab.

(2) In the *Start Slide Show* group, click the **From Beginning** button.

(3) Exit the presentation by pressing the [Esc] key on the keyboard.

c. Start a presentation from the current slide:

(1) Click the **Slide Show** tab.

(2) In the *Start Slide Show* group, click the **From Current Slide** button.

d. Navigate through the presentation using the keyboard:

    (1) To advance to the next slide: press `←Enter` or the **Spacebar.**

    (2) To go to the previous slide: press `←Backspace`.

    (3) To jump to a specific slide: type the number of the slide and press `←Enter`.

    (4) To exit the presentation: press `Esc`.

e. Navigate through your presentation using only the mouse:

    (1) To advance to the next slide: click the mouse or right-click and select **Next.**

    (2) To go to the previous slide: right-click and select **Previous.**

    (3) To jump to a specific slide: right-click, point to **Go to Slide,** and select the name of the slide.

    (4) To exit the presentation: right-click and select **End Show.**

6. Print presentations and handouts.

a. Print the presentation:

    (1) Click the **File** tab to open Backstage view; then click the **Print** tab.

    (2) In the *Settings* section, click the **Color** button and select **Grayscale** to change the color option for the presentation.

    (3) Click the **Print** button to print your slides.

b. Customize *Handout Masters:*

    (1) Click the **View** tab.

    (2) In the *Master Views* group, click the **Handout Master** button.

    (3) In the *Placeholders* group, click the **Date** check box to remove the date from the printed handout.

c. Preview and print outlines, handouts, and notes:

    (1) Click the **File** tab to open Backstage view; then click the **Print** tab.

    (2) In the *Settings* section, click the second button, and select **Outline.**

    (3) Click the **Print** button and print your handouts.

    (4) Save the presentation.

challenge yourself 1

In this challenge, you will use the skills learned in Chapter 4 to manage and deliver an existing presentation.

1. Open an existing presentation:

a. Open Microsoft PowerPoint 2010.

b. Navigate to the location of your PowerPoint 2010 student files.

c. Open *Ch4_Chall1_FamilyReunion.pptx.*

d. Save the file as *[your initials]*`PP_Challenge_4-3.`

2. Delete, reorder, copy, and paste slides, and use the Office Clipboard.

a. Delete a slide:

    (1) Delete **Slide 6.**

    (2) Click the **Undo** button to redisplay the slide.

b. Reorder and copy slides:

    (1) Move **Slide 7** before **Slide 6.**

    (2) Copy **Slide 7** and paste it between **Slide 1** and **Slide 2**

3. Define a custom show and hide a slide:

    a. Define a new *Custom Slide Show* entitled `Basic` using **Slides 1, 3, 4, 5, 6, 7,** and **8.**

    b. View the custom show.

    c. Hide **Slide 2.**

4. Add hyperlinks and comments:

    a. On **Slide 5,** select the text **Select a theme** and hyperlink it to **Slide 6.**

    b. On **Slide 5,** select the **Photographer** text and add a **New Comment:** `Ask Uncle David`

5. Rehearse timings and use navigation tools:

    a. Rehearse the timings.

    b. Start a presentation from the beginning.

    c. Start a presentation from the current slide.

    d. Navigate through the presentation using the keyboard from slide to slide and directly to *Slide 5.*

    e. Navigate through your presentation using only the mouse.

6. Print presentations and handouts:

    a. Print the presentation in black and white.

    b. Print the *Handouts* **4 to a page.**

    c. Save the presentation.

challenge yourself **2**

In this challenge, you will use the skills learned in Chapter 4 to manage and deliver an existing presentation.

1. Open an existing presentation:

    a. Open Microsoft PowerPoint 2010.

    b. Navigate to the location of your PowerPoint 2010 student files.

    c. Open *Ch4_Chall2_Coffee.pptx.*

    d. Save the file as *[your initials]*`PP_Challenge_4-4.`

2. Delete, reorder, copy, and paste slides, and use the Office Clipboard.

    a. Delete a slide:

        (1) Delete **Slide 5.**

        (2) Click the **Undo** button to redisplay the slide.

    b. Reorder and copy slides:

        (1) Move **Slide 6** before **Slide 5.**

        (2) Copy **Slide 6** and paste it between **Slide 1** and **Slide 2.**

3. Define a custom show and hide a slide:

    a. Define a new *Custom Slide Show* entitled `Basic` using **Slides 1, 3, 4, 5,** and **6.**

    b. View the custom show.

    c. Hide **Slide 2.**

4. Add hyperlinks and comments:

    a. On **Slide 5,** select the text **Service with a smile** and hyperlink it to **Slide 6.**

    b. On **Slide 5,** select the **Work with local farmers** text and add a **New Comment:** `Check with farmers association`

5. Rehearse timings and use navigation tools:

   a. Rehearse the timings.

   b. Start a presentation from the beginning.

   c. Start a presentation from the current slide.

   d. Navigate through the presentation using the keyboard from slide to slide and directly to *Slide 5*.

   e. Navigate through your presentation using only the mouse.

6. Print presentations and handouts:

   a. Print the presentation in black and white.

   b. Print the *Handouts* **4 to a page.**

   c. Save the presentation.

on your own

You are charged with holding the initial meeting for the local block watch committee and want to create an introductory presentation to share with your neighbors.

1. Navigate to the location of your PowerPoint 2010 student files.

2. Open *Ch4_OYO_Blockwatch.pptx*.

3. Save the file as *[your initials]*`PP_OnYourOwn_4-5.`

4. Delete **Slide 5.**

5. Click the **Undo** button to redisplay the slide.

6. Move **Slide 6** after *Slide 8*.

7. Copy **Slide 8** and paste it between **Slide 2** and **Slide 3.**

8. Define a new *Custom Slide Show* entitled `Basic` using all but **Slide 3.**

9. View the custom show.

10. Hide **Slide 2.**

11. On **Slide 6,** select the text **SMART** and hyperlink it to **Slide 8.**

12. On **Slide 4,** select the **Safety** text and add a **New Comment:** `Top Priority`

13. Rehearse the timings.

14. Start a presentation from the beginning.

15. Start a presentation from the current slide.

16. Navigate through the presentation using the keyboard from slide to slide and directly to *Slide 5*.

17. Navigate through your presentation using only the mouse.

18. Print the presentation in black and white.

19. Print the *Handouts* **4 to a page.**

20. Save the presentation.

fix it

You have been assigned the task of fixing an existing presentation based on the skills learned in Chapter 4.

1. Using PowerPoint 2010, open *Ch4_Fixit_Students.pptx*.

2. Save the file as *[your initials]*`PP_FixIt_4-6.`

3. Move **Slide 6** before **Slide 5.**

4. Copy **Slide 6** and paste it between **Slide 1** and **Slide 2.**

5. Define a new *Custom Slide Show* entitled Basic using all but **Slide 2.**

6. View the custom show.

7. Hide **Slide 2.**

8. On **Slide 3,** select the text **Preparation** and hyperlink it to **Slide 5.**

9. On **Slide 6,** select the **Responsibility** text and add a **New Comment:** Learner success with learner responsibility

10. Rehearse the timings.

11. Start a presentation from the beginning.

12. Start a presentation from the current slide.

13. Navigate through the presentation using the keyboard from slide to slide and directly to *Slide 5.*

14. Navigate through your presentation using only the mouse.

15. Print the presentation in black and white.

16. Print the *Handouts* **4 to a page.**

17. Save the presentation.

chapter 5

Exploring Advanced Graphics, Tables, and Charts

In this chapter, you will learn the following skills:

Skill **5.1**   Applying Artistic Effects to Pictures

Skill **5.2**   Removing the Background from Pictures

Skill **5.3**   Correcting Pictures

Skill **5.4**   Changing the Color of Pictures

Skill **5.5**   Cropping Graphics

Skill **5.6**   Compressing Pictures

Skill **5.7**   Resetting Pictures

Skill **5.8**   Aligning Text in Tables

Skill **5.9**   Inserting and Deleting Rows and Columns in Tables

Skill **5.10** Modifying Charts

Skill **5.11** Animating Charts

Skill **5.12** Creating Multipart Animations

Skill **5.13** Setting Animation Timings

Skill **5.14** Creating an Action Button

Skill **5.15** Recording a Slide Show

Skill **5.16** Editing Audio on a Slide

Skill **5.17** Editing Video on a Slide

Skill **5.18** Creating a Photo Album

skills

> Learn to modify pictures using the new picture effects available in PowerPoint 2010

> Make a presentation file size smaller by changing the compression settings for images

> Align text in tables and insert rows and columns

> Modify charts including layouts, styles, and animating a chart

> Create a multipart animation and adjust the animation timings

> Add an action button to a slide

> Record the slide show, including narration

> Edit audio and video from within the PowerPoint application

> Create a photo album of digital photographs

introduction

In this chapter, students will learn more advanced skills for working with graphics, tables, and charts. They will learn about the new picture effects available in PowerPoint 2010. They will learn to modify tables and charts, as well as learn animation techniques, including animating charts, creating a multipart animation, and working with animation timings. Students will also learn how to edit audio and video clips from inside PowerPoint. Finally, students will learn how to create a slide show of digital photographs using PowerPoint's Photo Album feature.

5.1 Applying Artistic Effects to Pictures

PowerPoint 2010 comes with a number of new commands for working with pictures and graphics. These commands allow you to modify pictures using tools that in the past were only available through image editing applications.

One of the new graphic tools in PowerPoint 2010 is the **Artistic Effects** command. The *Artistic Effects* command applies a graphic filter to an image. These filters mimic a wide variety of artistic tools including paint strokes, pencil strokes, watercolors, mosaics, blurs, and glows.

To apply an artistic effect to a picture:

1. Select the image you want to apply the artistic effect to.
2. Click the **Format** tab under *Picture Tools*.
3. In the *Adjust* group, click the **Artistic Effects** button.
4. Select an option from the gallery to apply it to the picture.

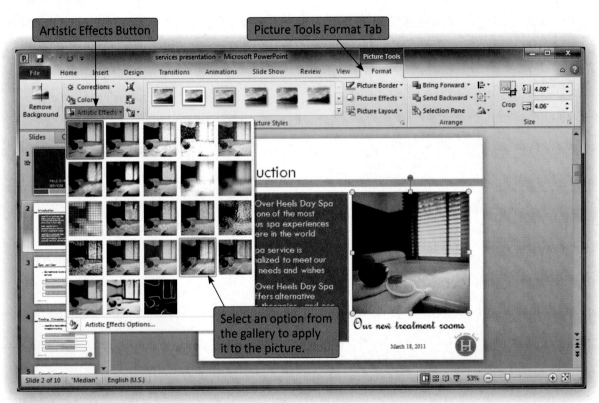

FIGURE PP 5.1

tips & tricks

If you have Live Preview enabled, when you roll your mouse over an option in the gallery, the effect is previewed on the selected image.

tell me **more**

The *Artistic Effects* command can only be used on photographs not on illustrations.

5.2 Removing the Background from Pictures

One way to modify a picture is to remove the background from the picture. To remove the background from a picture, PowerPoint analyzes the picture and calculates which areas are the background. PowerPoint then marks the background areas for removal. The resulting effect is as if you had traced the main part of the picture and then erased the background, leaving you with an outline of the picture.

To remove the background from a picture:

1. Select the image you want to remove the background from.

2. Click the **Format** tab under *Picture Tools*.

3. In the *Adjust* group, click the **Remove Background** button.

4. The *Background Removal* tab displays.

5. Adjust the marked area until the image appears as you want it.

6. Click the **Keep Changes** button to remove the background from the image.

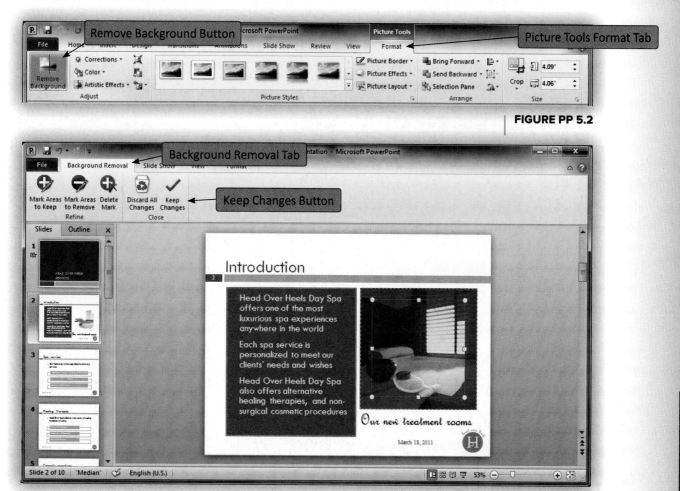

FIGURE PP 5.2

FIGURE PP 5.3

---

tips & tricks

Click the **Discard All Changes** button to close the *Background Removal* tab and not change the picture.

try **this**

You can also press ⏎Enter on the keyboard to accept the changes.

tell me **more**

You can modify the area marked for removal from the *Refine* group on the *Background Removal* tab:

> **Mark Areas to Keep**—allows you to draw lines indicating areas not to delete when the background is removed.

> **Mark Areas to Remove**—allows you to draw lines indicating areas to delete when the background is removed.

> **Delete Mark**—removes lines you have added marking areas to keep or remove.

5.3 Correcting Pictures

After you have added a picture to a presentation, you may find that it does not appear quite the way you want. It may appear too dark or too light, or it could appear slightly blurry. You can correct problems in pictures from the *Picture Tools Format* tab.

To correct a picture:

1. Select the image you want to modify.

2. Click the **Format** tab under *Picture Tools*.

3. In the *Adjust* group, click the **Corrections** button.

4. The gallery displays how the selected image will appear with the correction applied.

5. Select an option from the gallery to make the change.

FIGURE PP 5.4

When you make corrections, you are changing the following properties for a picture:

Brightness—makes the overall picture darker or lighter.

Contrast—changes the range of color intensity within the picture. A picture with high contrast will have bolder colors, while a picture with low contrast will have more muted colors.

Softness—removes hard edges, giving the picture a smoother feel.

Sharpness—removes any blurriness, giving the picture a crisper feel.

tips & tricks

The *Corrections* gallery displays the preset options for correcting images. If you want to adjust the picture manually, you should use the *Format Picture* dialog box. To open the *Format Picture* dialog box, click **Picture Corrections Options**. . . at the bottom of the *Corrections* gallery.

tell me **more**

If the picture you want to change is a drawing, you can adjust the brightness and contrast. If the picture you want to change is a photograph, you can adjust the sharpness of the image in addition to the brightness and contrast.

5.4 Changing the Color of Pictures

Another graphic effect you can apply to a picture in Power-Point is to **recolor** the image. When you color an image, PowerPoint takes the image and applies a color overlay. All colors are removed from the image and replaced with shades of one color. The resulting effect is as if you were looking at the image through colored glass.

To recolor a picture:

1. Select the image you want to recolor.
2. Click the **Format** tab under *Picture Tools.*
3. In the *Adjust* group, click the **Color** button.
4. The gallery displays how the selected image will appear with the color applied.
5. Select an option from the gallery to apply it to the picture.

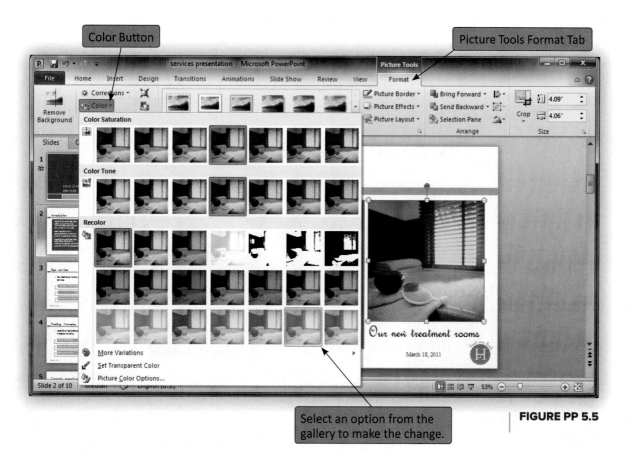

FIGURE PP 5.5

---

tips & tricks

> You can choose to make any color in the picture transparent. Click **Set Transparent Color** at the bottom of the gallery. Click any part of the image that has the color you want to make transparent. PowerPoint makes all matching areas of the image transparent.

> Point to *More Variations* at the bottom of the gallery to choose from other colors in the presentation's color theme.

5.5 Cropping Graphics

When you add an image to a presentation, you may only want to show part of the image. You could edit the picture in an image editing application, or you could use the *Crop* tool in PowerPoint to trim the picture.

To crop a picture:

1. Select the image you want to crop.
2. Click the **Format** tab under *Picture Tools*.
3. In the *Size* group, click the **Crop** button.
4. PowerPoint displays black lines around the edges of the image. These are cropping handles.
5. Point to a cropping handle. When the cursor changes to one of the crop cursors, click and drag toward the center of the image.
6. Press ←Enter to accept the changes.

Notice the size of the objects in the image does not change. When you **crop** an image, it is as if you are removing part of the image, hiding it from sight.

FIGURE PP 5.6

tips & tricks

When you crop an image, the entire image remains as part of the presentation. The cropped areas are simply hidden from sight. If you want to restore part of an image, use the *Crop* tool to expand the cropped area and the previously hidden area will be visible. If you know you will not need to restore the image in the future, you can remove the cropped areas of pictures by compressing the images in your presentation.

tell me **more**

Click the **Crop** drop-down arrow for more cropping options. Other cropping options include:

> **Crop to Shape**—allows you to crop an image using any of PowerPoint's built-in shapes as an outline.

> **Aspect Ratio**—crops the image to a rectangular shape with a ratio of a specific width by height.

> **Fill**—resizes the cropped picture so it fills the entire picture area while keeping the aspect ratio the same.

> **Fit**—resizes the picture to fit inside the picture area while keeping the aspect ratio the same.

5.6 Compressing Pictures

The more images you add to a presentation, the larger the presentation's file size will become. Before sending a presentation out to others, it is a good practice to reduce the file size as much as possible. When you compress the pictures in a presentation, you can choose the target output for the presentation: *Print (220 ppi), Screen (150 ppi),* or *E-mail (96 ppi).* PPI stands for pixels per inch. The higher the PPI, the less the images will be compressed. The lower the PPI, the more the images will be compressed, resulting in a smaller file size, but potentially lesser quality images. One way to reduce the file size of a presentation is to change the target output for all the images in the presentation.

To change the default target output for images in a presentation:

1. Click the **File** tab to open Backstage view.
2. Click the **Options** button.
3. In the *PowerPoint Options* dialog box, click the **Advanced** button.
4. In the *Image Size and Quality* section, verify the **Do not compress images in file** option is not checked.
5. Click the **Set default target output to:** arrow and select an option.
6. Click **OK** in the *PowerPoint Options* dialog box.

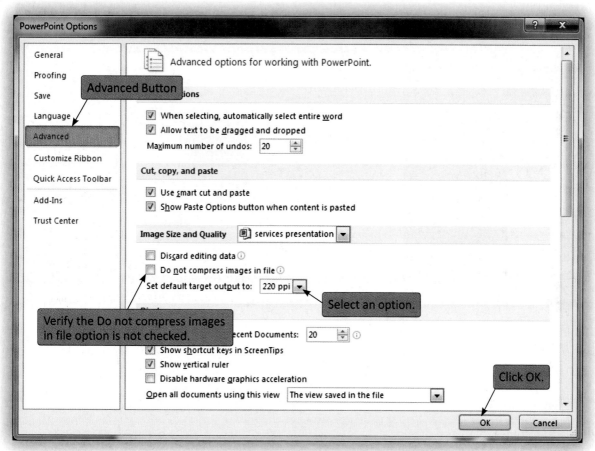

FIGURE PP 5.7

You can also change the target output for all images in a presentation through the *Compress Pictures* dialog box:

try this

1. Select a picture in the presentation.
2. Click the **Format** tab under *Picture Tools.*
3. In the *Adjust* group, click the **Compress Pictures** button.
4. Uncheck the *Apply only to this picture* option.
5. In the *Target output:* section, select a compression option.
6. Click **OK.**

5.7 Resetting Pictures

If you have made several changes to an image and decide to undo the changes you made, you could use the *Undo* command to revert the picture to its original state, or you could use the **Reset Picture** command. The *Reset Picture* command removes all PowerPoint formatting applied to the picture, and reverts the picture to the state it was before any formatting was applied.

To reset a picture:

1. Click the **Format** tab under *Picture Tools*.
2. In the *Adjust* group, click the **Reset Picture** button.
3. Any PowerPoint formatting you added to the picture is removed.

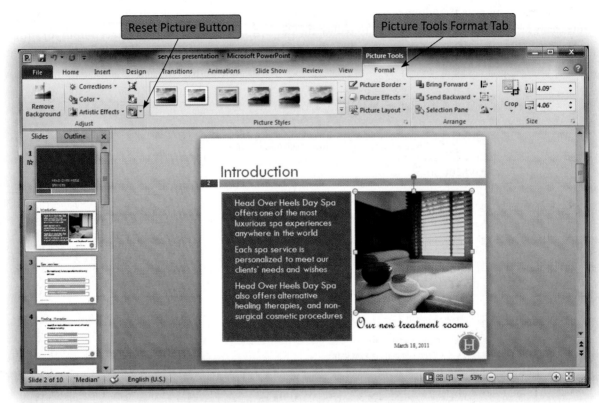

FIGURE PP 5.8

tips & tricks

Clicking the **Reset Picture** button does not revert the image to the original size. If you want to remove the formatting and change the picture back to the size it was when you first added it to the document, click the arrow next to the *Reset Picture* button and select **Reset Picture & Size.**

try **this**

To reset a picture, removing any formatting you added in PowerPoint, you can also click the **Reset Picture** button arrow and select **Reset Picture.**

5.8 Aligning Text in Tables

Horizontal alignment refers to how text is aligned with regard to the left and right margins of a cell. *Left* alignment aligns the text on the left side, leaving the right side ragged. *Center* alignment centers each line of text relative to the cell margins. *Right* alignment aligns the text on the right side, leaving the left side ragged.

To change the horizontal alignment of text in a cell:

1. Click in the cell you want to change.

2. Click the **Layout** tab under *Table Tools.*

3. In the *Alignment* group, click one of the horizontal alignment buttons:

Align Text Left

Center

Align Text Right

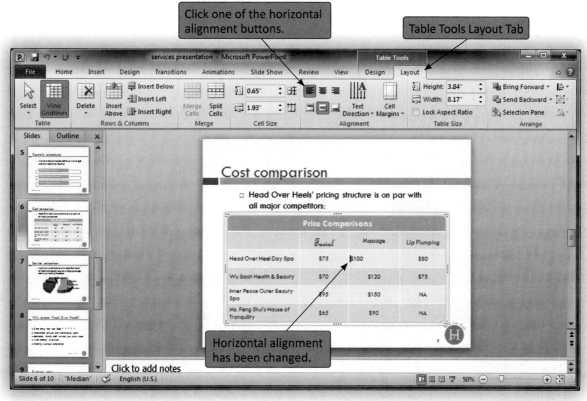

FIGURE PP 5.9

Vertical alignment refers to how text is aligned with regard to the top and bottom of a cell. *Top* alignment places the text at the top of the cell. *Middle* alignment places the text in the middle of the cell. *Bottom* alignment places the text at the bottom of the cell.

To change the vertical alignment of text in a cell:

1. Click in the cell you want to change.
2. Click the **Layout** tab under *Table Tools.*

3. In the *Alignment* group, click one of the vertical alignment buttons:

   Align Top

   Center Vertically

   Align Bottom

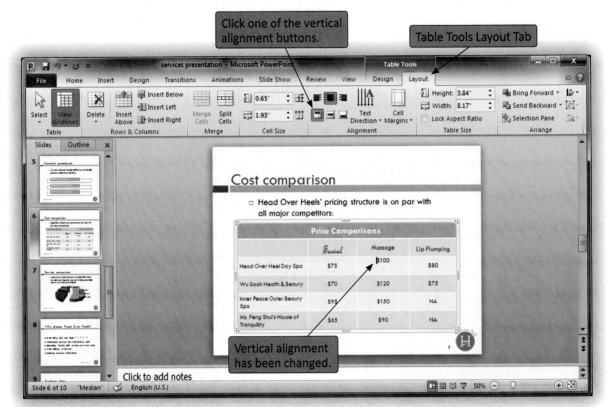

FIGURE PP 5.10

tell me **more**

In addition to changing the alignment of text in cells, you can also change the text direction. There are four built-in options for changing the text direction in cells:

Horizontal—displays text horizontally across the cell.

Rotate all text 90°—displays text vertically in the cell. The text is rotated 90 degrees clockwise from the horizontal position.

Rotate all text 270°—displays text vertically in the cell. The text is rotated 90 degrees counterclockwise from the horizontal position.

Stacked—displays the text vertically, one letter stacked above the other.

try **this**

You can also change the alignment of text in cells from the *Home* tab. In the *Paragraph* group, click the **Align Text Left, Center,** or **Align Text Right** to change the horizontal alignment of text in a cell. Click the **Align Text** button and select an option from the menu to change the vertical alignment of text in a cell.

The following keyboard shortcuts can be used to apply horizontal alignment:

> Align left = Ctrl + L
> Center = Ctrl + E
> Align Right = Ctrl + R

5.9 Inserting and Deleting Rows and Columns in Tables

Once you have created a table, you often find you need more rows or columns. You can easily insert additional rows and columns from the *Table Tools* contextual tabs.

When you place the cursor in a table, the *Table Tools* contextual tabs display. These tabs are called contextual tabs because they only display when a table is the active element. The *Design* tab contains tools to change the look of the table, such as shading and borders. The *Layout* tab contains tools to change how information is displayed in the table, such as row and column commands.

To insert an additional row and column:

1. Click the **Layout** tab under *Table Tools.*
2. To insert a new row, click the **Insert Above** button or the **Insert Below** button.
3. To insert a new column, click the **Insert Left** button or the **Insert Right** button.

To delete a row or column:

1. Click in the row or column you want to delete.
2. Click the **Layout** tab under *Table Tools.*
3. Click the **Delete** button and select an option.

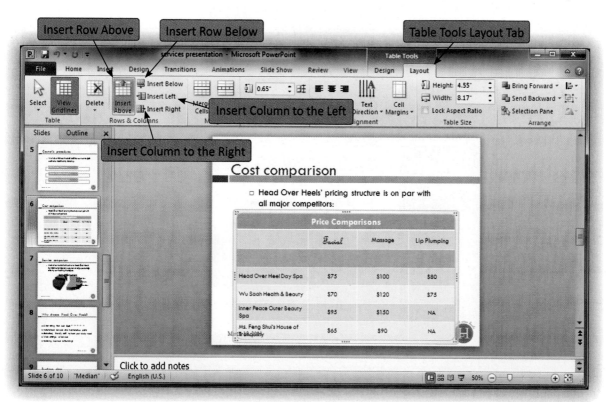

FIGURE PP 5.11

tips & tricks

A quick way to insert a new row at the end of a table is to place the cursor in the last cell in the last row and then press the Tab↹ key. A new row is automatically added to the table, with your cursor in its first cell.

try **this**

To insert rows and columns, you can right-click in a cell, point to **Insert,** and select **Insert Rows Above, Insert Rows Below, Insert Columns to the Left,** or **Insert Columns to the Right.**

tell me **more**

Another way to add rows and columns to tables is to copy an existing row or column and then paste it into the table. To copy and paste a row, first select the row you want to copy and click the **Copy** button. Next, place your cursor in the first cell of the row below where you want the copied row to appear. Click the **Paste** button to insert the copied row. You can use the same method to copy and paste columns in tables as well.

5.10 Modifying Charts

When you insert a chart, PowerPoint displays the *Chart Tools* contextual tabs. These tabs provide easy access to all the chart design, layout, and formatting tools. From the *Design* tab, you can change the chart layout or style using the predefined **Quick Layouts** and **Quick Styles**. Quick Layouts apply combinations of labels, titles, and data tables, while Quick Styles apply combinations of colors, line styles, fills, and shape effects that coordinate with the presentation theme.

Changing the layout and style of a chart can make a dramatic impact.

To change the chart layout using a Quick Layout:

1. Click the **Design** tab under *Chart Tools*.
2. In the *Chart Layouts* group, click one of the chart layouts, or click the **More** button ▾ to see all the chart layouts available.

To change the chart style using a Quick Style:

1. Click the **Design** tab under *Chart Tools*.
2. In the *Chart Styles* group, click the style you want to use, or click the **More** button ▾ to see all the chart styles available.

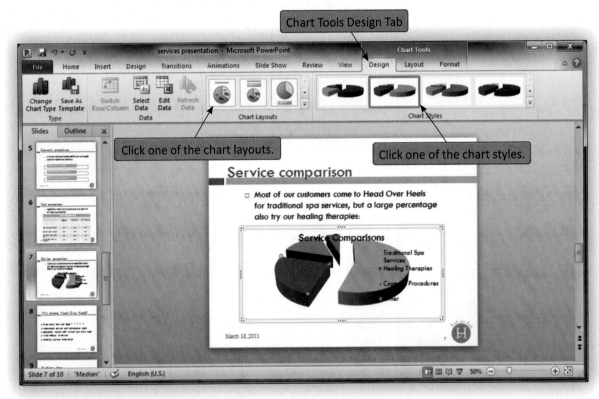

FIGURE PP 5.12

tell me **more**

The *Chart Tools Layout* tab allows you to change chart layout elements manually. The *Chart Tools Format* tab allows you to change chart style elements manually.

5.11 Animating Charts

When you add a chart to a slide, by default it appears as a static object. One way to help your information come to life for your audience is to animate the chart. Depending on the animation scheme you have chosen, you can animate the chart as one object or you can apply the animation scheme to individual parts of the chart.

To animate a chart:

1. Select the chart you want to animate.
2. Click the **Animations** tab.
3. In the *Animation* group, click the **More** button and select an animation scheme.
4. Click the **Effects Option** button and select **By Series** to have the animation applied to individual data series.

FIGURE PP 5.13

tips & tricks

You can further modify the chart animation through the *Animation* task pane. Click the **Animation Pane** button, in the *Advanced Animation* group, to display the *Animation* task pane. From the task pane, you can change the order in which the objects animate on the slide. You can also control when animations play and for how long.

tell me **more**

When you add an animation to an object, a number appears next to the object on the slide. This number indicates the order in which objects will be animated. Notice that if you animate a chart as one object, the number 1 appears next to the chart. However, if you animate the chart by category, several numbers appear next to the chart indicating that there are multiple animations applied to the object.

5.12 Creating Multipart Animations

Animating objects in a presentation can help your slides come to life for your audience. For example, you can design an image to fly in from off-screen when you click the slide. But what if you want to add a similar exit effect to the same image? In PowerPoint, you can add multiple animations to a single object.

To add additional animations to an object:

1. Select the object to which you want to add additional animations.

2. Click the **Animations** tab.

3. In the *Advanced Animations* group, click the **Add Animations** button.

4. Select an option from gallery.

When you add animations to a slide, PowerPoint displays a number next to each animated object. These numbers indicate the order in which the objects will be animated.

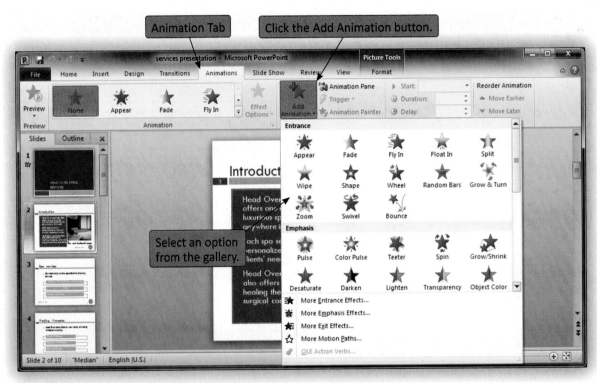

FIGURE PP 5.14

---

tips & tricks   If you do not see an animation effect in the gallery that you want to use, click one of the options on the menu at the bottom of the gallery to open a dialog box with more animation schemes to choose from.

5.13 Setting Animation Timings

When you apply an animation to an object in PowerPoint, the animation is set to play immediately and for a default length of time. But what if you want a pause before the animation plays? Or have the animation play more quickly or slowly than the default length of time? You can control both when and for how long an animation plays.

To control animation timings:

1. Select the animated object.
2. Click the **Animations** tab.
3. In the *Timing* group, enter the number of seconds for the animation to play in the *Animation Duration:* box.
4. In the *Animation Delay:* box, enter the number of seconds to wait before the animation starts.

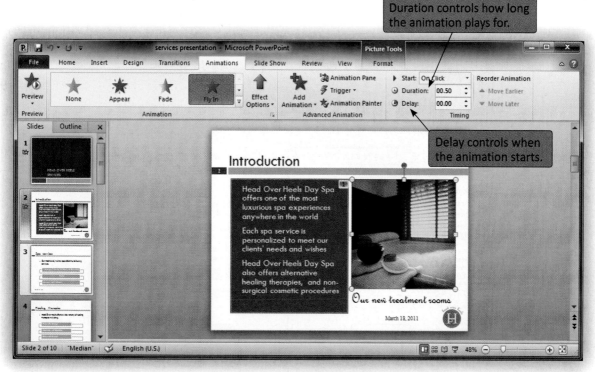

Duration controls how long the animation plays for.

Delay controls when the animation starts.

FIGURE PP 5.15

tips & tricks

By default animations are set to play when you click the slide. To have the animation automatically play when the slide appears, click the **Start:** arrow and select **With Previous**.

tell me **more**

Increasing the duration will make the animation play more slowly. Decreasing the duration will make the animation faster.

try **this**

To set the length of time for the duration or delay, you can also click the up and down arrow controls.

5.14 Creating an Action Button

An **action button** is a button you add to a slide that performs a set function. Action buttons are used in Slide Show view. You can use action buttons to navigate between slides or to open a program.

To create an action button:

1. On the *Home* tab, in the *Drawing* group, click the **Shapes** button.
2. At the bottom of the gallery is the *Action Buttons* section. Select an option from the gallery.
3. Click on the slide where you want the action button to appear.
4. The *Action Settings* dialog box opens.
5. Click the *Hyperlink to:* arrow, and select where you want the button to navigate to when clicked.
6. Click **OK.**

Each action button option in the *Shapes* gallery is designed for a specific purpose. There are buttons that are used to navigate within a presentation (such as the *Next, Previous,* and *Home* buttons), and there are buttons which are used to access additional content (such as the *Information, Movie, Document,* and *Sound* buttons).

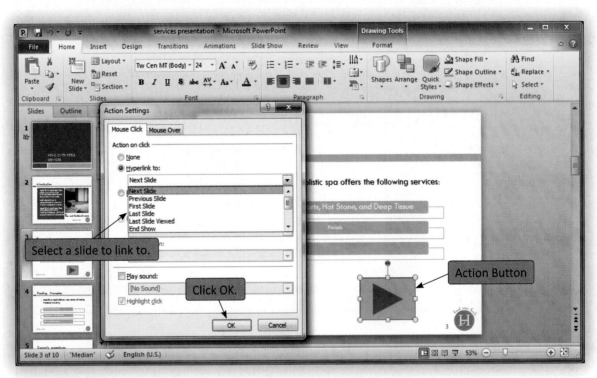

FIGURE PP 5.16

tips & tricks

You can have the action button play a sound when clicked. Select the check box next to *Play sound:*. Click the menu arrow, and select a sound to play when the action button is clicked.

tell me **more**

You can set the action button to perform the function when the button is clicked or when the mouse rests over the button.

try **this**

To add an action button to a slide, on the *Insert* tab, in the *Illustrations* group, click the **Shapes** button and select an option from the *Action Buttons* section.

5.15 Recording a Slide Show

Rather than presenting a slide show live, you can choose to record your slide show, including the timings and narrations. When you play the recorded slide show, PowerPoint will automatically play the recorded narration and navigate through the slides using the timings you created when you recorded the slide show.

Note: In order to record your narration, you will need to have a microphone or headset with a microphone attached to your computer. Please be sure the microphone/headset is plugged in and working before doing the following steps.

To record a slide show:

1. Click the **Slide Show** tab.

2. In the *Set Up* group, click the **Record Slide Show** button.

3. The *Record Slide Show* dialog box opens.

4. Verify the *Slide and animation timings* and the *Narrations and laser pointer* check boxes are selected.

5. Click the **Start Recording** button.

6. When the first slide appears, begin your presentation. Work through your presentation as if you were presenting to an audience.

7. Click the **Pause** button if you want to stop the timer.

8. Click the **Next** button to advance to the next slide.

9. Continue narrating each slide, clicking the **Next** button to advance the slides, until you reach the end of the presentation.

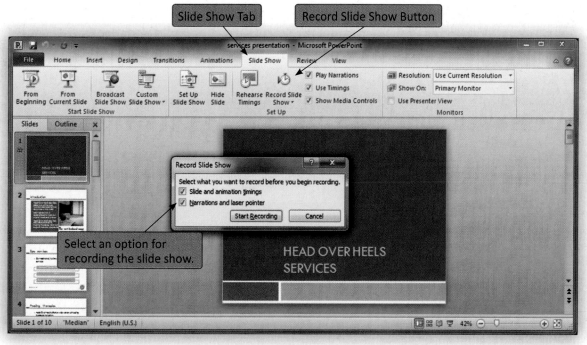

Slide Show Tab

Record Slide Show Button

Select an option for recording the slide show.

FIGURE PP 5.17

When you record a presentation, PowerPoint will use the timings and narration you recorded as the default playback options for the presentation. To change these options, on the *Slide Show* tab, in the *Set Up* group, click the **Set Up Slide Show** button. In the *Set Up Show* dialog box, click the **Manually** radio button in the *Advance slides* section to advance the slides yourself. In the *Show options* section, select the **Show without narration** check box to run the presentation without the narration.

> To remove timings from a presentation, click the **Record Slide Show** button arrow, point to **Clear,** and select **Clear Timings on All Slides.**

> To remove narration from a presentation, click the **Record Slide Show** button arrow, point to **Clear,** and select **Clear Narrations on All Slides.**

tips & tricks

5.16 Editing Audio on a Slide

When you add audio to a slide, you may find that you need to have it start at a different point or end at an earlier point. In past versions of PowerPoint, you needed an audio editing program to edit the start and end points of the audio. In PowerPoint 2010, you can edit audio within PowerPoint by using the tools available on the *Playback Audio Tools* tab.

To edit audio on a slide:

1. Click the speaker icon on the slide with audio you want to edit.
2. Click the **Playback** tab under *Audio Tools.*
3. Click the **Trim Audio** button.

4. The *Trim Audio* dialog box appears. The dialog includes a visual representation of the audio file along a timeline.
5. On the left side of the timeline is the green *Start Time* indicator. Click and drag the indicator to the right to have the audio begin at a later point.
6. On the right side of the timeline is the red *End Time* indicator. Click and drag the indicator to the left to have the audio stop playing at an earlier point.
7. Click the **Play** button to play the trimmed audio piece.
8. Click **OK** to accept the changes and trim the audio.

Trim Audio Button — Audio Tools Playback Tab

FIGURE PP 5.18

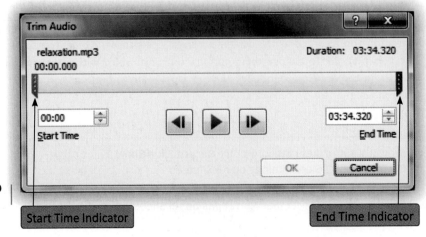

Start Time Indicator — End Time Indicator

FIGURE PP 5.19

from the perspective of . . .

MIDDLE SCHOOL PRINCIPAL

It's always tough to go back to school after summer break; but teachers are more enthusiastic about the upcoming year when they see images of their students displayed in our "Welcome Back" presentation. They especially love it when the students have included audio of their favorite experiences from the prior school year.

tips & tricks

By default the audio clip icon is displayed in the presentation. On the *Playback* tab, select the **Hide During Show** check box not to have the icon appear on your slides.

tell me **more**

When you select an audio clip on a slide, the *Audio Tools* contextual tabs automatically display. The *Playback* tab is called a contextual tab, because it only displays when an audio clip is the active element. The *Playback* tab contains tools for adding bookmarks, fading the audio in and out, looping the audio, and controlling the volume.

try **this**

You can also enter when you want the audio to begin playing in the *Start Time* box. Similarly, you can enter when you want the audio to stop playing in the *End Time* box.

5.17 Editing Video on a Slide

Just as you can modify the end and start times of audio clips you add to slides, you can also modify when a video begins and ends. You can edit videos within PowerPoint by using the tools available on the *Playback Video Tools* tab.

To edit a video on a slide:

1. Select the video you want to edit.
2. Click the **Playback** tab under *Video Tools*.
3. Click the **Trim Video** button.
4. The *Trim Video* dialog box appears. The dialog includes a preview of the video above a timeline for the video.

5. On the left side of the timeline is the green *Start Time* indicator. Click and drag the indicator to the right to have the video begin at a later point.
6. On the right side of the timeline is the red *End Time* indicator. Click and drag the indicator to the left to have the video stop playing at an earlier point.
7. Click the **Play** button to play the trimmed video piece.
8. Click **OK** to accept the changes and trim the video.

FIGURE PP 5.20

tips & tricks

> Select the **Hide While Not Playing** check box not to show the video on the slide until it plays.

> Select the **Play Full Screen** check box to have the video take over the screen when played.

tell me more

When you select a video clip on a slide, the *Video Tools* contextual tabs automatically display. The *Playback* tab is called a contextual tab, because it only displays when a video clip is the active element. The *Playback* tab contains tools for adding bookmarks, fading the video in and out, looping the video, and controlling the volume.

try this

You can also enter when you want the video to begin playing in the *Start Time* box. Similarly, you can enter when you want the video to stop playing in the *End Time* box.

5.18 Creating a Photo Album

Have you ever wanted to create a PowerPoint presentation of pictures you downloaded from your digital camera or cell phone? PowerPoint's **Photo Album** feature does just that. From the *Photo Album* dialog box, you can import your digital photographs and add captions and effects to each image. The *Photo Album* feature then creates a new presentation based on the information you entered, allowing you to further modify the presentation using the robust formatting tools available in PowerPoint 2010.

To create a photo album:

1. On the *Insert* tab, in the *Images* group, click the **Photo Album** button.

2. The *Photo Album* dialog box opens.

3. Click the **File/Disk** button.

4. In the *Insert New Pictures* dialog box, select the picture you want to include in the photo album and click the **Insert** button.

5. Continue adding pictures to the photo album.

6. Click the **New Text Box** button to add a text slide between images in the photo album.

7. Click the **Create** button to create the photo album as a new presentation.

FIGURE PP 5.21

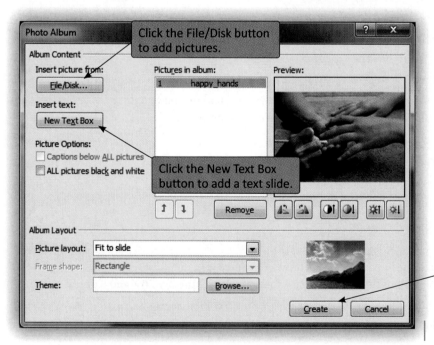

FIGURE PP 5.22

tips & tricks

Use the up and down arrows below the *Pictures in album* box to reorder the images in the photo album. Click the **Remove** button to remove an image from the photo album.

tell me **more**

When you create a photo album, PowerPoint automatically creates a title slide for the photo album. By default, the title slide includes the title and a byline. PowerPoint gives the presentation the title "Photo Album" and pulls the Author property for the presentation to use as the byline.

projects

Skill Review 5.1

In this review, you will use the skills learned in Chapter 5 to edit an existing presentation.

1. Open Microsoft PowerPoint 2010.
2. On the *File* tab, click **Open.**
3. In the *Open* dialog box, navigate to the location of your PowerPoint 2010 student files.
4. Find *bellascafe.pptx,* and double-click the file to open it.
5. On the *File* tab, click the **Save As** option.
6. Change the file name to `[your initials]PP_SkillReview_5-1`, and then click **Save.**
7. Add artistic effects to pictures:
   a. Go to **Slide 4,** and select the picture of the oranges.
   b. On the *Picture Tools Format* tab, in the *Adjust* group, click the **Artistic Effects** button.
   c. In the *Artistic Effects* gallery, click the **Glow Diffused** option.
   d. In *Picture Styles* group, click the **Picture Effects** button, point to *Shadow,* and select **Perspective Diagonal Upper Left.**
   e. Click outside the text box to deselect the picture.
8. Crop pictures:
   a. Go to **Slide 3,** and select the picture of the vegetables.
   b. On the *Picture Tools Format* tab, in the *Size* group, click the **Crop** button.
   c. Click and drag the cropping tools that surround the image until the image of the bread in the plastic bag in the top corner is not visible.
   d. Click the **Crop** button again.
9. Change the color of a graphic:
   a. Be sure the picture on *Slide 3* is still selected.
   b. In the *Adjust* group, click the **Color** button.
   c. In the *Color Saturation* area, click **Saturation: 200%.**
10. Correct and compress pictures:
    a. Select the recropped vegetable image on *Slide 3.* In the *Adjust* group click the **Corrections** button, and choose the option **Brightness +20% and Contrast −20%.**
    b. While picture is still selected, click **Compress Pictures** in the *Adjust* group.
    c. Under target output, select the **Screen Option (150 ppi)** button.
    d. Click **OK.**
11. Remove background from pictures:
    a. Go to **Slide 1** and select the picture.
    b. On the *Picture Tools Format* tab, in the *Adjust* group, click the **Remove Background.**
    c. Click the **Keep Changes** button in the *Close* group.
12. Modify a chart:
    a. Select **Slide 6,** and select the chart.
    b. Click the *Chart Tools Design* tab. In the *Chart Layouts* group, select **Layout 3.**

13. Add animation and multipart animation to a chart:

    a. Click the **Animations** tab.

    b. In the *Animation* group, click the **Float In** option.

    c. In the *Advanced Animation* group, click the **Add Animation.**

    d. In the *Emphasis* section, click the **Teeter** animation.

14. Add an action button:

    a. Select **Slide 7.**

    b. Click the **Insert** tab. In the *Illustrations* group, click the **Shapes** button.

    c. Go down to the button choices, and click the small icon of the *house (Action Button: Home)* in the *Action Button* choices.

    d. Go to the right corner of *Slide 7*, and draw the size of the action button you would like by clicking and dragging. Please note: The button should be a small image.

    e. Click **OK.**

    f. In Slide Show view, clicking this button will take you to the first slide of your show.

15. Insert rows, columns, and cells in tables:

    a. On *Slide 4*, select the table in the center of the slide.

    b. Put your insertion point in the cell that says *Fri.*

    c. Click the **Layout** tab. In the *Rows and Columns* group, click the **Insert Right** button.

    d. Type `Sat` in the new cell header that was added for the column.

    e. Next, select the cell below and type: `Steak Salad`

    f. Click the **Layout** tab. Click the **Insert Below** button.

    g. Click the first cell in row 2.

    h. Next, type `Fruit & Nut` under the *Caesar* row.

16. Align text in a table:

    a. Select the data in the table by dragging or by using the selection arrow.

    b. Click the **Layout** tab under *Table Tools.*

    c. In the *Alignment* group, click the **Center** option.

17. Insert and edit audio on a slide:

    a. If necessary, switch to Normal view.

    b. Go to **Slide 1.**

    c. Click the **Insert** tab. In the *Media* group, click the **Audio** button arrow and select *Clip Art Audio.*

    d. Within the *Clip Art* pane, type the words `Classical Fast` in the *Search for* box, and click the **Go** button.

    e. Click **Classical Fast.wav.**

    f. The audio will be placed on the slide.

    g. Go to the audio image, and drag it to the left corner of the slide.

    h. Click the **Playback** tab. In the *Editing* group, click the **Trim Audio** button.

    i. Click the red line to the far right of the recording area. Drag the line to the left of the screen until you see the numbers *00.09.997.* If you have trouble, then enter 00.09.997 in the *End Time* box.

    j. Click **OK.**

18. Save and close the slide show.

Skill Review **5.2**

In this review, you will use the skills learned in Chapter 5 to edit an existing presentation.

1. Open Microsoft PowerPoint 2010.
2. On the *File* tab, click **Open.**
3. In the *Open* dialog box, navigate to the location of your PowerPoint 2010 student files.
4. Find *NL_breakfast.pptx,* and double-click the file to open it.
5. On the *File* tab, click the **Save As** option.
6. Change the file name to `[your initials]PP_SkillReview_5-2` and then click **Save.**
7. Change the color of a graphic:
    a. Go to **Slide 1,** and select the picture of the bay.
    b. On the *Picture Tools Format* tab, in the *Adjust* group, click the **Color** button.
    c. Click **Temperature: 8800 k** in the *Color Tone* category.
8. Remove background from pictures:
    a. Go to **Slide 2,** and select the picture of the flower.
    b. In the *Adjust* group, click the **Remove Background** button.
    c. On the *Remove Background* tab, in the *Close* group, click the **Keep Changes** button.
9. Correct and compress pictures:
    a. With the flower image on *Slide 2* selected, in the *Adjust* group, click the **Corrections** button and choose the option **Brightness +40% and Contrast +20%.**
    b. While picture is still selected, click **Compress Pictures** in the *Adjust* group.
    c. Under target output, select the **Screen Option (150 ppi)** button.
10. Add artistic effects to pictures:
    a. On *Slide 6,* select the picture of the salmon on the left of the slide.
    b. On the *Picture Tools Format* tab, in the *Adjust* group, click the **Artistic Effects** button.
    c. In the *Artistic Effects* gallery, click **Plastic Wrap.**
11. Add a multipart animation to a chart:
    a. Select **Slide 7,** and select the chart.
    b. Click the **Animations** tab.
    c. In the *Animation* group, select **Fly In.**
    d. In the *Advanced Animation* group, click the **Add Animation** button.
    e. In the *Emphasis* choices, click the **Pulse** animation.
12. Crop graphics:
    a. Go to **Slide 8,** and select the picture of the cookies.
    b. Click the **Format** tab under *Picture Tools.* In the *Size* group, click the **Crop** button.
    c. Drag the corner of the picture until the fireplace is no longer in the picture.
    d. Deselect the picture to apply the cropping.
13. Add an action button:
    a. Select **Slide 9.**
    b. Click the **Insert** tab. In the *Illustrations* group, click the **Shapes** button.

c. Go down to the button choices, and click the small icon of the *left arrow (Action button: Back or Previous)* in the *Action Button* choices.

d. Go to the right corner of *Slide 9,* and draw the size of the action button you would like. Please note: The button should be a small image.

e. Click **OK.**

f. In Slide Show view, clicking this button will take you to the previous slide.

14. Insert rows, columns, and cells in tables:

a. On *Slide 4,* select the table in the center of the slide.

b. Put your insertion point in the table in the cell that says *Specifics.*

c. Click the **Layout** tab, and in the *Rows & Columns* group, click the option **Insert Right.**

d. Type `Price` in the new cell header that was added for the column.

e. Next, select the cell below, and type: `$199` for Cliff Room pricing.

f. Next type `$250` for Ocean Room.

g. Next type `$250` for Coral Room.

h. Click in the *Coral Room* text in row 4.

i. Click the **Layout** tab. In the *Rows & Columns* group, click the **Insert Below** button.

j. Next, type `Starfish Room` under the *Coral Room* row.

k. Press the **Tab** key and type: `Queen size, garden view`

l. Press the **Tab** key and type: `$150`

m. Move the table up by clicking and dragging to be sure it fits within the black borders.

15. Edit video on a slide:

a. On *Slide 3,* click the video image.

b. Click the **Playback** tab, and then click the **Trim Video** button. Go to the red line, and drag the red line until the video ends on the bouquet of flowers on the table (approximately 00.07.001 seconds long).

c. Click **OK.**

d. In the *Video Options* group, click the box for **Loop until Stopped.**

e. Deselect the *Loop until Stopped* choice, and click the box for **Rewind after Playing.**

16. Save and close the slide show.

challenge yourself 1

In this challenge, you will use the skills learned in Chapter 5 to create a presentation for Sally's Bakery Shoppe.

1. Open Microsoft PowerPoint 2010.

2. Create a new presentation using the *Oriel* theme.

3. Save the file as `[your initials]PP_Challenge_5-3.`

4. Use the **Normal View** button to add or edit content.

5. On Slide 1:

   a. Type the title: **Sally's Pastry Shoppe**

   b. In the subtitle box, add the text: **Product Presentation**

6. Now you will be adding the rest of the slides. Add a bulleted slide, and type **What We Are Known For** as the title of the slide. Type in the following bulleted items:

   • **Cookies**

   • **Scones**

   • **Brownies**

   • **Biscotti**

   • **Apple Crisp**

   • **Chocolate Lava Cake**

7. Add the *applecrisp.jpg* image from your data file folder. Resize the image and remove the background.

8. Create a new slide and type its title: **Hours of Operation**

9. Create the following table below the title, center the table text, and apply a table design of your choice.

DAYS OF WEEK	HOURS
Monday - Friday	9 am - 5 pm
Saturday	9 am - 3 pm
Sunday	9 am - 12 pm

10. Insert the following column into the table between the two existing columns:

MANAGER
Jill
Janice
Diane

11. Center the text in the new column.

12. Create a slide, and type the title: **Specialty Biscotti**

13. Add the *biscottis.jpg* picture to the slide, and resize it if necessary so it is centered on the screen. Apply the *Paint Brush* artistic effect to the picture. Recolor the picture using the *Blue, Accent color 2 Light* option, and compress the image for display on a Web page.

14. Create a new slide with bar graph of your choice based on the data below. Title the slide: **Top Sellers by $000s**

PRODUCT	2012
Brownies	30
Cookies	20
Biscotti	15

15. Animate the bar graph with the *Fly In* animation. Modify the animation so each part of the data series is animated as a separate piece.

16. Create a slide, and type the title **Our Cookies** and add the *sugar.avi* video. Trim the video from the end so it is 2.5 seconds in length.

17. Save and close the presentation.

In this challenge, you will use the skills learned in Chapter 5 to create a presentation for Laura's Floral Boutique.

1. Open Microsoft PowerPoint 2010.
2. Create a new presentation using the *Opulent* theme.
3. Save the file as **[your initials]PP_Challenge_5-4.**
4. Use the **Normal View** to add or edit content.
5. On Slide 1:
   a. Type the title: **Laura's Floral Boutique**
   b. In the subtitle box, add the text: **Spring is Here**
6. Add a bulleted slide, and type **Our Flowers** as the title of the slide. Type in the following bulleted items:
   - **Tulips**
   - **Daisies**
   - **Peonies**
7. Add the *flower.jpg* image from your data files folder. Resize the image and remove the background.
8. Create a new slide, and type its title: **Flowers Pricing**
9. Create the following table below the title, and center the table text. Apply a table design of your choice.

CLOTHING	RETAIL
Tulips	$6.99 per flat
Daisies	$2.99 per flat
Peonies	$2.00 per flat

10. Insert the following column into the table between the two existing columns:

COLORS
Yellow
Red
Pink

11. Center the new column.
12. Create a slide, and type the title: **Our Flowers Are in Bloom!**
13. Add the *flower.jpg* to the slide, and resize it if necessary so it is centered on the slide. Apply the *Marker* artistic effect to the picture. Recolor the picture using the *Purple, Accent color 2 Light* option.
14. Adjust the image so it is 20% lighter with 40% more contrast.
15. Create a new slide with a bar graph of your choice based on the data below. Title the slide: **Top Sellers by Pieces**

PRODUCT	2012
Tulips	800
Daisies	900
Peonies	950

16. Apply the *Wipe In* and *Wipe Out* animation effects to the chart.
17. Create a slide, and type the title **We provide landscaping as well . . .** Add the *nursery.avi* video and trim the video from the end so it is 4.315 seconds in length.
18. Save and close the presentation.

on your own

You have been asked to create an informative presentation on the topic of mobile devices in the classroom for your university. Research the iPad and what it has to offer for students at your school.

Create a presentation that includes the following information:

1. Title of slide and your name on the first slide.
2. Include a slide that has the specifications of the iPad.
3. Research ways that iPads are currently being used in classrooms. Create a new slide, add a table, and enter three ways iPads are being used for educational purposes. Center the table text.
4. On a new slide, add two iPad images, and apply artistic effects to them. Crop, recolor, and compress the images.
5. Insert a new slide and create a chart based upon the data you find about the number of apps available for the iPad versus two other competing tablets. Apply a multipart animation to it.
6. Add an action button on the last slide in your presentation that will return you to the first slide.
7. Save the file as *[your initials]*`PP_OnYourOwn_5-5.` Close the presentation

fix it

You have been assigned to fix a presentation.

1. Using Microsoft PowerPoint 2010, open *jsam_financial_fix.pptx*.
2. Save the file as *[your initials]*`PP_FixIt_5-6.`
3. On *Slide 1*, crop the pond image and recolor it.
4. Add a column between the two columns on *Slide 4*, and type the information below:

   `Extension`
   `505`
   `506`
   `508`
   `509`

5. Center the text in the table.
6. Create a new slide with a chart after *Slide 3* with each of the average percentage returns on investment for this year (For example, *Stock 10%, Mutual Funds 15%, 401k 10%*).
7. Apply an entrance and an exit animation to the chart elements.
8. Modify the audio on *Slide 1* so it loops.
9. Add an action button to a slide of your choice.
10. Save and close the file.

chapter **6**
Polishing and Finishing the Presentation

In this chapter, you will learn the following skills:

Skill **6.1**   Adding Slides from Another Presentation

Skill **6.2**   Applying Character Effects

Skill **6.3**   Aligning Text

Skill **6.4**   Adding Columns to Text Placeholders

Skill **6.5**   Changing Line Spacing

Skill **6.6**   Using the Format Painter

Skill **6.7**   Clearing Formatting

Skill **6.8**   Using Animation Painter

Skill **6.9**   Modifying the Slide Master

Skill **6.10** Adding New Layouts and Placeholders to the Slide Master

Skill **6.11** Checking for Compatibility with Previous Versions of PowerPoint

Skill **6.12** Saving Slides as Graphics

Skill **6.13** Saving a Presentation as a PDF

Skill **6.14** Saving a Presentation as a Template

Skill **6.15** Packaging a Presentation for CD

Skill **6.16** Broadcasting a Presentation

Skill **6.17** Publishing Slides to a Slide Library

Skill **6.18** Saving a Presentation as a Video

> Add slides from another presentation

> Format text and slides including aligning text, applying character effects, and changing line spacing

> Use the Format Painter to copy and paste text formatting

> Use the Animation Painter to copy and paste animation settings

> Modify the slide master

> Save slides and presentations in a variety of ways, including as video, PDF, a graphic, template, and compatible file

> Package a presentation for a CD

> Broadcast a presentation

> Publish slides to a Slide Library

skills

introduction

In this chapter, students will learn the advanced skills necessary to finalize a professional looking PowerPoint 2010 presentation. They will learn to add slides from another presentation and modify the slide master. Formatting techniques in this chapter, such as aligning text, applying character effects, changing spacing, and using the Format Painter, provide ways to enhance a presentation. Students will also learn to save their presentations in different formats for different audiences, including video, graphics, templates, and PDF files. Finally, students will learn how to share their presentation in various ways such as packaging it as a CD, broadcasting it, or publishing the slides to a Slide Library.

6.1 Adding Slides from Another Presentation

If you have a slide containing detailed information, such as a chart of sales figures or a table of revenue projections, you may find you want to use the slide in more than one presentation. You could manually re-create the slide, including adding all the information, or you can add the slide from the original presentation into the new presentation. You can add slides from one presentation to another through the **Reuse Slides** task pane.

To add slides from another presentation:

1. On the *Home* tab, in the *Slides* group, click the **New Slide** button arrow and select **Reuse Slides. . .**

2. The *Reuse Slides* task pane appears.

3. Click the **Browse** button and select **Browse File. . .**

4. In the *Browse* dialog box, navigate to the presentation you want to reuse slides from and select the file.

5. Click the **Open** button.

6. A list of slides appears.

7. Click the slide you want to add to the presentation.

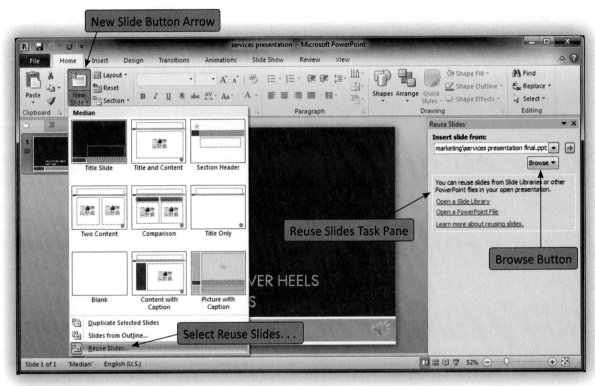

FIGURE PP 6.1

---

try **this**

To open the *Browse* dialog box, you can also click the **Open a PowerPoint File** link in the *Reuse Slides* task pane.

6.2 Applying Character Effects

When you add text to a slide, it is formatted according to the slide design. But what if you want the text to look different from the preset design? You can call attention to text in your presentation by using the bold, italic, underline, strikethrough, or shadow effects. Remember, these effects are used to emphasize important text, and should be used sparingly.

To add character effects to your text, on the *Home* tab, in the *Font* group:

Bold—click the **Bold** button **B**.

Italic—click the **Italic** button *I*.

Underline—click the **Underline** button **U**.

Shadow—click the **Shadow** button **S**.

Strikethrough—click the **Strikethrough** button abc.

When text has the bold, italic, underline, shadow, or strikethrough effect applied to it, the button highlights on the Ribbon. To remove the effect, click the highlighted button, or press the appropriate keyboard shortcut.

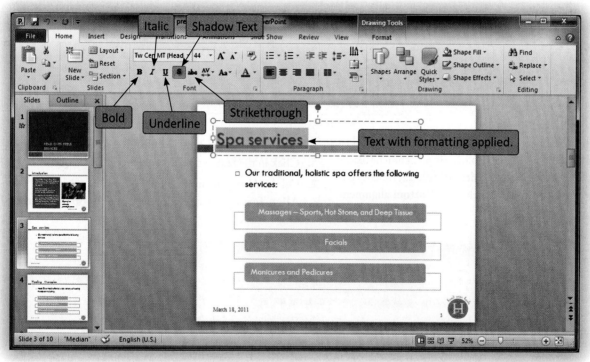

FIGURE PP 6.2

Character spacing refers to the amount of horizontal space that appears between characters when you type. In some cases, you will want to make the characters closer together to fit better on-screen. In other cases, you will want to make the characters farther apart for a visual effect. To change the spacing of the characters in text, in the *Font* group, click the **Character Spacing** button and select an option.

You can also apply character effects through the *Font* dialog box. To open the *Font* dialog box, click the **dialog launcher** in the *Font* group on the *Home* tab.

tips & tricks

To apply character effects, you can also use the following keyboard shortcuts:

> **Bold** = Ctrl + B
>
> **Italic** = Ctrl + I
>
> **Underline** = Ctrl + U
>
> To apply the bold or italic effect, you can also:

1. Right-click the text you want to change.

2. Click the **Bold** or **Italic** button on the Mini toolbar.

try **this**

6.3 Aligning Text

Text alignment refers to how text is lined up with regard to the left and right edges of a slide.

> **Left alignment** aligns the text on the left side, leaving the right side ragged.
> **Center alignment** centers each line of text relative to the edges of the slide.
> **Right alignment** aligns the text on the right side, leaving the left side ragged.
> **Justified alignment** evenly spaces the words, aligning the text on the right and left sides.

To change the alignment of text:

1. Click in the text you want to change.
2. On the *Home* tab, in the *Paragraph* group, click an alignment button.
   Align Text Left
   Center
   Align Text Right
   Justify

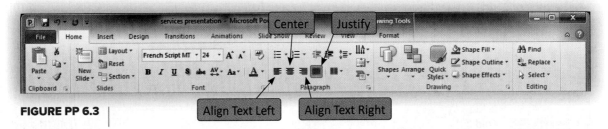

FIGURE PP 6.3

Vertical alignment refers to how text is aligned with regard to the top and bottom of the placeholder. **Top** alignment places the text at the top of the placeholder. **Middle** alignment centers the text vertically in the placeholder. **Bottom** alignment places the text at the bottom of the placeholder.

To change the vertical alignment of text:

1. Click in the text you want to change.
2. On the *Home* tab, in the *Paragraph* group, click the **Align Text** button and select an option: **Top, Middle,** or **Bottom.**

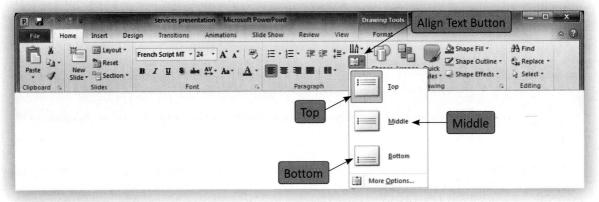

FIGURE PP 6.4

tips & tricks

When creating presentations, it is important to use consistent text alignment on every slide. For example, if a slide's title area is center-aligned, then every title throughout the presentation should also be center-aligned.

tell me more

Bulleted and numbered lists are typically left-aligned. When you apply left alignment to a list, the bullets and numbers align vertically, giving your slide a precise, organized appearance.

try this

To align text, you can also use the following keyboard shortcuts:

Align Left = Ctrl + L
Center = Ctrl + E
Align Right = Ctrl + R
Justify = Ctrl + J

To left-align, center, or right-align text, you can right-click the text and click an alignment button on the Mini toolbar.

6.4 Adding Columns to Text Placeholders

When you add a list to a slide, the items in the list are displayed in a single column. This is fine if you have a few items in the list, but what if your list includes more items than will easily fit in a single vertical column? You can apply columns to text, giving you the flexibility of displaying lists across a slide.

To apply columns to text:

1. Select the text placeholder containing the list you want to convert.

2. On the *Home* tab, in the *Paragraph* group, click the **Columns** button and select an option: **One Column, Two Columns,** or **Three Columns.**

After you have applied the columns to the text placeholder, you can resize the text placeholder, making it wider or shorter to even out the number of items in each column.

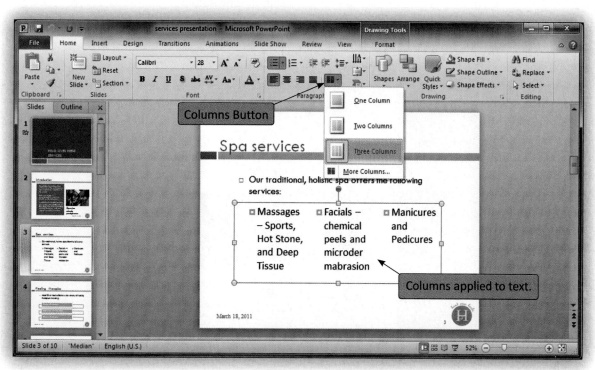

FIGURE PP 6.5

tips & tricks

In the *Columns* dialog box, you can increase the number of columns to more than three. You can also control the spacing between the columns of text on the slide. To open the *Columns* dialog box, click the **Columns** button and select **More Columns. . .**

tell me more

Applying columns to text is a feature that was introduced in PowerPoint 2007. In older versions of PowerPoint, you needed to create a separate placeholder for each column of text to achieve the same effect. Although this method achieved the same visual effect, it made it cumbersome to add, delete, or reorder items in the placeholders.

6.5 Changing Line Spacing

Line spacing is the white space between lines of text. The default line spacing in Microsoft PowerPoint 2010 is single spacing. This line spacing is a good choice to use for the items on a slide. Other commonly used spacing options include double spacing and 1.5 spacing. When you increase the line spacing, you are adding more white space between the items on the slide.

To change line spacing:

1. Select the text you want to change.
2. On the *Home* tab, in the *Paragraph* group, click the arrow next to the *Line Spacing* button.
3. Select the number of the spacing you want.

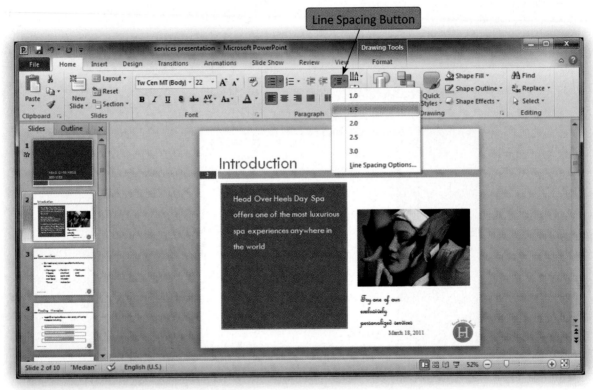

FIGURE PP 6.6

6.6 Using the Format Painter

PowerPoint 2010 gives you the ability to apply complex formatting to objects. If you want to use the same formatting for more than one object, you could select the second object and reapply all the effects to create the final result, or you could use **Format Painter** to copy the formatting from one object to another.

To use Format Painter:

1. Select the object that has the formatting you want to copy.

2. On the *Home* tab, in the *Clipboard* group, click the **Format Painter** button.

3. Click the object that you want to apply the formatting to.

4. The formats are automatically applied to the second object.

If you want to apply the formats more than once, double-click the **Format Painter** button when you select it. It will stay on until you click the **Format Painter** button again or press Esc to deselect it.

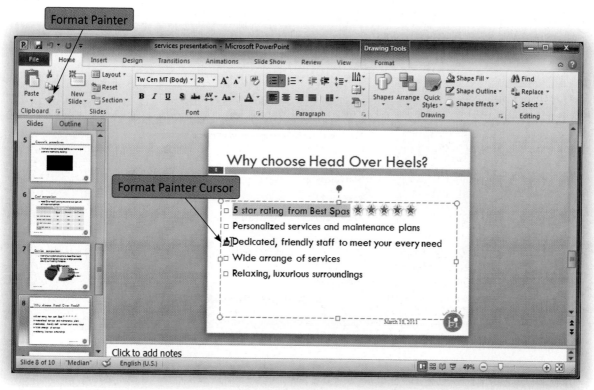

FIGURE PP 6.7

tips & tricks

If you are copying formatting from a text box, click in the text (so the text box appears with a dashed line around it) to copy and paste the formatting of just the text. Select the text box (so it appears with a solid line around it) to copy and paste the formatting of the entire text box.

try **this**

To activate Format Painter, you can also right-click the text with formatting you want to copy and click the **Format Painter** button on the Mini toolbar. If you are copying the formatting on a picture, you will not see the Mini toolbar.

6.7 Clearing Formatting

After you have applied a number of character formats and effects to text, you may find that you want to return your text to its original formatting. You could perform multiple *Undo* commands on the text, or you could use the **Clear All Formatting** command. The *Clear All Formatting* command removes any formatting that has been applied to text, including character formatting, text effects, and styles, and leaves only plain text.

To remove formatting from text:

1. Select the text you want to remove the formatting from.
2. On the *Home* tab, in the *Font* group, click the **Clear All Formatting** button.

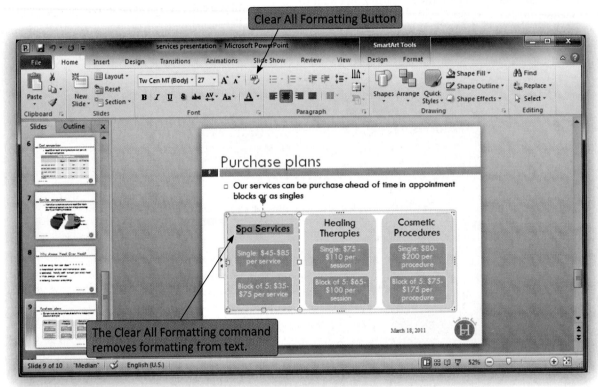

FIGURE PP 6.8

---

tips & tricks

If you clear the formatting from text and then decide that you want to keep the formatting that was removed, you can use the *Undo* command to apply to the previous formatting to the text.

6.8 Using Animation Painter

Animations can become complex very quickly. You can invest a lot of time working on an animation to get it just right. What if you want to use those same animation effects on another slide? In past versions of PowerPoint, you would need to re-create the animation. PowerPoint 2010 includes a new feature called the Animation Painter. The Animation Painter works similarly to the Format Painter, but instead of copying and pasting formatting, the Animation Painter copies and pastes the animations that have been applied to an object.

To use the Animation Painter to copy and paste animations:

1. Select the object that has the animation you want to copy.

2. Click the **Animations** tab.

3. In the *Advanced Animations* group, click the **Animation Painter** button.

4. Click the object that you want to apply the animation to.

5. The animation is automatically applied to the second object.

If you want to apply the animation more than once, double-click the **Animation Painter** button when you select it. It will stay on until you click the **Animation Painter** button again or press Esc to deselect it.

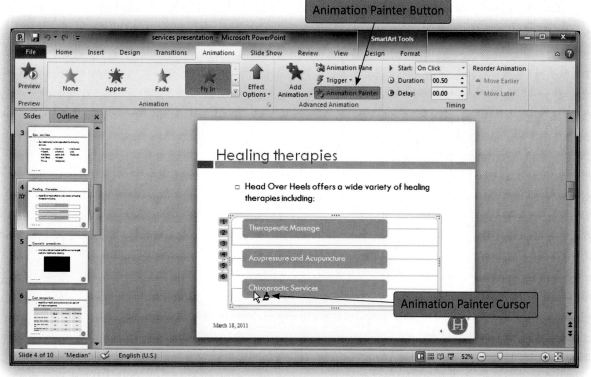

FIGURE PP 6.9

To remove an animation, on the *Animations* tab, in the *Animation* group, click the **None** option in the gallery.

tips & tricks

6.9 Modifying the Slide Master

The slide master controls the look of elements in a presentation. By default, a presentation has one slide master containing several prebuilt layouts. But what if you want to adjust one of the layouts to better suit your needs? In Slide Master view, you can modify the slide master's layouts. You can resize and move placeholders, as well as change other formatting, such as the theme or bullets styles.

To work with the slide master, click the first slide thumbnail in the *Slides* pane on the left side of the PowerPoint window. To work with one of the prebuilt layouts, click one of the thumbnails under the slide master thumbnail. You will notice

a dotted line connecting the slide master thumbnail with its associated layout thumbnails.

To change the theme of a slide master:

1. Click the **View** tab.
2. In the *Master Views* group, click the **Slide Master** button.
3. On the *Slide Master* tab, in the *Edit Theme* group, click the **Themes** button and select an option from the gallery. Every layout under the slide master has the new theme applied to it.

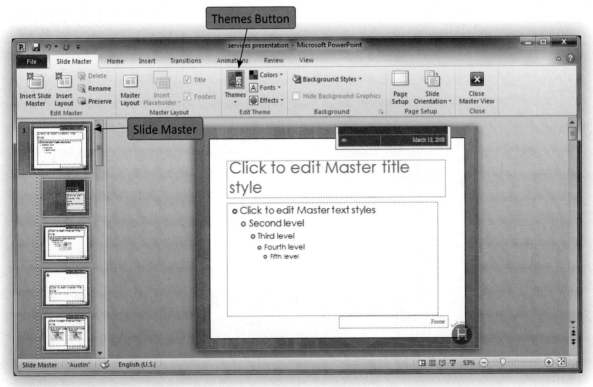

FIGURE PP 6.10

To change placeholders in a layout:

1. In Slide Master view, select a layout from the *Slides* pane on the left.
2. Select a placeholder, and resize the placeholder by clicking and dragging one of the resize handles ⊖.

3. To move a placeholder, select the placeholder. When the cursor changes to the move cursor ✛, click and drag the placeholder to the new location and release the mouse button.

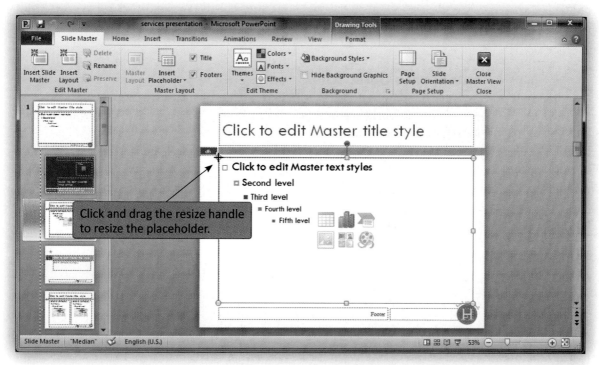

FIGURE PP 6.11

To change the bullet style for a layout:

1. In Slide Master view, select a layout from the *Slides* pane on the left.

2. Select the placeholder containing the bullets you want to change.

3. Click the **Home** tab.

4. In the *Paragraph* group, click the **Bullets** button and select an option from the gallery.

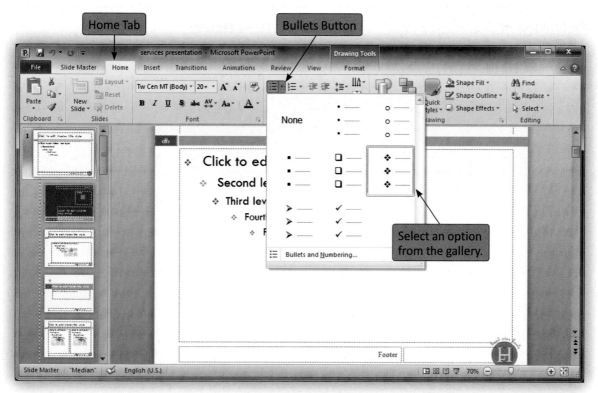

FIGURE PP 6.12

from the perspective of . . .

MARKETING DIRECTOR
Branding company media is easy with the use of the slide master. Our company logo is now part of every presentation produced by our employees. When they need to do a presentation, we've got a template to handle it!

tips & tricks

If you no longer want a layout to be available, select the layout and click the **Delete Slide** button in the *Edit Master* group. Be aware, PowerPoint will only allow you to delete layouts that are not in use in the presentation.

tell me **more**

Some changes you make, such as the theme, will be applied to every layout under the slide master. Other changes, such as changing the bullet style, will only apply to the selected layout. If you want to change the bullet styles for all layouts under a slide master, you should change the style on the master itself, not one of the layouts.

6.10 Adding New Layouts and Placeholders to the Slide Master

The slide master for a presentation comes with a number of prebuilt layouts for you to use. In addition to using these standard layouts, you can add your own layouts and then format and add placeholders to the layouts.

To add a new layout to the slide master:

1. On the *Slide Master* tab, in the *Edit Master* group, click the **Insert Layout** button.

2. A new layout is added under the selected slide master.

FIGURE PP 6.13

The default placeholders in slide layouts are content placeholders. Content placeholders include buttons for adding a wide variety of content types including tables, charts, pictures, clips, and SmartArt. But what if you want to include a layout that only allows one type of content to be added through the placeholder? You can add content-specific placeholders to any layout. PowerPoint includes the following placeholder types for you to add to layouts:

	Content	Creates a content placeholder with buttons for adding a table, chart, SmartArt, picture, clip art, or media file.
	Text	Creates a placeholder for adding text. Includes the bullet styles for five levels of bullets.
	Picture	Creates a placeholder with a button that opens the *Insert Picture* dialog box.
	Chart	Creates a placeholder with a button that opens the *Insert Chart* dialog box.
	Table	Creates a placeholder with a button that opens the *Insert Table* dialog box.
	SmartArt	Creates a placeholder with a button that opens the *Choose a SmartArt Graphic* dialog box.
	Media	Creates a placeholder with a button that opens the *Insert Video* dialog box.
	Clip Art	Creates a placeholder with a button that displays the *Clip Art* task pane.

To add a placeholder to the slide master:

1. Select the layout you want to add the placeholder to.

2. On the *Slide Master* tab, in the *Edit Master* group, click the **Insert Placeholder** button arrow and select an option.

3. The cursor changes to the crosshair cursor ✛.

4. Click on the slide layout where you want the placeholder to appear.

FIGURE PP 6.14

tips & tricks

After you have added a placeholder, you can resize the placeholder by clicking and dragging one of the resize handles ⚲. Click and drag toward the center of the placeholder to make the placeholder smaller. Click and drag away from the center of the placeholder to make the placeholder larger. To move a placeholder, select the placeholder. When the cursor changes to the move cursor ✛, click and drag the placeholder to the new location and release the mouse button.

tell me **more**

When you switch back to Normal view, the new layout you added to the slide master will be available from the *New Slide* and *Slide Layout* buttons.

6.11 Checking for Compatibility with Previous Versions of PowerPoint

Some features in PowerPoint 2010 are not available in previous versions of the application. If a presentation uses one of the new features, opening it in a previous version of PowerPoint may have unintended consequences. For example, if you apply Quick Styles to images in a presentation, the styles will be converted to a static image in PowerPoint 2003. If you are sharing a presentation created in PowerPoint 2010 with someone who may be using an earlier version of PowerPoint, you should check the presentation for compatibility issues.

To check your presentation to see if it contains elements that are not compatible with earlier versions of Microsoft PowerPoint:

1. Click the **File** tab.
2. The *Info* tab in Backstage view opens automatically. Click the **Check for Issues** button, and then click **Check Compatibility.**
3. The *Compatibility Checker* dialog box opens. The Compatibility Checker lists the items in your presentation that may be lost or downgraded if you save the presentation in an earlier Microsoft PowerPoint format. For each item, the dialog lists the number of times the issue occurs in the presentation (*occurrences*).
4. Review the compatibility issues, and then click **OK** to close the Compatibility Checker.

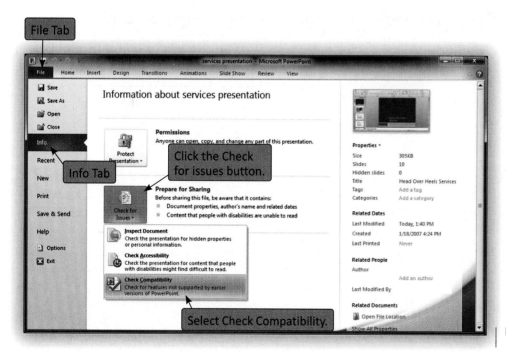

FIGURE PP 6.15

Note: Running the **Compatibility Checker** does not change your presentation. It only lists the items that will lose functionality when the presentation is saved in an earlier Microsoft PowerPoint format. It is up to you whether or not you want to make any changes to the presentation.

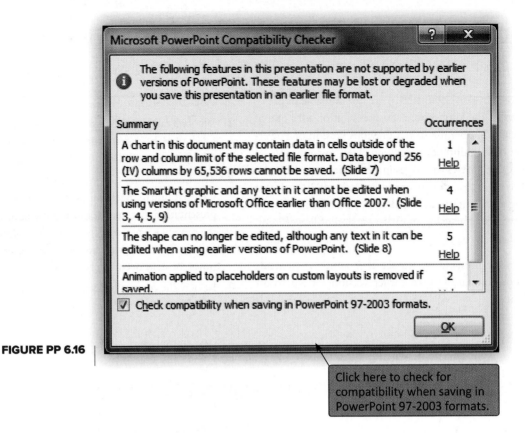

FIGURE PP 6.16

Click here to check for compatibility when saving in PowerPoint 97-2003 formats.

tips & tricks

If you often share presentations with people using an older version of Microsoft PowerPoint, you can set Compatibility Checker to run every time you save the presentation. Open the *Compatibility Checker* dialog, and then click the **Check compatibility when saving** check box to add a check mark. Click **OK**.

tell me **more**

There are few compatibility issues between PowerPoint 2010 and PowerPoint 2007, but there may be quite a number of compatibility issues between PowerPoint 2010 and PowerPoint 97-2003.

6.12 Saving Slides as Graphics

You may find that you want to include a picture of a slide in another document, such as a marketing plan created in Word. In PowerPoint, you can save an individual slide as a picture and then insert that image into a Word document.

To save a slide as a graphic:

1. Click the **File** tab.
2. Click **Save As.**
3. In the *Save As* dialog box, click the **Save as type:** arrow and select a graphic format (see below for a list of graphic file formats).
4. Click **Save.**
5. PowerPoint displays a message box asking if you want to save all the slides in the presentation or just the current slide. Click the **Current Slide Only** button to save the slide as a graphic.

FIGURE PP 6.17

There are a number of graphic file formats for you to choose from:

.jpg (or JPEG)	Joint Photographic Experts Group
.gif	Graphics Interchange Format
.bmp	Windows Bitmap
.png	Portable Network Graphics
.tif (or tiff)	Tagged Image File Format

Select the graphic format you want to save the slide as.

Click Save.

FIGURE PP 6.18

tips & tricks

If you want to save every slide in the presentation as an image, click the **Every Slide** button in the message box. When you save all the slides at once, PowerPoint automatically creates a folder and saves an image file for each slide in the presentation. The folder will have the same name as the presentation.

tell me **more**

When you save a slide as a picture, the slide becomes a static image. This means if you have animated objects designed to appear and disappear on the slide, all the objects will be visible. The saved image will look like the slide in Normal view rather than Slide Show view.

6.13 Saving a Presentation as a PDF

One way to publish a presentation in a static format is to save the presentation as a PDF file. **PDF** stands for *portable document file,* which is Adobe's custom format for displaying forms and documents in a Web browser. When you save a file in PDF format, the slides are converted into static pages with each slide on a separate page. All the formatting you applied to the presentation (including fonts, images, and styles) is preserved, but transitions and animations are not part of the PDF file. PDF files can be read by any computer with Adobe's Acrobat Reader installed, but they cannot be changed by those reading the file.

To save a presentation as a PDF:

1. Click the **File** tab.
2. Click **Save & Send.**

3. Under *File Types,* click the **Create PDF/XPS Document** button.
4. Under *Create a PDF/XPS Document,* click the **Create PDF/XPS** button.
5. In the *Publish as PDF or XPS* dialog box, navigate to where you want to save the file.
6. Click in the *File name:* box and type a file name.
7. Click the **Publish** button.
8. PowerPoint saves the file and opens it in Adobe Reader.

An **XPS (XML Paper Specification)** file is another file format that creates a static document of a presentation, and is easily readable but not easily editable. XPS files can be opened with Microsoft's XPS Viewer, which comes installed with Windows Vista and Windows 7.

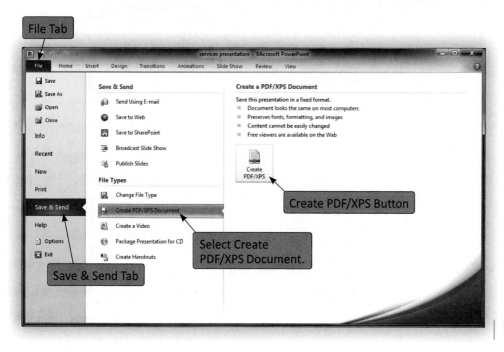

FIGURE PP 6.19

tips & tricks

You can also send a presentation through e-mail as a PDF file:

1. On the *Save & Send* tab, verify the **Send Using E-mail** option is selected.
2. Click the **Send as PDF** button.
3. Your default e-mail program opens with the subject line filled in and the presentation in PDF format attached.

tell me more

In order to read PDF files, your computer must have the Adobe Reader program installed. This program can be downloaded for free from Adobe's site:

1. Open your browser and navigate to http://get.adobe.com/reader/.
2. Click the **Download Now** button.
3. In the *Security Warning* dialog box, click **Install**.
4. The install program launches. When the program has finished installing, click **OK**.

6.14 Saving a Presentation as a Template

A **template** is a presentation with predefined settings that you can use as a pattern to create a new file of your own. Power-Point comes with a number of built-in templates that you can use to create presentations, or you can create your own templates and save them to use to create other presentations.

To create a template, first create a new blank presentation. Modify the slide master, adding new layouts and editing existing layouts for the slides you will add to the template. Add a new slide for each type of content slide you will have in the presentation. For example, create a title slide, a text with image slide, a chart slide, a SmartArt slide, a video slide, and so on. Create the bare bones of each slide—do not add content to the slides. Format the slides and presentation including applying a theme, creating a background for the slides, formatting text, and adding slide transitions. Once you have created the template, you will need to save it for future use.

To save a template:

1. Click the **File** tab.
2. Click **Save As.**
3. Click the **Save as type:** arrow and select **PowerPoint Template (*.potx).**
4. The *Save As* dialog box automatically navigates to the *Templates* location.
5. Click in the *File name:* box and type a file name.
6. Click the **Save** button.

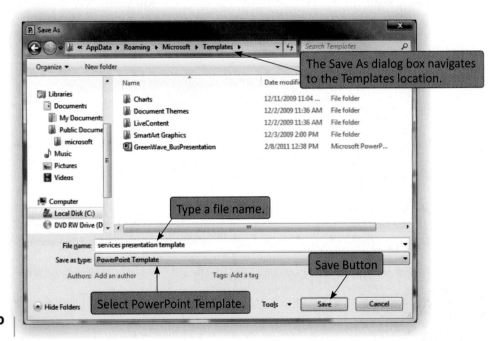

FIGURE PP 6.20

To create a new presentation from a presentation template you created:

1. Click the **File** tab.

2. Click **New.**

3. Under *Available Templates and Themes,* click the **My templates** button.

4. The template you saved now appears in the *New Presentation* dialog box.

5. Click the template to select it, and click **OK.**

The template you saved now appears in the New Presentation dialog box.

FIGURE PP 6.21

When you save a template to the default template location, the template will only be available locally on your machine. If you want other people to be able to use the template, you should save the template in a location that is accessible to others, such as a shared network drive.

tips & tricks

6.15 Packaging a Presentation for CD

PowerPoint's **Package for CD** feature allows you to copy your presentation to a CD directly from inside PowerPoint. The PowerPoint viewer is included by default, allowing you to run your presentation from any computer.

To use the Package for CD feature:

1. Place a blank CD-R or CD-RW in your computer's CD drive.
2. Click the **File** tab.
3. Click **Save & Send.**
4. Under *File Types,* click **Package Presentation for CD.**
5. Under *Package Presentation for CD,* click the **Package for CD** button.
6. The *Package for CD* dialog box opens.
7. Type the name of the CD in the *Name the CD:* box.
8. Click the **Copy to CD** button.

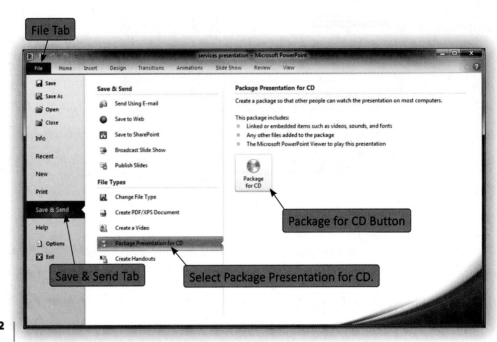

FIGURE PP 6.22

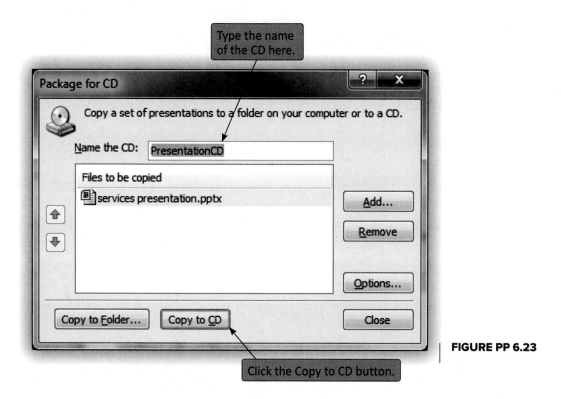

FIGURE PP 6.23

You can also package your presentation to a folder. You can then send the presentation via e-mail or a removable storage medium, such as a USB flash drive. When sending a presentation through e-mail, be aware that the larger the packaged presentation is, the longer it will take for the recipient to download the presentation. Therefore, only include the PowerPoint viewer and embedded fonts if absolutely necessary.

tips & tricks

> Click the **Add. . .** button in the *Package for CD* dialog box to copy more than one presentation to the CD.

> Click the **Options. . .** button in the *Package for CD* dialog box to change the options for including linked files and embedding True Type fonts. In the *Options* dialog box you can also add passwords for opening the presentation and modifying the presentation.

tell me **more**

When you place the CD in a CD drive, the autorun feature will automatically launch the PowerPoint viewer and run the presentation.

6.16 Broadcasting a Presentation

A new feature in PowerPoint 2010 is the ability to **broadcast** your presentation across the Internet. When you broadcast a presentation, you send others a link to a specific URL. Your audience members open a Web browser and navigate to the URL you provided to watch the presentation live as you show it.

To broadcast a presentation:

1. Click the **Slide Show** tab.

2. In the *Start Slide Show* group, click the **Broadcast Slide Show** button.

3. The *Broadcast Slide Show* dialog box opens.

4. Click the **Start Broadcast** button.

5. Log in to the broadcast service.

6. PowerPoint creates a URL for others to view the broadcast. Copy the link and send it to whomever you want to watch the broadcast. Be sure to let your audience know the date and time when you will be showing the presentation.

7. Click the **Start Slide Show** button to begin the presentation and broadcast it live.

Broadcast Slide Show Button

Slide Show Tab

FIGURE PP 6.24

PowerPoint Broadcast Service selected.

Click Start Broadcast to begin presentation and broadcast it live.

FIGURE PP 6.25

tips & tricks

When you are broadcasting a presentation, PowerPoint locks the presentation and will not allow you to make any changes. PowerPoint also displays the *Broadcast* tab. This tab is only available when you are broadcasting a slide show and provides you with tools for working with the presentation while broadcasting. To end the broadcast, on the *Broadcast* tab, in the *Broadcast* group, click the **End Broadcast** button.

tell me **more**

In order to broadcast a presentation you must have a broadcast service. The broadcast service is where the presentation is hosted, giving others access to the presentation. Your organization may have a broadcast service available through its SharePoint server, or you can use the PowerPoint Broadcast Service, available to anyone with a Windows Live ID.

try **this**

To open the *Broadcast Slide Show* dialog box, you can also:

1. Click the **File** tab.
2. Click **Save & Send.**
3. Under *Save & Send,* click **Broadcast Slide Show.**
4. Under *Broadcast Slide Show,* click the **Broadcast Slide Show** button.

6.17 Publishing Slides to a Slide Library

One way to share slide layouts with others is through a **Slide Library**. A Slide Library is located on a server and contains slides that have been uploaded for others to view and use in their presentations. Using Slide Libraries for creating presentations can help ensure presentation designs are consistent and up to date across large organizations.

To publish slides to a Slide Library:

1. Click the **File** tab.
2. Click **Save & Send.**

3. Under *Save & Send,* click **Publish Slides.**
4. Under *Publish Slides,* click the **Publish Slides** button.
5. In the *Publish Slides* dialog box, click the check boxes next to the slides you want to publish.
6. Enter the location of the Slide Library in the *Publish To:* box.
7. Click **Publish.**

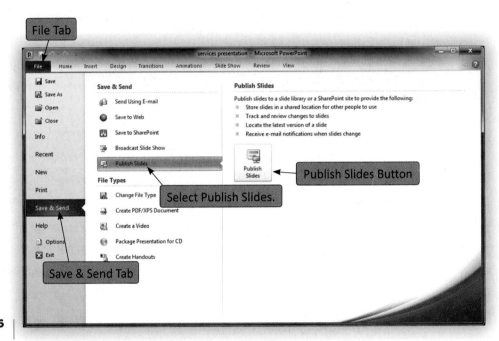

FIGURE PP 6.26

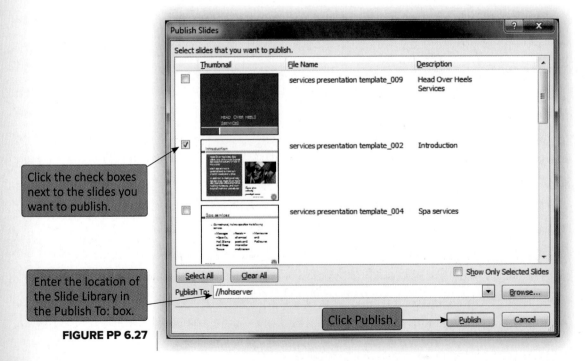

FIGURE PP 6.27

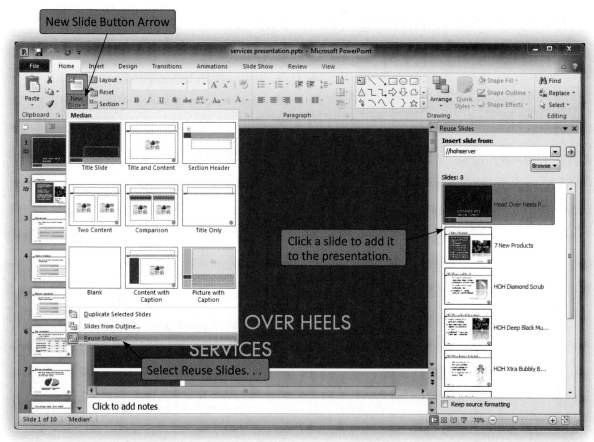

FIGURE PP 6.28

To add a slide from a Slide Library to a presentation:

1. On the *Home* tab, in the *Slides* group, click the **New Slide** button and select **Reuse Slides. . .**

2. The *Reuse Slides* task pane appears.

3. In the *Insert slide from:* box, type the location of the Slide Library and click the arrow button.

4. A list of slides appears.

5. Click the slide you want to add to the presentation.

tips & tricks

When you use a slide from a Slide Library in your presentation, the slide maintains a link to the original slide in the library. If the original slide is modified in any way, you will be notified of the change when you open the presentation, and you can choose to update the slide, add the changed slide to your presentation, or keep the slide as it currently appears in the presentation.

tell me **more**

The Slide Library feature is only available in the Microsoft PowerPoint Professional Plus 2010 version. In addition, in order to have a Slide Library, the server where the Slide Library is to be stored must be running either Office SharePoint Server 2007 or Microsoft SharePoint Server 2010.

try **this**

To open the *Publish Slides* dialog box, you can also right-click a slide thumbnail and select **Publish Slides** from the menu.

6.18 Saving a Presentation as a Video

Another new feature in PowerPoint 2010 is the ability to save a presentation as a video. Saving a presentation as a video gives you the ability to deliver a fully formatted, self-running slide show that others can view. The video will include all the transitions and animations you have added, as well as timings and narration you may have recorded. By saving the presentation as a video, you can deliver the presentation through e-mail, via the Web, or to mobile devices.

To save a presentation as a video:

1. Record the slide show including narration. For more information on how to record a slide show, see the skill *Recording the Slide Show* in Chapter 5.

2. Click the **File** tab.

3. Click **Save & Send.**

4. Under *File Types,* click **Create a Video.**

5. Under *Create a Video,* click the **Computer & HD Displays** button and select a display option.

6. Click the **Create Video** button.

7. The *Save As* dialog box opens with *Windows Media Video (*.wmv)* selected as the file type.

8. Navigate to the location where you want to save the video.

9. In the *File name:* box, enter a name for the video.

10. Click **Save.**

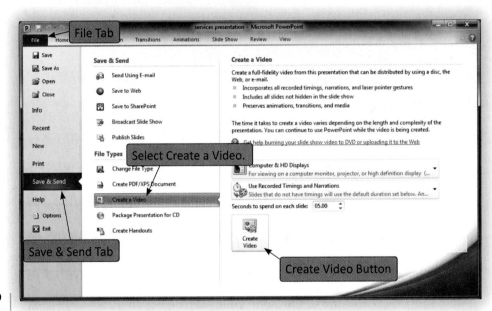

FIGURE PP 6.29

Different devices have differently video playback capability. Computers and HD displays are able to play videos at a higher resolution. If the video presentation is to be played across the Internet or on a standard DVD, you will want to save it at the medium setting. Video presentations can also be played on mobile devices, but you should set the display option to the lowest setting. Be aware that at this size, some text in your presentation may not be legible.

tips & tricks

If you do not want to use the recorded timings and narration in the video, click the **Use Recordings and Narration** button and select **Don't Use Recordings and Narration.**

tell me more

PowerPoint saves the video files in the .wmv (Windows Media Video) file format. This is a digital video format that can be read by most personal computers. You can also install third-party add-ins to PowerPoint to give you the ability to save presentations in other video formats, such as QuickTime or AVI.

projects

Skill Review 6.1

In this review, you will use the skills learned in Chapter 6 to edit a presentation.

1. Open Microsoft PowerPoint 2010.

   a. On the *File* tab, click **Open.**

   b. In the *Open* dialog box, navigate to the location of your PowerPoint 2010 student files.

   c. Find *Harry_Landscaping.pptx,* and double-click the file to open it.

   d. On the *File* tab, click the **Save As** option.

   e. Change the file name to **[your initials]PP_SkillReview_6-1**, and then click **Save.**

2. Add a slide from another presentation:

   a. Select **Slide 5.**

   b. On the *Home* tab, in the *Slides* group, click the **New Slide** button arrow and select **Reuse Slides.**

   c. Click the **Browse** button and select **Browse File. . .**

   d. Navigate to the location of your PowerPoint 2010 student files, and select the *Gardening Today.pptx* file.

   e. In the *Reuse Slides* task pane, click the **Our flowers. . .** slide to insert it as the sixth slide in the presentation.

   f. Close the *Reuse Slides* task pane.

3. Create a multipart animation:

   a. Go to **Slide 2** and click the text placeholder.

   b. Click the **Animation** tab.

   c. In the *Animations* group, click the **More** button in the *Animation* gallery.

   d. Under *Entrance,* select **Shape.**

   e. In the *Advanced Animation* group, click the **Add Animation** button.

   f. Under *Exit,* select **Shape.**

4. Use the Format Painter:

   a. Go to **Slide 3** and click in the second bulleted item.

   b. On the *Home* tab, in the *Clipboard* group, click the **Format Painter** button.

   c. Click and drag across the first bulleted item.

5. Align text:

   a. Go to **Slide 2,** and click the text placeholder.

   b. On the *Home* tab, in the *Paragraph* group, click the **Center** button.

6. Change the line spacing:

   a. With the text placeholder still selected, on the *Home* tab, in the *Paragraph* group, click the **Line Spacing** button, and select **1.5.**

7. Copy an animation from one object to another with the Animation Painter:

   a. With the text placeholder still selected, click the **Animations** tab.

   b. In the *Advanced Animation* group, click the **Animation Painter** button.

   c. Click on **Slide 3.**

   d. Click the text placeholder to apply the copied animation style.

8. Modify the slide master:

  a. Click the **View** tab.

  b. In the *Master Views* group, click the **Slide Master** button.

  c. Click the first thumbnail in the left pane that has the number *1* next to it.

  d. Click the image that is in the left corner, and drag it to the right side of the slide.

  e. While still in Slide Master view and on the first slide, click inside the first bulleted text.

  f. Click the **Home** tab. In the *Paragraph* group, click the drop-down arrow to the right of the *Bullets* button.

  g. Click the second option in the second row, **Hollow Square Bullets.**

  h. Click the **Slide Master** tab. Click the **Close Master View** button.

9. Check for compatibility issues with previous versions:

  a. Click the **File** tab.

  b. On the *Info* tab, click the **Check for Issues** button.

  c. Select **Check Compatibility.**

  d. Click **OK** in the dialog box.

10. Publish the presentation as a PDF:

  a. Click the **File** tab.

  b. Click **Save & Send.**

  c. Under *File Types,* click **Create PDF/XPS File.**

  d. Click the **Create PDF/XPS** button.

  e. Click the **Publish** button.

  f. The presentation opens in *Adobe Reader.* Close *Adobe Reader* and return to PowerPoint 2010.

11. Save the presentation as a video:

  a. Click the **File** tab.

  b. Click **Save & Send.**

  c. Under *File Types,* click **Create a Video.**

  d. Click the **Computer & HD Displays** button and select **Internet & DVDs.**

  e. Click the **Create Video** button.

  f. Type in a file name, `[your initials]PP_Video_6_1.`

  g. Click the **Save** button.

12. Save and close the PowerPoint presentation.

Skill Review **6.2**

In this review, you will use the skills learned in Chapter 6 to edit a presentation.

1. Open Microsoft PowerPoint 2010.

2. On the *File* tab, click **Open.**

3. In the *Open* dialog box, navigate to the location of your PowerPoint 2010 student files.

4. Find *sm_financial.pptx,* and double-click the file to open it.

5. On the *File* tab, click the **Save As** option.

6. Change the file name to *[your initials]*`PP_SkillReview_6-2`, and then click **OK**.

   a. Select **Slide 5.**

   b. On the *Home* tab, in the *Slides* group, click the **New Slide** button arrow and select **Reuse Slides.**

   c. Click the **Browse** button and select **File. . .**

   d. Navigate to the location of your PowerPoint 2010 student files, and select the *marketing_present.pptx* file.

   e. In the *Reuse Slides* task pane, click the **Our motto is. . .** slide to insert it as the sixth slide in the presentation.

   f. Close the *Reuse Slides* task pane.

7. Use the Format Painter:

   a. Go to **Slide 3,** and click in the text *We provide:.*

   b. On the *Home* tab, in the *Clipboard* group, click the **Format Painter** button.

   c. Click and drag across the title of *Slide 4* to apply the copied formatting.

8. Align text:

   a. Go to **Slide 2,** and highlight the paragraph.

   b. On the *Home* tab, in the *Paragraph* group, click the **Align Left** button.

9. Change the line spacing:

   a. On the *Home* tab, in the *Paragraph* group, click the **Line Spacing** button.

   b. Click **1.5.**

10. Add a placeholder to the slide master:

    a. Click the **View** tab. In the *Master Views* group, click the **Slide Master** button.

    b. Select the second thumbnail in the *Slide* pane on the left.

    c. In the *Master Layout* group, click the drop-down arrow below the *Insert Placeholder* button.

    d. Click **Picture.**

    e. Click and drag across the lower-right corner of the slide to add the placeholder to the layout.

    f. Click the **Close Master View** button.

11. Save a slide as a graphic:

    a. Click **Slide 6.**

    b. Click the **File** tab.

    c. Click **Save As.**

    d. In the *Save As* dialog box, click the arrow to the right of *Save as type:* box, and click **JPEG File Interchange Format.**

    e. Click **Save.**

    f. Click the **Current Slide Only** button.

12. Check for compatibility issues with previous versions:

    a. Click the **File** tab.

    b. On the *Info* tab, click the **Check for Issues** button.

    c. Select **Check Compatibility.**

    d. Click **OK** in the dialog box.

13. Package the presentation for CD:

   a. Insert a blank CD-R or CD-RW into the CD drive.

   b. Click the **File** tab and click **Save & Send.**

   c. Under *File Types,* click **Package Presentation for CD.**

   d. Click the **Package for CD** button on the right pane.

   e. Click **Copy to CD.**

   f. Click **Yes** in the message box that appears.

14. Save and close the PowerPoint presentation.

challenge yourself **1**

In this challenge, you will use the skills learned in Chapter 6 to format a presentation and save it as various types of files.

1. Open Microsoft PowerPoint 2010.

2. Navigate to the location of your PowerPoint 2010 student files.

3. Open *Insurance.pptx,* and save it as **[your initials]PP_Challenge_6-3.**

4. Reuse a slide from an existing presentation:

   a. Display the *Reuse Slides* task pane, and open the *People_We_Serve.pptx.*

   b. Add **Slide 2** from this show after the last slide in *[your initials]PP_Challenge_6-3.*

5. Apply the *Split* entrance animation and the *Split* exit animation to the bulleted list on *Slide 2.*

6. Use the animation painter to apply the animations from the bulleted list on *Slide* 2 to the bulleted lists on *Slide 3* and *Slide 4.*

7. Apply character effects and text alignment:

   a. Select the bulleted list text on *Slide 2,* and change the font to Arial, 24 pt.

   b. Left-align the text.

   c. Change the line spacing to 1.5.

8. Copy the formatting from the bulleted list on *Slide 2* and apply the formatting to the bulleted lists on *Slide 3* and *Slide 4.*

9. Save your presentation:

   a. Save the presentation as a series of graphics. Save the slides in the PNG format.

   b. Save the presentation as a PDF.

   c. Close Acrobat Reader and return to PowerPoint.

10. Save and close the PowerPoint presentation.

challenge yourself **2**

In this challenge, you will use the skills learned in Chapter 6 to format a presentation.

1. Open Microsoft PowerPoint 2010.

2. Navigate to the location of your PowerPoint 2010 student files.

3. Open *Alices_Bags.pptx,* and save it as **[your initials]PP_Challenge_6-4.**

4. Reuse a slide from an existing presentation:

   a. Display the *Reuse Slides* task pane, and open the *Specialize_Bag.pptx*.

   b. Add **Slide 2** from this show after the last slide in *[your initials]PP_Challenge_6-4.*

5. Apply character effects and text alignment:

   a. Select the bullet points on *Slide 3,* and change the font size from 24 pt. to 32 pt.

   b. Right-align the bullet points on *Slide 3.*

   c. Change the line spacing to be double-spaced.

6. Use the Format Painter to copy the formatting from the bulleted list on *Slide 3* and apply the formatting to the bulleted list on *Slide 2.*

7. Modify the slide master:

   a. Change the bullets in the slide master to use the *Star Bullets* option.

   b. Add a media placeholder to the seventh layout under the slide master (the blank layout).

8. Use the Compatibility Checker to find any issues with previous versions of PowerPoint.

9. Save your presentation for distribution:

   a. Package it for a CD.

   b. Save the presentation as a video for delivery on mobile devices.

10. Save and close the PowerPoint presentation.

on your own

You have been asked to create a PowerPoint slide show on QR codes and how they may be used in your field or major.

1. Navigate to the location of your PowerPoint 2010 student files.

2. Open *QR_Codes.pptx.*

3. Save the file as **[your initials]PP_OnYourOwn_6-5.**

4. Apply the *Civic* theme.

5. Add **Slide 2** from *QR_Code_Reuse.pptx,* and make it the last slide in the presentation.

6. Apply an entrance and an exit animation of your choice to the bulleted list on *Slide 3.*

7. Use the Animation Painter to copy the animation from *Slide 3* and apply it to all the other bulleted lists in the presentation.

8. Change the font size of the bulleted list on *Slide 3* to be at least 30 pt., and change the line spacing to 1.5.

9. Use the Format Painter to copy the formatting from the bulleted list on *Slide 3* and apply it to all the other bulleted lists in the presentation.

10. Format the title text on the slide master by applying character formatting and changing the font size and color.

11. Save the fourth slide as a graphic in the PNG format.

12. Check the presentation for compatibility issues with previous versions of PowerPoint.

13. Save the presentation as a video for delivery on the Internet.

14. Package the presentation for a CD.

15. Save and close the PowerPoint presentation.

fix it

You have been asked to fix a presentation based on the skills learned in Chapter 6.

1. Using Microsoft PowerPoint 2010, open *Digital_Self.pptx*.
2. Save the file as *[your initials]*`PP_FixIt_6-6`.
3. Add the second slide from *Are_You_Digital_Final.pptx* to the end of the presentation.
4. Clear the formatting from the title on *Slide 1*.
5. Bold the title on the slide master.
6. Change line spacing of the bulleted item on *Slide 2* to 1.5.
7. Apply a multipart animation to the bulleted item on *Slide 2*.
8. Use the Animation Painter to apply the animation to the bulleted list on *Slide 3*.
9. Use the Format Painter to copy the formatting from the bulleted item on *Slide 2* and apply it to the bulleted list on *Slide 3*.
10. Save the fourth slide as a graphic in the JPEG format.
11. Check for compatibility issues with previous versions of PowerPoint.
12. Save the presentation as a video for delivery on mobile devices.
13. Package the presentation for a CD.
14. Save and close the PowerPoint presentation.

glossary

a

Action button: A button you add to a slide that performs a set function.

Animation: Movement of an object or text in a presentation. The four basic animation schemes are *Entrance, Emphasis, Exit,* and *Motion Paths.*

Animation Painter: Tool that copies and pastes an animation from one object to another.

Artistic Effects: Application of different graphic filters to an image. These filters mimic a wide variety of artistic tools, including paint strokes, pencil strokes, watercolors, mosaics, blurs, and glows.

b

Background: The graphic element that fills a slide. Backgrounds can be solid colors, textures, or images.

Brightness: Control of how dark or light a picture appears.

Broadcast: Method for delivering presentations via the Internet.

Bulleted list: List type used to organize information that does not have to be displayed in a particular order.

c

Cell: The intersection of a row and column in a table.

Character effects: Effects applied to text to alter its appearance. Effects include bold, italic, underline, shadow, and strikethrough.

Chart: A graphic that transforms numerical data into a more visual representation.

Clear All Formatting: Command that removes any formatting that has been applied to text, including character formatting, text effects, and styles and leaves only plain text.

Clip art: Copyright-free illustrations, photographs, audio clips, and video clips that are made available through PowerPoint to use in presentations.

Close command: Command that removes a presentation from your computer screen but leaves the PowerPoint application open.

Color theme: A set of colors that complement each other and are designed to work well in a presentation. A color theme will change the color of backgrounds, placeholders, text, tables, charts, Smart-Art, and drawing objects in a presentation.

Column: A vertical arrangement of text on-screen. Text at the bottom of one column continues on to the top of the next column.

Comment: A small text note that is added to a slide that is not meant to be a part of the presentation.

Compatibility Checker: Tool that checks for conflicts between the current presentation and previous versions of PowerPoint.

Content placeholder: A special type of placeholder that provides a quick way to add a variety of material to presentations, including tables, charts, SmartArt diagrams, pictures, clip art, and videos.

Contextual tabs: Ribbon tabs that contain commands specific to the type of object selected and are only visible when the commands might be useful.

Contrast: Feature that changes the range of color intensity within a picture.

Copy: Command that places a duplicate of the selected text or object on the Office Clipboard without changing the file.

Crop: Remove part of an image, hiding it from sight.

Custom slide show: A slide show that runs inside another slide show. Custom slide shows can be accessed through the *Custom Show* menu in Slide Show view or through a hyperlink.

Cut: Command that removes the selected text or object from the file and places it on the Office clipboard for later use.

e

Embedded object: Independent object that is pasted into a presentation. Double-clicking an embedded object will open the object inside the PowerPoint presentation, using the source program but not the source file.

Enhanced ScreenTip: A ScreenTip that displays not only the name of the command but also the keyboard shortcut (if there is one) and a short description of what the button does and when it is used.

Exit command: Command that removes a presentation from your computer screen and closes the PowerPoint application.

f

File tab: Ribbon tab located at the far left side that opens Microsoft Office Backstage view.

Find: Command that locates specific instances of text in a presentation.

Font: A set of characters of a certain design. The font is the shape of the character or number as it appears on-screen.

Footer: Text that appears on every slide or handout. Typically, a footer appears at the bottom of a slide or handout.

Format Painter: Tool that copies and pastes formatting styles from one object to another.

g

Gridlines: A series of dotted vertical and horizontal lines that divide the slide into small boxes. Used as visual markers for aligning placeholders and graphics.

Group: Subsection of a tab on the Ribbon; organizes similar commands together.

h

Handout: A printout of a presentation with anywhere from one to nine slides per page and with areas for taking notes.

Handout Master view: Master view where the printed version of a presentation is modified.

Handout masters : Master that controls how the slides in a presentation look when printed.

Header: Text which appears on every slide or handout. Typically, a header appears at the top of a handout.

Highlighter tool: Slide show tool that adds color behind text on slides in Slide Show view and emphasizes parts of a slide.

Home tab: Ribbon tab that contains the most commonly used commands for PowerPoint.

Horizontal alignment: Position of text with regard to the left and right edges of a cell or placeholder.

Hyperlink: Text or a graphic that can be clicked to open another file or jump to another place in the presentation.

k

Keyboard shortcuts: Keys or combinations of keys that when pressed execute a command.

l

Layout: Template for arranging elements on a slide.

Line spacing: The white space between lines of text.

Linked object: Dependent object that is pasted into a presentation. Double-clicking a linked object will open the source file in the original application for editing.

Live Preview: The display of formatting changes in a file before actually committing to the change.

m

Master views: Contain universal settings for the presentation, and include the Slide Master view, the Handout Master view, and the Notes Master view.

Metadata: Information describing a file, including keyword tags, the file title, and the author.

Microsoft Office Backstage view: *File* tab that contains the commands for managing and protecting files, including *Save, Open, Close, New,* and *Print.* Backstage replaces the *Office Button* menu from Office 2007 and the *File* menu from previous versions of Office.

Mini toolbar: Toolbar that provides access to common commands for working with text and graphics. When you select text and leave the mouse over the text, the Mini toolbar fades in.

Movie: A multimedia clip which includes moving images and sounds.

n

New command: Command that creates a new file in an Office application without exiting and reopening the program.

Normal view: The view where content is created and edited. Normal view consists of the *Slide* and *Outline* tabs, *Slide* pane, and *Notes* pane.

Notes Master view: View that controls how the printed notes pages will look.

Notes masters: Master that controls the look of notes when printed along with the slides.

Notes Page view: The view where notes are displayed along with slides in a presentation.

Notes pages: The printed copy of the slide with its associated note.

Numbered list: List type used to organize information that must be presented in a certain order.

o

Office Clipboard: Task pane that displays up to 24 copied or cut items for use in the current presentation or any other Office application.

Outline tab: Feature that displays only the text from the slides in a presentation in an outline format. Use the *Outline* tab to enter and edit text directly in the outline.

p

Package for CD: Allows you to copy your presentation to a CD directly from inside PowerPoint. The PowerPoint viewer is included by default, allowing you to run your presentation from any computer.

Paste: Command that inserts text or an object from the Office Clipboard into a file.

Paste Special: Command that inserts objects from other Office applications into PowerPoint. Objects can be pasted as linked or embedded objects.

PDF (portable document file): Adobe's custom file format that preserves the formatting of the document and is easily readable, but not easily editable.

Pen tool: Slide show tool used to underline or circle important points in Slide Show view as they are discussed.

Photo Album: Feature that allows you to create a presentation of digital images with captions.

Placeholders: A container on a slide that holds text or other content, such as a table, chart, or image.

PPI: Acronym for pixels per inch; used to measure picture resolution when compressing images in presentations.

Presentation: A multimedia slide show that combines text, images, charts, audio, video, animations, and transitions to convey information.

Presentation properties: Information about a presentation, such as the location of the presentation, the size of the file, when the presentation was created and when it was last modified, the title, and the author.

Protected View: Read-only format that protects your computer from becoming infected by a virus or other malware.

q

Quick Access Toolbar: Toolbar located at the top of the application window above the *File* tab. The Quick Access Toolbar gives quick one-click access to common commands.

Quick Layout: Combinations of labels, titles, and data tables applied to charts.

Quick Style: Formatting element that gives a presentation a more polished, graphical look without a lot of work. Quick Styles include fills, borders, shadows, reflections, and picture shapes.

r

Reading view: The view that runs the presentation within the PowerPoint application window.

Recolor command: Command that removes all colors from a picture and replaces them with shades of one color.

Redo: Command that reverses the *Undo* command and restores the file to its previous state.

Rehearse timings: Feature that runs the presentation while recording the time spent on each slide.

Replace: Command that is used with the *Find* command to insert specified text in a file with new text.

Reset Picture: Command to remove all PowerPoint formatting applied to a picture, reverting the picture to its state before any formatting was applied.

Reuse Slides task pane: Task pane that allows you to add slides from other presentations or from a Slide Library.

Ribbon: Graphic interface across the top of the application window that organizes common features and commands into tabs.

s

Screenshot: An image of what is currently displayed on the computer screen (such as an open application window or of a Web page).

ScreenTip (hyperlinks): A bubble with text that appears when the mouse hovers over a hyperlink. Typically, a ScreenTip provides a description of the hyperlink.

ScreenTip (Ribbon): A small information box that displays the name of the command when the mouse hovers over a button on the Ribbon.

Sections: Smaller groups of slides within a presentation to help better organize the content.

Shape: A drawing object that can be quickly added to a presentation.

Sharpness: Feature that removes any blurriness from a picture, giving it a crisper feel.

Shortcut menu: List of commands that appears after an area of the application window is right-clicked.

Slide: A unit within a presentation. Each slide contains content, including text, graphics, audio, and video.

Slide library: Slides that have been uploaded to a server for others to view and use in their presentations.

Slide master: A slide template that is used throughout a presentation to create a consistent look and feel.

Slide Show view: The view that displays the slides full-screen and displays the presentation as the audience will see it.

Slide Sorter view: The view that displays a grid of thumbnail pictures of the slides in a presentation, and is useful in rearranging the order of slides in a presentation.

Slides tab: Tab that displays thumbnails of all the slides in a presentation. Use the *Slides* tab to quickly navigate between slides and rearrange the slide order of presentation.

SmartArt: Visual diagram containing graphic elements with text boxes for entering information.

Softness: Feature that removes hard edges from a picture, giving it a smoother feel.

Sound files: Music or sound effects that can be added to slides.

Speaker notes: Hidden notes you add to slides through the *Notes* pane.

Spelling checker: Analyzes your entire presentation for spelling errors, and presents any errors in a dialog box, enabling you to make decisions about how to handle each error or type of error in turn.

t

Tab: Subsection of the Ribbon that organizes commands into related groups.

Table: Content element that helps organize information by rows, which display horizontally, and columns, which display vertically.

Tags: Keywords describing the file.

Template: A file with predefined settings that can be used as a pattern to create a new file.

Text boxes: Boxes that are added to the slide layout to enter text anywhere on the slide.

Text placeholders: Predefined areas in slide layouts where text is entered.

Theme: A group of formatting options that is applied to an entire presentation. Themes include font, color, and effect styles that are applied to specific elements of a presentation. In PowerPoint, themes also include background styles.

Theme effects: Aspect of the theme that controls how graphic elements appear.

Transition: An effect that occurs when one slide leaves the screen and another one appears.

U

Undo: Command that reverses the last action performed.

V

Vertical alignment: Position of text with regard to the top and bottom of a cell or placeholder.

W

WordArt: Predefined graphic styles that are applied to text. These styles include a combination of colors, fills, outlines, and effects.

X

XPS (XML paper specification): Microsoft's file format that preserves the formatting of the document and is easily readable but not easily editable. XPS files can be opened with Microsoft's XPS Viewer, which comes installed with Windows Vista and Windows 7.

Z

Zoom slider: Slider bar that controls how large or small slides are displayed in the *Slide* pane. It is located at the right side of the status bar at the bottom of the application window.

index

a

Action button, PP-36, PP-124
Action Settings dialog box, PP-124
Add
      clip art, PP-38
      comments, PP-93
      hyperlink, PP-92
      movies, PP-42
      picture, PP-40
      screenshot, PP-39
      sections, PP-9
      shape, PP-36
      slides, PP-8, PP-138
      SmartArt, PP-35
      sound, PP-41
      text, PP-25, PP-37
      WordArt, PP-30 to PP-31
Add Animation button, PP-74
Add Section, PP-9
Adding columns to text placeholders, PP-141
Adding slides from another presentation, PP-138
Advanced Animation gallery, PP-73
Align button, PP-71
Aligning, PP-71, PP-72
Aligning text, PP-117 to PP-118, PP-140
Animating charts, PP-121
Animation, PP-73, PP-74, PP-121 to PP-123, PP-145
Animation Painter, PP-145
Animation Pane button, PP-74
Animation task pane, PP-121
Animation timings, PP-123
Applying columns to text, PP-141
Artistic Effects, PP-110
Aspect ratio, PP-69, PP-114
Audio, PP-126 to PP-127
Audio Tools contextual tab, PP-41
Audio Tools Playback tab, PP-126
Author property, PP-xvii

b

Background, PP-60
Background Removal tab, PP-111
Background Styles button, PP-60
Background Styles gallery, PP-60
Backstage, PP-vi
Balance, PP-xii
Basic custom slide show, PP-90
Basic shapes, PP-36
Block arrow, PP-36
.bmp, PP-153

Bold, PP-139
Bottom alignment, PP-140
Brightness, PP-112
Broadcast Slide Show dialog box, PP-160, PP-161
Broadcasting a presentation, PP-160 to PP-161
Bullet style, PP-147, PP-148
Bulleted list, PP-26 to PP-27
Bullets and Numbering dialog box, PP-27
Bullets button, PP-27, PP-147

c

Callout, PP-36
CD/USB flash drive, package for, PP-158 to PP-159
Cell, PP-33
Center alignment, PP-140
Changing the order of slides, PP-87
Character effects, PP-139
Character spacing, PP-139
Chart, PP-34, PP-120, PP-121
Chart Layouts, PP-120
Chart Styles, PP-120
Chart Tools Design tab, PP-120
Chart Tools Format tab, PP-120
Chart Tools Layout tab, PP-120
Check Compatibility, PP-151, PP-152
Choose a SmartArt Graphic dialog box, PP-35
Clear All Formatting, PP-144
Clear Table button, PP-64
Clip art, PP-38
Clipboard, PP-xviii, P-89
Clipboard dialog launcher, PP-89
Close, PP-xxv
Color button, PP-113
Color theme, PP-58
Columns dialog box, PP-141
Comments, PP-93
Compatibility Checker, PP-151, PP-152
Compress Pictures, PP-115
Content placeholder, PP-32
Content-specific placeholders, PP-149
Contextual tabs, PP-vi
Contrast, PP-112
Convert to SmartArt Graphic button, PP-35
Copy, PP-xviii, PP-88
Corrections button, PP-112
Corrections gallery, PP-112
Create Video button, PP-164
Cropping handle, PP-114
Custom slide show, PP-90, PP-97
Custom theme, PP-57
Customizing PowerPoint, PP-xi
Cut, PP-xviii

d

Date and time, PP-13
Decrease indent button, PP-27
Default chart type, PP-34
Define Custom Show dialog box, PP-90
Delete Comment button, PP-93
Delete Slide, PP-86
Design principles, PP-xii
Distinction, PP-xii
Dos and don'ts, PP-xii
Drawing Tools Format contextual tab, PP-31
Duplicate, PP-88

e

E-mail, PP-155, PP-159
Edit Shape button, PP-65
Editing text, PP-6
Effect Options button, PP-11
Embedded objects, PP-xix
Emphasis animations, PP-73
Enable Editing, PP-xiv
Enhanced ScreenTip, PP-ix
Entrance animations, PP-73
Equation shape, PP-36
Exit animations, PP-73
Exiting PowerPoint, PP-xxvi

f

File size, PP-115
Find, PP-xxi
Flow, PP-xii
Flowchart, PP-36
Font, PP-61
Font Color button, PP-61
Font dialog box, PP-139
Font Size box, PP-61
Footer, PP-13
Format Painter, PP-143
Format Picture dialog box, PP-112
Format Shape dialog box, PP-65
Formatting
    aligning, PP-71, PP-72
    animations, PP-73, PP-74
    background, PP-60
    clearing, PP-144
    color theme, PP-58
    font, PP-61
    gridlines, PP-68
    grouping, PP-71, PP-72
    Quick Styles. *See* Quick Styles
    rotating, PP-71
    ruler, PP-68
    sizing, PP-69, PP-70
    SmartArt, PP-66
    text box, PP-62, PP-63
    theme, PP-57
    theme effects, PP-59
Frame Slides, PP-100

g

.gif, PP-153
Graphic effects, PP-59
Graphic file formats, PP-153
Grid and Guides dialog box, PP-68
Gridlines, PP-68, PP-72
Group, PP-vi
Group button, PP-71
Grouping, PP-71, PP-72

h

Handout, PP-100
Handout master, PP-12
Handout Master button, PP-99
Handout Master view, PP-5, PP-99
Handouts layout, PP-100
Header, PP-13
Header & Footer button, PP-13
Heading 1 style, PP-28
Heading 2 style, PP-28
Help, PP-xxiv
Help toolbar, PP-xxiv
Hide Slide button, PP-91
Highlighter, PP-96
Home tab, PP-vi
Hyperlink, PP-92
Hyperlinked custom slide show, PP-90

i

Increase indent button, PP-27
Insert. *See* Add
Insert Audio dialog box, PP-41
Insert Chart dialog box, PP-34
Insert Hyperlink dialog box, PP-92
Insert Layout button, PP-149
Insert Movie dialog box, PP-42
Insert Picture dialog box, PP-40
Insert Placeholder button, PP-25, PP-70, PP-149, PP-150
Insert SmartArt Graphic button, PP-35
Insert Video button, PP-42
Italic, PP-139

j

.jpg, PP-153
Justified alignment, PP-140

k

Keyboard shortcuts, PP-vi to PP-vii

l

Last Viewed, PP-97
Layout, PP-146 to PP-150

Layout button, PP-29
Left alignment, PP-140
Line, PP-36
Line spacing, PP-142
Linked objects, PP-xix
List
        bulleted, PP-26 to PP-27
        columns, PP-141
        multilevel, PP-27
        numbered, PP-26 to PP-27
Live Preview, PP-x

m

Master view, PP-5
Microsoft Access, PP-iv
Microsoft Excel, PP-iii, PP-34
Microsoft Office 2010, PP-iii to PP-v
Microsoft Office Backstage view, PP-vi
Microsoft PowerPoint, PP-iv
Microsoft PowerPoint Help, PP-xxiv
Microsoft Word, PP-iii
Middle alignment, PP-140
Mini toolbar, PP-ix
Motion Path animations, PP-73
Movie, PP-42
Moving a graphic, PP-36
Multilevel list, PP-27
Multipart animations, PP-122

n

New, PP-xv
New Comment button, PP-93
New presentation
        blank presentation, PP-xv
        template, PP-xvi
New Slide button, PP-8
New Slide button arrow, PP-138
Normal view, PP-4
Notes and Handouts tab, PP-13
Notes master, PP-12
Notes Master view, PP-5, PP-12, PP-15
Notes Page button, PP-14, PP-15
Notes Page option, PP-100
Notes Page view, PP-5
Notes pane, PP-3
Notes view, PP-14
Numbered list, PP-26 to PP-27
Numbering button, PP-27

o

Office Clipboard, PP-xviii, PP-89
Office.com, PP-38
Office Home and Business, PP-v
Office Home and Student, PP-v
Office Professional, PP-v

Open, PP-xiii
Outline tab, PP-7

p

Package for CD, PP-158
Page Options button, PP-100
Paragraph dialog box, PP-142
Paste, PP-xviii, PP-88
Paste Special, PP-xix
PDF file, PP-155
Pen, PP-96
Photo Album, PP-40, PP-129
Photograph slide shows, PP-40
Picture, PP-40, PP-67
        Artistic Effects, PP-110
        compress, PP-115
        corrections, PP-112
        crop, PP-114
        recolor, PP-113
        remove background, PP-111
        reset, PP-116
        transparency, PP-113
Picture Quick Styles, PP-67
Picture Styles gallery, PP-67
Picture Tools contextual tab, PP-39
Placeholder, PP-146, PP-149, PP-150
        content, PP-32
        edit, PP-6
        move, PP-6
        resize, PP-6, PP-70
        text, PP-25
        type, PP-3, PP-25, PP-149
.png, PP-153
Pointer Options button, PP-96
PowerPoint Options dialog box, PP-xi, PP-115
PPI, PP-115
Presentation, PP-3
        broadcast, PP-160, PP-161
        close, PP-xxv
        design, PP-xii
        open, PP-xiii
        package for CD/USB flash drive, PP-158 to PP-159
        properties, PP-xvii
        save, PP-xxiii, PP-155, PP-156 to PP-157
Presentation Properties, PP-xvii
Presentation tools, PP-96
Presenter view, PP-15
Print
        comments/ink markup, PP-100
        handout, PP-100
        Handout Master view, PP-99
        notes, PP-100
        options, PP-98
        outline, PP-100
        previewing slides, PP-98, PP-99
        slides (presentation), PP-98
        speaker notes, PP-15
Print tab (Backstage view), PP-98, PP-100
Protected View, PP-xiv
Publish Slides dialog box, PP-162, PP-163
Publishing slides to Slide Library, PP-162 to PP-163

q

Quick Access toolbar, PP-viii
Quick Layouts, PP-120
Quick Styles, PP-120
    picture, PP-67
    shape, PP-65
    table, PP-64
    text box, PP-63
    WordArt, PP-31

r

Reading view, PP-4, PP-5
Record Slide Show, PP-125
Rectangle, PP-36
Recurrence, PP-xii
Redo, PP-xx
Rehearse Timings, PP-94, PP-96
Remove Background button, PP-111
Remove Hyperlink button, PP-92
Remove Section, PP-9
Rename Section, PP-9
Replace, PP-xxi
Reset button, PP-10
Reset Picture, PP-116
Resize. *See* Sizing
Resize handle, PP-36, PP-62, PP-69
Ribbon, PP-vi
Right alignment, PP-140
Right-click shortcut menu, PP-vii
Rotate button, PP-71
Rotate handle, PP-36
Ruler, PP-68

s

Sans serif fonts, PP-61
Save & Send tab, PP-158, PP-162, PP-164
Save as
    graphic, PP-153 to PP-154
    PDF, PP-155
    template, PP-156 to PP-157
    video, PP-164
Save As dialog box, PP-xxiii, PP-153, PP-156
Scale to Fit Paper, PP-100
Screen Clipping tool, PP-39
Screenshot, PP-39
Screenshot gallery, PP-39
ScreenTip, PP-ix, PP-92
Section, PP-9
Security warnings, PP-xiv
Serif fonts, PP-61
Shadow, PP-139
Shape, PP-36, PP-37, PP-65
Shape Effects button, PP-62
Shape Fill button, PP-62
Shape Outline button, PP-62
Shape Styles gallery, PP-62, PP-63, PP-65

Shapes button, PP-36
Shapes gallery, PP-36
Sharpness, PP-112
Show Markup button, PP-93
Shortcut menus, PP-vii
Sizing
    image, PP-69
    placeholder, PP-70
Slide, PP-3
    change the slide order, PP-87
    copy, PP-88
    delete, PP-86
    hide/unhide, PP-91
    number, PP-13, PP-87
    paste, PP-88
Slide background, PP-60
Slide layout, PP-8, PP-10
Slide Library, PP-10, PP-162 to PP-163
Slide master, PP-12, PP-146 to PP-150
Slide Master tab, PP-12
Slide Master view, PP-5
Slide number, PP-13, PP-87
Slide pane, PP-3
Slide show
    custom, PP-90, PP-97
    exit, PP-96
    last viewed slide, PP-97
    navigation, PP-96, PP-97
    next/previous slide, PP-96
    notations, PP-96
    record, PP-125
    start, PP-95
Slide show navigation, PP-96
Slide Show toolbar, PP-97
Slide Show view, PP-4, PP-5
Slide Sorter view, PP-4, PP-87
Slide transitions, PP-11
Slides tab, PP-6, PP-7
SmartArt, PP-35, PP-66
SmartArt Tools contextual tab, PP-66
Softness, PP-112
Sound, PP-41
Sound files, PP-41
Sound icon, PP-41
Spacing
    character, PP-139
    line, PP-142
Speaker notes, PP-14 to PP-15
Spelling checker, PP-xxii
Stars and banners, PP-36
Starting the slide show, PP-95
Strikethrough, PP-139

t

Tab, PP-vi
Table, PP-33, PP-64
    aligning text, PP-117 to PP-118
    insert/delete rows/columns, PP-119
Table Quick Styles gallery, PP-64
Template, PP-xii, PP-xvi, PP-156

10/20/30 rule, PP-xii
Text, PP-25
Text alignment, PP-117 to PP-118, PP-140
Text box, PP-25, PP-62, PP-63
Text direction, PP-119
Text placeholder, PP-25
Theme, PP-57, PP-58
Theme Color button, PP-58
Theme Colors gallery, PP-58
Theme effects, PP-59
Themes button, PP-57, PP-146
Themes gallery, PP-57
.thmx, PP-57
Thumbnail, PP-6
.tif, PP-153
Timing, PP-94
Top alignment, PP-140
Transform gallery, PP-31
Transitions, PP-11
Transparent Color, PP-113
Trim Audio dialog box, PP-126
Trim Video dialog box, PP-128
Trust Center, PP-xiv
Trusted Locations, PP-xiv

U

Underline, PP-139
Undo, PP-xx

USB flash drive, package for, PP-158 to PP-159
User interface, PP-vi

V

Vertical alignment, PP-140
Video, PP-128
Video Tools Playback tab, PP-128
View, PP-4 to PP-5

W

.wmv, PP-164
Word document, PP-28 to PP-29
WordArt, PP-30 to PP-31
WordArt Quick Styles, PP-30

X

XPS file, PP-155

Z

Zoom bar, PP-5

photo credits